NORTH CAROLINA
NATURE WRITING

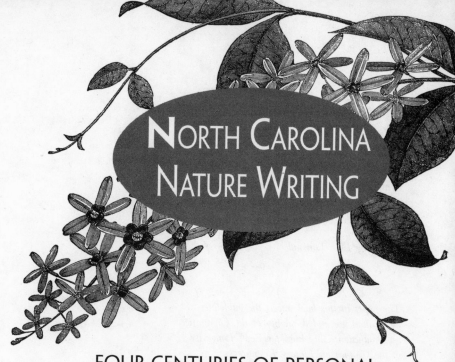

NORTH CAROLINA NATURE WRITING

FOUR CENTURIES OF PERSONAL NARRATIVES AND DESCRIPTIONS

Edited by Richard Rankin

JOHN F. BLAIR, PUBLISHER
Winston-Salem, NC

Design by Liza Langrall

*The paper in this book meets the guidelines
for permanence and durability of the Committee
on Production Guidelines for Book Longevity
of the Council on Library Resources.*

Library of Congress Cataloging-in-Publication Data
    North Carolina nature writing : four centuries of personal narratives
    and descriptions / [edited] by Richard Rankin.
        p.   cm.
    Includes index.
    ISBN 0-89587-151-3 (alk. paper)
    1. Natural history—North Carolina. 2. Nature. 3. North
Carolina. I. Rankin, Richard.
QH105.N8N65 1996
508.756—dc20   96-2640

Contents

INTRODUCTION

*N*ature writing in North Carolina is a literary tradition that has evolved over a span of more than three hundred years. During that time, Europeans and their American descendants have set in motion a process of agricultural and industrial growth that has profoundly altered the face of nature. Attitudes toward nature have also changed over this time as a seemingly inexhaustible wilderness has been cleared and cultivated, and the harmful consequences of this unrestrained development have become apparent. In response, conservationists, environmentalists, and ecologists in this century have attempted to limit and, in some cases, to halt development occurring at the expense of nature, and to redefine *progress* so the quality of the environment is included in the definition. All of these changes are reflected in the essays in this anthology.

Because the human encounter with the environment is the subject of nature writing, it is important to understand the variety of natural habitats in this state. The Natural Heritage Program identifies 104 distinct natural communities that occur in the three major sections of North Carolina—the mountains, piedmont, and coastal plain. These include habitats as diverse as the "fraser fir forests" of the mountains and the "salt flats" of the coast. The accounts of early naturalists like William Brewster, John Lawson, and William Hilton provide wonderful descriptions of many of these natural areas in their virgin state, and also provide the basis for a comparison with the current condition of the same habitats.

When ornithologist William Brewster travelled to the mountains of western North Carolina in 1881, much of the ancient forest had already been cut, and second-growth forest was succeeding it. But a rhododendron swamp near Highlands, North Carolina, was an exception.

> The road after leaving the village plunged down a steep slope and entered a superb rhododendron swamp where many of these shrubs attained a height of 25 ft. They grew in such tangled thickets that it was impossible for anything larger than a cat to get through them and their glossy evergreen foliage presented the appearance of a solid wall of dark green, semitropical in aspect. They formed the undergrowth of a forest of superb hemlocks, many of which were three or four feet in diameter and seventy or eighty feet high. The ground beneath was a spongy morass carpeted with green moss . . . and rich in beautiful ferns.

Brewster also described an awesome ancient cove forest near Black Mountain.

> The open hardwood forest stretched away as far as the eye could reach, the ground open, smooth, and perfectly free from

undergrowth, with scanty tufts of coarse wild grass or occasional ferns and numerous decaying logs forming the only obstructions. Everywhere it was densely shaded by the canopy of foliage supported, a hundred feet or more overhead by the sturdy shafts of the oaks, hickories, chestnuts, tulip trees, beeches, sugar maples, and black walnuts. Many of these trees were six or seven feet in diameter at the base and their trunks often rose perfectly smooth and straight to at least fifty feet before reaching the first branch. I saw some that must have been at least 125 ft. high. They stood usually about one hundred feet apart and altogether formed the finest forest I have seen east of the Wabash River.

If Brewster could return to the North Carolina mountains today, he would enter a world vastly different from a hundred years ago. Mountain resorts have proliferated, allowing more and more tourists and seasonal residents to enjoy the natural splendor, but also disturbing fragile environments. At the highest elevations, above 5500 feet, the spruce and fir forests are sick and dying, and scientists debate whether acid rain from pollution, the wooly balsam aphid, a combination of the two, or something as yet unidentified is the cause. The chestnuts are gone from the deciduous forest, a victim of blight. Except for a few sanctuaries like the Joyce Kilmer Memorial Forest, the ancient growth has been cut. Vast stretches of second growth remain healthy, but development advances and encroaches.

Changes in the natural environment of the piedmont are even more pronounced than in the mountains. When John Lawson trekked through this region in 1701, the trees were so tall that he "saw plenty of Turkies, but pearch'd upon such lofty Oaks, that our Guns would not kill them, tho' we shot very often, and our Guns were very good." The piedmont has been cleared of much of the original oak-hickory forest, except in a last wild corridor along certain streams and rivers. Cities and towns create pockets of intensive development that drastically transform the landscape. In rural areas, a patchwork of cultivated fields and old fields fills the land. These old fields are in various stages of succession that will, in time, cover them with broomstraw, loblolly pines, and finally, oak and hickory again.

In 1663, William Hilton paddled up the Cape Fear River through North Carolina's coastal plain and found oaks with trunks extending sixty feet before the first branch appeared. Today there are still wild stretches on the river, but large-scale agriculture and timber operations have cleared many of the great forests of the region. The beaches that Hilton saw were unpopulated—now they are crowded, and coastal growth strains the carrying capacity of nature. Undisturbed salt marshes once teeming with aquatic life are becoming less pristine. The maritime forests of live oak, laurel oak, and loblolly pine continue to disappear, particularly at the ocean front.

Hopefully, the foregoing discussion of the state's habitats and how they have changed over the centuries will create a map in the mind of the reader so that the accounts and essays in this anthology can be placed in their proper context. It is also important for the reader to understand the particular types of nature writing included in this book. The literature of nature is a rich genre, with several different categories. According to Thomas J. Lyons in *This Incomperable Lande*, nature writing "has three main dimensions to it: natural history information, personal responses to nature, and philosophical interpretations of nature. The relative weight or interplay of these three aspects determines all the permutations and categories within the field." These "dimensions" can be manifested in different forms. In nature guides and manuals, the natural history information, or the "facts of nature," are the main purpose. The feelings of the author are hidden. At the other extreme, the subjective experience of the author can be emphasized to such a degree that consideration of nature is overshadowed. The narratives selected for this book strike a balance between the personal and the descriptive. The writer is both a participant and an observer in the outdoors.

The earliest explorers in North Carolina who left nature writings were those associated with the expeditions of William Hilton and John Lawson. These explorers clearly studied nature to gauge the prospects of future settlement. They were good commercial capitalists who were constantly imagining how the land might be brought into productive use, and their writings have a promotional flavor. They were keen observers and recorders nevertheless. Their accounts are extremely valuable because they bring the modern reader into contact with virgin wilderness. The Native Americans had tread softly upon the land.

A new generation of naturalists arose by the middle of the eighteenth century, and some of the most distinguished came to North Carolina. Influenced by the Newtonian scientific revolution, they believed in an orderly, rational world. Their field of study was natural history, and it was broad enough to include ethnology, geology, botany, astronomy, and paleontology. From the work of John Bartram in the mid-1700s to the early career of Asa Gray before 1840, these individuals were part of an international scientific community that was attempting a systematic description of American plants and animals. The binomial method of Swedish botanist Carolus Linnaeus provided an ideal way of classifying flora and fauna. Within the wide bounds of natural history, many gravitated toward a specialty, with botany and ornithology becoming particularly popular.

As the antebellum period closed, changes were in motion that would give rise to the new field of biology—a field that would eclipse natural history. Evolutionary theory revolutionized thought. The microscope shifted study from the field to the laboratory. Professional biologists were devoted to narrow research, and their outlet for expression was the scientific journal.

In contrast to the increasingly scientific character of biological research, nature writing after the Civil War was directed at a more general audience. Perhaps the popularity of nature writing lies in its ability to satisfy a need to be connected to nature. A need that has become increasingly difficult in a modern, industrial society. Many nature writers, such as H.H. Brimley and John K. Terres, brought considerable scientific knowledge to their task, but their writings remain accessible to an interested reader. Most contemporary nature writing shows the strong influence of the humanities. And some of it, for example, the works of Donald Culross Peattie and Harry Middleton, has considerable literary polish and style.

Certain themes do distinguish contemporary nature writing from the work of the early natural historians. First, the influence of the environmental movement and the growth of ecological consciousness, as expressed by writers such as Rachel Carson, can be seen clearly in the later writings of Jan DeBlieu and Harry Middleton. Middleton's awareness of the way acid rain harms trees and trout streams, and DeBlieu's discussion of the effect of habitat loss on sea turtle populations both demonstrate a profound concern for the delicate interrelationship between living things and their environment.

A second defining characteristic of recent nature writing is that it often involves the intensive study of a smaller place. H.H. Brimley, Paul Koepke, and John K. Terres all became intimately familiar with fairly small pieces of land. Careful study and long association with a modest-sized parcel is replacing the grand treks of Lawson, Bartram, André Michaux and, to a lesser extent, Gray, Brewster, and Bradford Torrey. In this respect, nature writing parallels the development of "bio-regional" environmentalism, which attempts to preserve small, local habitats.

Lastly, the regenerating powers of nature are emphasized in much modern writing. For John Muir—here, as in so much else, ahead of his time—nature was transcendent. It was the place where "the Word made flesh" indwells in plants, trees, animals, rocks, and rivers. For other writers, such as John K. Terres and Harry Middleton, transcendence is downplayed, but nature is a preserve where jaded moderns can go to restore numbed senses and to regain a sense of primitive vitality.

I hope that this book will provide readers with a greater appreciation of North Carolina's natural history, and perhaps, encourage some to become active in conserving natural areas in the state. James R. Troyer in *Nature's Champion*, the biography of B.W. Wells, a twentieth-century North Carolina pioneer in the field of ecology, concludes his book with what he believes would be Wells's advice to our generation: "Make progress . . . for the betterment of humankind, but respect the meshwork of the earth. Stride purposefully ahead, but stride softly: hear the trees, the grass, the flowers; read the land, the air, the waters; honor all nature, of which we are but part."

It was impossible for the earliest colonial explorers and settlers to imagine progress apart from the subjugation of nature. As we approach the twenty-first century, many North Carolinians recognize the need to balance the productive potential of the earth and environmental health and wholeness. Nature writing represents a literature of inspiration and hope for those who would conserve our natural heritage.

NORTH CAROLINA
NATURE WRITING

*I*N 1662, WILLIAM HILTON (1617-1675), a veteran sailor, led an expedition to explore the southeastern coast from Florida to present-day North Carolina. Sailing on the ship *Adventure*, Hilton and his group of fellow New Englanders departed from Charleston, Massachusetts. After Hilton's initial attempt to enter the Cape Fear River was blown off course by a storm, he succeeded in guiding the ship into the river on 3 October. For several weeks thereafter, the group explored the branches and tributaries of the river — then known as the Charles River — as far inland as the present Northeast Cape Fear River.

The strongest candidate for authorship of this chronicle describing the region's flora and fauna is John Greene, a member of the group. The natural bounty of the region impressed the adventurers, and they were already imagining the potential for farm settlement.

Selection from

"CHRONICLE OF WILLIAM HILTON'S FIRST VOYAGE TO THE CAPE FEAR RIVER, 1663"

by John Greene (?)

*I*t was resolved, w[i]th all expedition possible to recover Cape fear, and to search ye entry into ye haven better; and fearing, our whole voyage would be lost, should we make no attempts, we laboured through contrary winds, and calmes, untill ye 3d of Oct., before we could arrive in to Cape Feare road, where being now come to an Anchor again, we Judged our early worke to discover, what might be there, and found it a large and deep road, having good bottom, and well secured from most dangerous winds, lying open between ye South; and ye West, (hardly so much) but after ye Masters mate and some others had spent most of ye day in ye long

Reprinted from "New Englanders at Sea: Cape Fear before the Royal Charter of 24 March 1662-1663," by Louise Hall. *New England Historical and Genealogical Register* 124 (April 1970): 88-108. Used by permission.

boat, more seriously to sound ye Entry in to ye Haven, and found in ye sholdest place 2. fathoms deep at low water on ye 4th octob. we weighed, and went into ye Haven, where was 5. 6. 7. 8. fathom water, and in a weeks time, spent w[i]th ye Indians, and in sounding ye River (now call'd Charles river [Cape Fear River]) and ye ship turning up always agst ye wind, we gott up 15. or 16. leagues in to ye river; and after in our long boate half of us went 15. leagues further, till at ye head of ye river we could not tell, w[hi]ch of ye many rivers to take, and so returned to our ship, and as we went and came, we found many faire and deep rivers, all ye way running in to this Charles river [Cape Fear River]: w[hi]ch abounds w[i]th Sturgeon, and variety of other well tested fish, w[hi]ch some of us have eaten off: There are severall sholds of Oisters, w[i]thin ye Havens mouth, but we saw none so big, as they are in New Engld, nor are they so muddy tasted. All ye way up ye river there are abundance of vast meddows, besides upland fields, [that] renders ye Contry fit to be calld a Land for Catle, whereby they [that] dwell there, may enjoy ye freedom from [that] toyle in other plantac[i]ons, where they are necessitated to provide hay. And there are besides greatt swamps laden w[i]th varieties of great Oakes, and other trees of all Sortes, and some very great Ciprus-trees, tall Cedars, Ash, maple, poplar, great bay-trees, willows, large grape-vines in abundance, and other fruites. [Y]e uplands are laden w[i]th all sorts of Canes, of w[hi]ch many are very great, walnuts and pine-trees: And ye Land hath generally great store off weeds and grasse. We found also some barren land, and other exceeding good land, most of it very easy to plow up. There is scarce a stone to be seene, only in 2. or 3. places by ye side of ye river we spied some rocks in a very sandy ground. We have seen india Corn stalks as big as a mans wrist, 11. or 12. foot long; and ye weeds thick:

Amongst it there is very good clay. We saw severall mulberry trees grow up and downe in ye wood, and some baggs of silk worms; some of us sawe bees swarming, though ye latter end of october. Few of us saw any mosquitos, and they [that] did, saw but few. Some of us supposed, we heard a kennel off wolves, one night in our travell. There appeared to us no kind off ratle-snakes: Some other snakes there be, w[hi]ch ye natives boyle w[i]th their victuals: ye indians here are very poor, and silly Creatures, divers of [them] are very aged; but they are not numerous: for in all our various travells for 3. weeks and more, we saw not 100 in all, they were very courteous to us, and affraid of us, but they are very theevish; By our best observac[i]on we cannot conceive this Climat and place admits of any considerable winter, if any at all, besides ye Considerac[i]on of ye many Palmettos growing na[tur]ally there, w[hi]ch renders it a summer Contry: we found ye trees some florishing, some blossom[in]g, and some falling. There are abundance of Deer, as appears by ye many tracks, w[hi]ch we cannot avoyd almost if we goe ashoare: We saw two run by us: There are store of Otters, and of fowles there is abundance, Gray and White geese, Ducks, Teale, Eagles, Goshawkes, Quayles, Doves, Crowes, Blackbirds, Gulls, Cormorants, Cranes, Hernes, Woodpeckers, Parrots, Parrokettos, Ox-eyes etc. [S]everall sorts of other fowles. We know no fruit or grain, [that] grows in New Engld, but will grow there very well; Besides potatoes; Oranges, Lemons, Plantins, Olives, Cotton-trees; and we know not, why ye Pine apple will not grow there; and also ye sugar-cane; for there are excellent tall and strong wilde canes in abundance: Tobacco must needs excell. There is reason to Judge, ye climat and Contry will yield two cropps a year. We conceive, many of ye premises may be brought in a few years to a very considerable trade by ye English, if prudently managed.

*I*N 1663, William Hilton sailed the *Adventure* on a second trip to Cape Fear, this time leaving from Barbados. Hilton, Captain Anthony Long, and Peter Fabian commanded the voyage, which made first landfall near Port Royal, South Carolina, before heading northward. The ship was again driven to sea by storm, but the expedition finally gained Cape Fear and dropped anchor on 12 October.

After waiting for favorable winds, the ship sailed upriver for two days and again lowered anchor. Then twelve men in a longboat set out for further exploration. The expedition remained on the river until 4 December. As in the earlier voyage, they enthusiastically noted "that we have seen facing on both sides of the River, and Branches of Cape-Fair aforesaid, as good Land, and as well Timbered, as any we have seen in any other part of the world, sufficient to accomodate thousands of our English Nation, lying commodiously by the said River."

The chronicle of this voyage has the names of all three commanders appended to it, so it is difficult to establish authorship.

Selection from

"CHRONICLE OF WILLIAM HILTON'S SECOND VOYAGE TO THE CAPE FEAR RIVER, 1663"

by Peter Fabian, William Hilton, and Anthony Long (?)

Sunday November the 8th, we lay still, and on *Monday* the 9th, went again up the main River [Cape Fear], being well stock'd with Provisions, and all things necessary, and proceeded upwards till *Thursday* noon, the 12th, at which time we came to a Place, where were two Islands in the Middle of the River; and by reason of the Crookedness of the River at that Place, several Trees lay cross both Branches, which stop'd the Passage of each Branch, so that we could proceed no farther with our Boat; but went up the River side by Land, some 3 or 4 Miles, and found the River wider and wider. So we return'd, leaving it, as far as we could see up a long Reach, running N.E. we judging ourselves near fifty Leagues North from the River's

Mouth. In our Return, we view'd the Land on both Sides the River, and found as good Tracts of dry, well-wooded, pleasant, and delightful Ground, as we have seen any where in the World, with abundance of long thick Grass on it, the Land being very level, with steep Banks on both Sides the River, and in some Places very high, the Woods stor'd every where, and great Numbers of Deer and Turkies, we never going on Shoar, but we saw of each Sort; as also great Store of Patridges, Cranes, and Conies, in several Places; we likewise heard several Wolves howling in the Woods, and saw where they had torn a Deer in Pieces. Also in the River we saw great Store of Ducks, Teal, Widgeon; and in the Woods, great Flocks of Parrakeeto's. The Timber that the Woods afford, for the most part, consists of Oaks of four or five Sorts, all differing in Leaves, but each bearing very good Acorns. We measur'd many of the Oaks in several Places, which we found to be, in Bigness, some Two, some Three, and others almost Four Fathom in Height, before you come to Boughs or Limbs; forty, fifty, sixty Foot, and some more; and those Oaks very common in the upper Parts of both Rivers; also a very tall large Tree of great Bigness, which some call *Cyprus*, the right Name we know not, growing in Swamps. Likewise Walnut, Birch, Beech, Maple, Ash, Bay, Willow, Alder, and Holly; in the lowermost Parts innumerable Pines, tall and good for Boards or Masts, growing, for the most part, in barren and sandy, but in some Places up the River, in good Ground, being mixt amongst Oaks and other Timbers. We saw Mulberry-Trees, Multitudes of Grape-Vines, and some Grapes which we eat of. We found a very large and good Tract of Land, on the N.W. Side of the River, thin of Timber, except here and there a very great Oak, and full of Grass, commonly as high as a Man's Middle, and in many Places to his Shoulders, where we saw many Deer, and Turkies; one Deer having very large Horns, and great Body, therefore call'd it *Stag-Park*. It being a very pleasant and delightful Place, we travell'd in it several Miles, but saw no End thereof. So we return'd to our Boat, and proceeded down the River, and came to another Place, some twenty five Leagues from the River's Mouth on the same Side, where we found a Place, no less delightful than the former; and as far as we could judge, both Tracts came into one. This lower Place we call'd *Rocky Point*, because we found many Rocks and Stones, of several Sizes, upon the Land, which is not common. We sent our Boat down the River before us; ourselves travelling by Land, many Miles. Indeed we were so much taken with the Pleasantness of the Country, that we travell'd into the Woods too far to recover our Boat and Company that Night. The next day being *Sunday,* we got to our Boat; and on *Monday* the 16th of *November,* proceeded down to a Place on the East-Side of the River, some 23 Leagues from the Harbour's Mouth, which we call'd *Turky-Quarters,* because we kill'd several Turkies thereabouts; we view'd the Land there, and found some Tracts of good Ground, and high, facing upon the River about one Mile inward, but backwards some two Miles, all Pine Land, but good Pasture Ground: We return'd to our Boat, and proceeded down some 2 or 3 Leagues, where we had formerly view'd, and found it a Tract of as good Land, as any we have seen, and had as good Timber on it. The Banks on the River being high, therefore we call'd it *High-Land-Point.* Having view'd that, we proceeded down the River, going on Shoar in several Places on both Sides, it being generally large Marshes, and many of them dry, that they may more fitly be call'd Meadows. The Wood-Land against them is, for the most part, Pine, and in some Places as barren, as ever we saw Land, but in other Places good Pasture-Ground.

JOHN LAWSON (1674–1711) was an English explorer who made a fifty-seven-day trek through the back country of what is now South Carolina and North Carolina. His party left Charleston, South Carolina, on 28 December 1700 and included five other colonists, three Indian men, and one Indian woman. Lawson's route in North Carolina began near what is now Charlotte and moved across the Piedmont, before finally arriving at Bath on the Pamlico River.

During the trip, Lawson kept a journal to record his observations on the land and its aboriginal inhabitants. In 1709, Lawson's journal, including additional material on the natural history of the region, was published as *A New Voyage to Carolina*. The work is justly regarded as a classic of early American literature.

The selections below include all the passages from the daily journal that deal with the natural history of North Carolina.

Selection from

A NEW VOYAGE TO CAROLINA

by John Lawson

On *Saturday* Morning, we all set out for *Sapona*, killing, in these Creeks, several Ducks of a strange Kind, having a red Circle about their Eyes, like some Pigeons that I have seen, a Top-knot reaching from the Crown of their Heads, almost to the middle of their Backs, and abundance of Feathers of pretty Shades and Colours. They prov'd excellent Meat. Likewise, here is good store of Wood-cocks, not so big as those in *England*, the Feathers of the Breast being of a Carnation-Colour, exceeding ours for Delicacy of Food. The Marble here is of different Colours, some or other of the Rocks representing most Mixtures, but chiefly the white having black and

Reprinted from *A New Voyage to Carolina*, by John Lawson. Edited by Hugh Talmage Lefler. Copyright © 1984 by the University of North Carolina Press. Used by permission of the publisher.

blue Veins in it, and some that are red. This day, we met with seven heaps of Stones, being the Monuments of seven *Indians*, that were slain in that place by the *Sinnagers*, or *Troquois*. Our *Indian* Guide added a Stone to each heap. We took up our Lodgings near a Brookside, where the *Virginia* Man's Horses got away; and went back to the *Kadapau's* [probably Catawba Indians].

This day, one of our Company, with a *Sapona Indian*, who attended *Stewart*, went back for the Horses. In the mean time, we went to shoot Pigeons, which were so numerous in these Parts, that you might see many Millions in a Flock; they sometimes split off the Limbs of stout Oaks, and other Trees, upon which they roost o' Nights. You may find several *Indian* Towns, of not above 17 Houses, that have more than 100 Gallons of Pigeons Oil, or Fat; they using it with Pulse, or Bread, as we do Butter, and making the Ground as white as a Sheet with their Dung. The *Indians* take a Light, and go among them in the Night, and bring away some thousands, killing them with long Poles, as they roost in the Trees. At this time of the Year, the Flocks, as they pass by, in great measure, obstruct the Light of the day.

On *Monday*, we went about 25 Miles, travelling through a pleasant, dry Country, and took up our Lodgings by a Hill-side, that was one entire Rock, out of which gush'd out pleasant Fountains of well-tasted Water.

The next day, still passing along such Land as we had done for many days before, which was, Hills and Vallies, about 10 a Clock we reach'd the Top of one of these Mountains, which yielded us a fine Prospect of a very level Country, holding so, on all sides, farther than we could discern. When we came to travel through it, we found it very stiff and rich, being a sort of Marl. This Valley afforded as large Timber as any I ever met withal, especially of Chestnut Oaks, which render it an excellent Country for raising great Herds of Swine. Indeed, were it cultivated, we might have good hopes of as pleasant and fertile a Valley, as any our *English* in *America* can afford. At Night, we lay by a swift Current, where we saw plenty of Turkies, but pearch'd upon such lofty Oaks, that our Guns would not kill them, tho' we shot very often, and our Guns were very good. Some of our Company shot several times, at one Turkey, before he would fly away, the Pieces being loaded with large Goose-shot.

Next morning . . . We travell'd, this day, about 25 Miles, over pleasant *Savanna* Ground, high, and dry, having very few Trees upon it, and those standing at a great distance. The Land was very good, and free from Grubs or Underwood. A Man near *Sapona* may more easily clear 10 Acres of Ground, than in some places he can one; there being much loose Stone upon the Land, lying very convenient for making of dry Walls, or any other sort of durable Fence. This Country abounds likewise with curious bold Creeks, (navigable for small Crafts) disgorging themselves into the main Rivers, that vent themselves into the Ocean. These Creeks are well stor'd with sundry sorts of Fish, and Fowl, and are very convenient for the Transportation of what Commodities this Place may produce. This Night, we had a great deal of Rain, with Thunder and Lightning.

Next Morning, it proving delicate Weather, three of us separated ourselves from the Horses, and the rest of the Company, and went directly for *Sapona* Town. That day, we pass'd through a delicious Country, (none that I ever saw exceeds it.) We saw fine bladed Grass, six Foot high, along the Banks of these pleasant Rivulets: We pass'd by the Sepulchres of several slain *Indians*. Coming, that day, about 30 Miles, we reach'd the fertile and pleasant Banks of *Sapona* River, whereon stands the *Indian* Town and Fort. Nor could all *Europe* afford a pleasanter Stream, were it inhabited by *Christians*, and cultivated by ingenious Hands. These *Indians* live in a clear Field, about a Mile square, which they would have sold me; because I talked sometimes of coming into those Parts to live. This most pleasant River may be something broader than the *Thames* at *Kingston*, keeping a continual pleasant warbling Noise, with its reverberating on the bright Marble Rocks. It is beautified with a numerous Train of Swans, and other sorts of Water-Fowl, not common, though extraordinary pleasing to the Eye. The forward Spring welcom'd us with her innumerable Train of small Choristers, which inhabit those fair Banks; the Hills redoubling, and adding Sweetness to their melodious Tunes by their shrill Echoes. One side of the River is hemm'd in with mountainy Ground, the other side proving as rich a Soil to the Eye of a knowing Person with us, as any this Western World can afford. We took up our Quarters at the King's Cabin, who was a good Friend to the *English*, and had lost one of his Eyes in their Vindication. . . .

Friday Morning, the old King having shew'd us 2 of his Horses, that were as fat, as if they had belong'd to the *Dutch* Troopers, left us, and went to look after his Bever-Traps, there being abundance of those amphibious Animals in this River, and the Creeks adjoining. Taken with the Pleasantness of the Place, we walk'd along the River-side, where we found a very delightful Island, made by the River, and a Branch; there being several such Plots of Ground environ'd with this Silver Stream, which are fit Pastures for Sheep, and free from any offensive Vermin. Nor can any thing be desired by a contented Mind, as to a pleasant Situation, but what may here be found; Every Step presenting some new Object, which still adds Invitation to the Traveller in these Parts. Our *Indian* King and his Wife entertain'd us very respectfully. . . .

On *Monday* Morning, our whole Company, with the Horses, set out from the *Sapona-Indian* Town, after having seen some of the Locust, which is gotten thereabouts, the same Sort that bears Honey. Going over several Creeks, very convenient for Water-Mills, about

8 Miles from the Town, we pass'd over a very pretty River, call'd Rocky River, a fit Name, having a Ridge of high Mountains running from its Banks, to the Eastward; and disgorging itself into *Sapona*-River; so that there is a most pleasant and convenient Neck of Land, betwixt both Rivers, lying upon a Point, where many thousand Acres may be fenced in, without much Cost or Labour. You can scarce go a Mile, without meeting with one of these small swift Currents, here being no Swamps to be found, but pleasant, dry Roads all over the Country. The Way that we went this day, was as full of Stones, as any which *Craven*, in the West of *Yorkshire*, could afford, and having nothing but *Moggisons* on my Feet, I was so lam'd by this stony Way, that I thought I must have taken up some Stay in those Parts. We went, this day, not above 15 or 20 Miles. After we had supp'd, and all lay down to sleep, there came a Wolf close to the Fire-side, where we lay. My Spaniel soon discover'd him, at which, one of our Company fir'd a Gun at the Beast; but, I believe, there was a Mistake in the loading of it, for it did him no Harm. The Wolf stay'd till he had almost loaded again, but the Bitch making a great Noise, at last left us and went aside. We had no sooner laid down, but he approach'd us again, yet was more shy, so that we could not get a Shot at him.

Next day, we had 15 Miles farther to the *Keyauwees*. The Land is more mountainous, but extremely pleasant, and an excellent Place for the breeding Sheep, Goats, and Horses; or Mules, if the *English* were once brought to the Experience of the Usefulness of those Creatures. The Valleys here are very rich. At Noon, we pass'd over such another stony River, as that eight Miles from *Sapona*. This is call'd *Heighwaree* [Uwharrie], and affords as good blue

15

Stone for Mill-Stones, as that from *Cologn*, good Rags, some Hones, and large Pebbles, in great abundance, besides Free-Stone of several Sorts, all very useful. I knew one of these Hones made use of by an Acquaintance of mine, and it prov'd rather better than any from *Old Spain*, or elsewhere. The Veins of Marble are very large and curious on this River, and the Banks thereof.

Five Miles from this River, to the N.W. stands the *Keyauwees* Town. They are fortify'd in, with wooden Puncheons, like *Sapona*, being a People much of the same Number. Nature hath so fortify'd this Town, with Mountains, that were it a Seat of War, it might easily be made impregnable; having large Corn-Fields joining to their Cabins, and a *Savanna* near the Town, at the Foot of these Mountains, that is capable of keeping some hundred Heads of Cattle. And all this environ'd round with very high Mountains, so that no hard Wind ever troubles these Inhabitants. Those high Clifts have no Grass growing on them, and very few Trees, which are very short, and stand at a great Distance one from another. The Earth is of a red Colour, and seems to me to be wholly design'd by Nature for the Production of Minerals, being of too hot a Quality, to suffer any Verdure upon its Surface. These *Indians* make use of Lead-Ore, to paint their Faces withal, which they get in the neighbouring Mountains. As for the refining of Metals, the *Indians* are wholly ignorant of it, being content with the *Realgar*. But if it be my Chance, once more to visit these Hilly Parts, I shall make a longer Stay amongst them: For were a good Vein of Lead found out, and work'd by an ingenious Hand, it might be of no small Advantage to the Undertaker, there being great Convenience for smelting, either by Bellows or Reverberation; and the Working of these Mines might discover some that are much richer.

At the Top of one of these Mountains, is a Cave that 100 Men may fit very conveniently to dine in; whether natural, or artificial, I could not learn. There is a fine Bole between this Place, and the

Saps. These Valleys thus hemm'd in with Mountains, would (doubt-less) prove a good place for propagating some sort of Fruits, that our Easterly Winds commonly blast. The Vine could not miss of thriving well here; but we of the Northern Climate are neither Artists, nor curious, in propagating that pleasant and profitable Veg-etable. Near the Town, is such another Current, as *Heighwaree* . . .

Leaving the rest of our Company of the *Indian*-Town, we travell'd, that day, about 20 Miles, in very cold, frosty Weather; and pass'd over two pretty Rivers, something bigger than *Heighwaree*, but not quite so stony. We took these two Rivers to make one of the Northward Branches of *Cape-Fair* River, but afterwards found our Mistake.

The next day, we travell'd over very good Land, but full of Free-Stone, and Marble, which pinch'd our Feet severely. We took up our Quarters in a sort of *Savanna*-Ground, that had very few Trees in it. The Land was good, and had several Quarries of Stone, but not loose, as the others us'd to be.

Next Morning, we got our Breakfasts of Parch'd Corn, having nothing but that to subsist on for above 100 Miles. All the Pine-Trees were vanish'd, for we had seen none for two days. We pass'd through a delicate rich Soil this day; no great Hills, but pretty Ris-ings, and Levels, which made a beautiful Country. We likewise pass'd over three Rivers this day; the first about the bigness of *Rocky* River, the other not much differing in Size. Then we made not the least Question, but we had pass'd over the North-West Branch of *Cape-Fair*, travelling that day above 30 Miles. We were much taken with the Fertility and Pleasantness of the Neck of Land between these two Branches, and no less pleas'd, that we had pass'd the River, which us'd to frighten Passengers from fording it. At last, deter-mining to rest on the other side of a Hill, which we saw before us; when we were on the Top thereof, there appear'd to us such another delicious, rapid Stream, as that of *Sapona*, having large Stones, about the bigness of an ordinary House, lying up and down the River. As the Wind blew very cold at N.W. and we were very weary, and hungry, the Swiftness of the Current gave us some cause to fear; but, at last, we concluded to venture over that Night. Accordingly, we stripp'd, and with great Difficulty, (by God's Assistance) got safe to the North-side of the famous *Hau*-River, by some called *Reatkin*; the *Indians* differing in the Names of Places, according to their several Nations. It is call'd *Hau*-River, from the *Sissipahau Indians*, who dwell upon this Stream, which is one of the main Branches of *Cape-Fair*, there being rich Land enough to contain some Thousands of Families; for which Reason, I hope, in a short time, it will be planted. This River is much such another as *Sapona*; both seeming to run a vast way up the Country. Here is plenty of good Timber, and especially, of a Scaly-bark'd Oak; And as there is Stone enough in both Rivers, and the Land is extraordinary Rich, no Man that will be content within the Bounds of Reason, can have any grounds to dislike it. And they that are otherwise, are the best Neighbours, when farthest of . . .

This Morning, we set out early, being four *English*-Men, besides several *Indians*. We went 10 Miles, and were then stopp'd by the Freshes of *Enoe*-River, which had rais'd it so high, that we could not pass over, till it was fallen. I enquir'd of my Guide, Where this River disgor'd it self? He said, It was *Enoe*-River, and run into a Place call'd *Enoe*-Bay, near his Country, which he left when he was a Boy; by which I perceiv'd, he was one of the *Cores* by Birth: This being a Branch of *Neus*-River . . . This River is near as large as *Reatkin*; the South-side having curious Tracts of good Land, the Banks high, and Stone-Quarries. The *Tuskeruros* being come to us, we ventur'd over the River, which we found to be a strong Current, and the Water about Breast-high. However, we all got safe to the North-Shore, which is but poor, white, sandy Land, and bears no Timber, but small shrubby Oaks. We went about 10 Miles, and sat down at the Falls of a large Creek, where lay mighty Rocks, the Water making a strange Noise, as if a great many Water-Mills were going at once. I take this to be the Falls of *Neus*-Creek, called by the *Indians, Wee quo Whom*. We lay here all Night . . .

We went, this day, above 30 Miles, over a very level Country, and most Pine Land, yet intermix'd with some Quantities of Marble; a good Range for Cattel, though very indifferent for Swine. We had now lost our rapid Streams, and were come to slow, dead Waters, of a brown Colour, proceeding from the *Swamps*, much like the Sluices in *Holland*, where the Track-*Scoots* go along . . .

We were forced to march, this day, for Want of Provisions. About 10 a Clock, we met an *Indian* that had got a parcel of Shad-Fish ready barbaku'd. We bought 24 of them, for a dress'd Doe-Skin, and so went on, through many *Swamps*, finding, this day, the long ragged Moss on the Trees, which we had not seen for above 600 Miles. In the Afternoon, we came upon the Banks of *Pampticough* [Pamlico], about 20 Miles above the *English* Plantations by Water, though not so far by Land. The *Indian* found a *Canoe*, which he had hidden, in which we all got over, and went about six Miles farther. We lay, that Night, under two or three Pieces of Bark, at the Foot of a large Oak. There fell abundance of Snow and Rain in the Night, with much Thunder and Lightning.

JOHN BARTRAM (1699–1777) was a pioneering American botanist. A Quaker who lived outside Philadelphia as an adult, Bartram traveled widely in colonial America collecting plants and studying insects, fish, and soil. Bartram also communicated with many famous Americans interested in natural history, collaborated with the eminent English horticulturist, Peter Collinson, and corresponded with most of the other celebrated European plantsmen. Carolus Linnaeus described him as the greatest "natural botanist" in the world.

Several of John Bartram's journals were published during his lifetime. The following selection is from the account of a 1765 trip to Lower Cape Fear, where Bartram's family once lived and where his brother, William, continued to live.

Bartram read widely, was essentially self-taught, and acquired a remarkable knowledge of nature. Spelling and consistent or correct capitalization were not his strengths. Capitalization has been corrected and made regular to make reading easier.

John was the father of the equally famous naturalist, William Bartram. Young William accompanied his father on this trip. William's description of the same region is very similar to his father's at points, and one wonders if the son did not rely on his father's journal to supplement his own observations.

Selection from

"DIARY OF A JOURNEY THROUGH THE CAROLINAS, GEORGIA, AND FLORIDA, 1765"

by John Bartram

S [JULY] 24. [1765] THERMOMETER 77.

*S*et out to Richard Singletary's. In ye way saw iron oar in a gravely cement. Then rode to observe a lovely species of onobrichis with large aromatick root & very regular branched stalk 3 foot high. People calls it here buck root & say it is very good for inward pains. I allso observed a large tree in ye bank of ye river, 8 foot long & 2 foot diameter, petrified to solid stone. It lay in a bank of sandy loam. Ye upper end lay 8 foot above ye surface of ye water, buried in sandy loam. Many more such like trees is found of very large dimentions in ye bank of ye river; for ye hicory trees grow very large here about. The trees common in this rich neck of land

Reprinted from "Diary of a Journey Through the Carolinas, Georgia, and Florida," by John Bartram [1765]. In *Transactions of the American Philosophical Society.* Philadelphia: The American Philosophical Society, 1942. Used by permission of the publisher.

is as follows: plane tree, tulup tree, black, red, & white oak, elm, sugar maple, ash, horn beam, poplor, sassafras, cornus [Dogwood], liquid amber [Sweet Gum], tupelo, water tupelo. Shrubs: fartle berry [Sparkleberry], stewartia [Silky Camellia], benjamin [Benzoin], cephalanthus [Buttonbush], halesia [Silverbell Tree], chiananthos [Old-man's Beard], mespilus of several kinds [Hawthorns, Choke-berries, or Shadbushes], celtis, white berried cornus [White Berried Dogwood], & a fine new genus. It thundred & rained much toward in ye evening ver[y] sharp & constant.

[JULY] 25.

Set out & travailed to ye lakes, by several cypress & bay swamps. Ye land on this side of ye river or no. east is not so good as ye land on ye no. west but much more sandy. We rode to a lake about one mile & half diameter each way, in which a prodigious numbers of fine colocasias [water chinquapins] in 8 or 10 foot water. Ye broad circular leaves was 16 inches or more diameter, lying flat upon ye water. Ye flower stalk shot above water 3 or 4 inches, produceing a cream colored flower nine inches diameter. Ye periant[h]ium is di-vided into four parts; five petals next are but half ye length of ye others which are sixteen. Ye apices are 70. Ye outwardmost are very broad at thair base & each circle is still narrower toward ye center. Here allso grows a very odd species of this genus which I take to be perenial. But I could not find any in its natural place of growth. What I saw was drove by storms on or near ye shore, broke off from its root. Ye stalk is scarsely so thick as a wheat straw. Very red & near ye surface of ye water sends forth ye pedicles of ye leaves 4 to 6 inches long, which enters ye center of an oval leafe very red on ye under side and 4 inches ye longest way & 3 ye shortest diam-eter more or less, out of ye alla of which shoots ye flower stem 4 or more inches long, produceing a perianthium divided in six parts. What flower it produces I cant say but there is 4 or 5 very hard ovall seeds as big as wheat grain contained in ye periantheum. All ye buds & leaves was surrounded with a thick transparent jelly much like ye white of an egg. It had a insipid tast . . .

[JULY] 29.

Foggy yet a fresh air. Thermometer 79 but rose at noon to 90. Rode to ye Wocoma [Waccamaw] lake, 14 mile distance; ye road very wet by reason of abundance of heavy rain & much savana ground. Greate variety of lovely plants & flowers & in generaly ye finest lofty pines I ever saw: ye negros was setting two tar kills: ye lake is 8 mile long & 5 broad & about 12 foot deep & very shoal toward ye borders in some places. Ye north east side is well inhabited being a bold shore & good land but ye so. west is very swampy. Ye outlet is at ye so. end into ye Wocoma [Waccamaw] river which runs a course of 50 mile & most of ye way very stil water. Ye lake abound with fish of several kinds as large cat fish, pearch, shad, & herings: much of ye great colocasia [Water Chinquapins] grows in it, & on ye borders grows elm, linden, ash, scarlet & red oak, large mirtle, pavia [Buckeye], cephalanthus [Buttonbush], hicory, wallnut, chiananthus [Old-man's Beard], maple, willow, white berried cornus [Swamp Dogwood], willow leaved oak, & plenty of ye broad leaved black oak, ye best oak for burning; ye banks is generaly 12 foot above ye surface of ye lake. Ye uper strata is a sandy virgin mould; next a very tenatious clay or marl, some red, some brown, 4 foot deep more or less; then some loose oister shels; then limestone full of several kind of sea shells as oisters, muscles, clams, schalops of monstrous size, cockles—all cememented in a solid mass to an unknown depth as I have observed at low water on our sea shores as well as on ye tops & sides of our high mountains near ye head of our great rivers. There is many clam shels of different sises cast on ye shore by ye waves, ye very same with our sea clams: very white: & perfect as if ye fish was just taken out but thay have lost ye fine violet color within side. If these was bread in this lake—as doubtles thay was—it must be long ago when ye sea flowed here: for ye lake is now very fresh & produceth now ye common fresh water muscle as all our rivers do. & ye river runs now near 50 mile fresh below ye lake in a straight line but above 100 in its winding. Another good branch of ye wocoma [Waccamaw] river is a great marsh a mile & half broad & seven long, surrounded with good land; ye inner part is exceeding black deep soil, to what depth is unknown; but toward ye east side it gradualy sholes to a tenatious clay; thence, to sandy virgin mould. Ye west side is more generaly steeper banks. Ye black part of ye marsh is yet rather too much repleat with salts to produce rice. Doubtless this formerly was a shallow lake which is in process of time filled up with ye gradual accumulation of soil from ye adjacent borders & ye rotting of vegitables. Its distance from ye before discribed lake is 7 or 8 mile. A fine branch runs thro it.

[JULY] 30.

This morning was clear & pleasant. Thermom. 80. Billy went down ye river with me alonge a bank 50 or 60 foot perpendicular to ye surface of ye water, to a steep bluf which continued near a mile: ye low land as usual being very broad on ye oposite side. This bluff was near 70 foot perpendicular: about ten from ye surface of ye ground was a strata of sea shels near rotton, but thair shape & dimentions very plain & close filled up with small broken fragments of shells being forced into ye least cavity by ye surging waves with numbers of very small intire ones: at noon thundred. thermom. 90. We went afternoon up ye river to a bluf shore on ye other side 40 foot above ye surface of ye river. Ye uper surface is virgin mould to 2 foot then 5 of very tenatious marl then great rocks in detached masses being a combination of many heterogenious materials: as various kinds of sea shels & I think belemnites, sea eggs, bills of birds, & wood or coal all cemented together with a calcarious cement; & some places a little feruginous, under which is a very black saline earth full of sea shels, near & deep under ye surface of ye river, not indurated nor perhaps ever will be for want of ye original marin salt. But ye greatest part of ye high bank on either side for 8, 9, or ten foot below ye surface is a very slipery black saline or sulphurious earth, lying in horisontal flakes of half a quarter of an inch thick, seperated by allmost invisible particles of fine sand & often a feruginous moisture ousing from between ye lamina; some places under a pr[o]jecting shelter & where ye sun shines hot: a saline matter, white & a little aluminous in tast, appears on ye surface. This earth, if it be brought away & spread on ye ground, it falls to powder as soon as it is dry, which indicates it to be a fine manure on ye sandy surface: it smels very strong like gunpowder & in it is dispersed numbers of yellow nodules which, when laid in a dry place, falls to vitriol: I cant see any esential difference in ye appearance of this mighty mass of saline earth in all our low countreys, & ye allum rocks near ye heads of our greatest rivers unless in ye induration, & that gradualy increaseth as we trace it higher up toward thair fountains even to ye foot of Alegany. There is other vast strata interspersed along ye steep banks to 10 or 12 foot in depth & as much from ye surface: as black as ye last &

25

mixed with shels but of much more sandy nature without any horisontal or perpendicular lamela but of a regular sandy texture in which is dispersed noduls as various in thair shapes as dimentions & very imperfect, either sand stone or limestone, yet a prety solid hard concreet; but seems as if many young ones was or had been forming round ye centtral one very iregularly & in different angles. . . .

[JULY] 31.

Pleasant morning. Thermomet. 76. Set out & rode about 30 mile up ye river over several branches of cypress & bay swamps but chiefly poorish soil, being sandy on ye surface, but soon came to a redish clay, in some places whiteish, produceing very fine lofty straight pines mixt with oaks & hicory & in moistish places liquid amber [sweet gum]. Ye oaks black, which is reconed ye best fire wood thay have; they call them black jacks; seldom grow above a foot diameter, very scruby, & of good use for timber for boats. Ye ashes are reconed ye strongest of all wood ashes. Its ye very same that grows in Jersey & all ye way to Carolina on poor ground. Thair other oaks is ye scarlet, red, white, both ye scruby sort & our common large white: thay have ye upland willow oak with a hoary leafe, & ye swamp willow with a narrow leafe. Ye pines are ye great long leafed, ye 2 & 3 leaf, ye narrow leaf, & ye broader three leafed pine. We kept about a mile distant from ye river.

AUGUST 1.

Set out stil up ye river. Came to a low bluff point but found no sea shells & consequently no limestone. Ye ground descended gradualy for a quarter of a mile, good soil to ye bluff; about 30 foot perpendicular to ye deep water; ye uper surface was virgin mould, then a hard blew clay which reached to or into ye river, consisting of lamella, some near perpendicular but most horisontaly, out of which in some places oused out a feruginous liquid; in this vast mass was interspersed numerous nodules of as various shapes as dimentions, of sulphurous concreets: some places where ye sand predominated ye feruginous sement had formed it into a brown or redish sand stone. But that which most agreeably surprised me was a bason of clear water from which ran a little current, of which I drank freely. It tasted at first quick & lively like one of ye german spaws, with an agreeable roughis[h] acid like alum: I then rode about a mile & half from ye river to an ould mill where ye steep banks was wore to a great depth. Here a large hicory tree lay horisontaly about 4 or 5 foot under ye surface of ye virgin mould. I dug under it & searched for its root, but ye tree seemed to be broke off from its root & ye end splintered & much rotted before it was petrified. & much of ye sulphurous marchasite had entered into ye cracks of ye splintered peices, which gave good fire on being struck with ye how, some of which it had quite surrounded but ye bark was not converted. Ye tree was two foot diameter & near 20 long. Some of ye iner part was rotten wood; which is a demonstration to me that it is onely ye solid wood that is converted into stone; some of ye marchasite adheared to ye bark, which was not alltered by it. I diligently observed ye black bank where it was sheltered from ye weather. There appeared a white matter on ye surface which tasted like allum & had ye exact appearance of ye allum rock on ye north branch of Potomack near Fort Cumberland. Onely that was hard & ye lamella was perpendicular, which answered to ye hills shape. We then set out to observe ye deep foundation of a new sawmill farther back from ye river, & in our way mounted upon a hill where we observed a very larg pine, blowed up by ye roots, about 4 foot diameter; about 8 foot of which was still left of ye main root & part of its bole. Ye rest was broke to pieces & most of it caried of. This tree, as it lay on dry sand, it was surrounded with cristall & ye outside was like spar. It was a little hollow near ye root; seemed all a body of hard stone. A little distance, in a road which had been wore deep by ye rains, lay two more large chunks of ye same kind. After which I went to where had been several rod square of sand dug, several feet deep, to make a dam withall. Thay dug to a strata of sand stone semented with a feruginous matter to prety large rocks of several ton weight. Amongst which a very large tree lay imbeded in ye strata, converted to a very hard brown or redish stone: when I came to ye mill, I found ye same strata of ye sulfurious black earth about 7 foot under ye surface, in thin flakes & a fine sand between, with little noduls or marchasites interspersed, like at ye river; & down ye stream I saw a chunk of many pound weight of wood with its root turned into hard stone. From which observations I would infer that most of this part of ye countrey covers this black sulphurious or vitriolick strata, which perhaps was once sea mud: & that prodigious numbers of these before mentioned stone trees is still embeded under ye surface of ye present vegitable mould, which in time may be exposed to sight like those discribed. . . .

[AUGUST] 5. THERMOMET. 77.

Lovely clear morning. Walked out to Donahoos Creek [Donohue's Creek] to search for fossils with Billy [son, William Bartram]. We found great variety in great rocks for two mile up it, of very large dimentions, on both sides of ye steep banks & bottom to within 8 or 9 foot of ye surface. Sometimes ye creek would plunge down between vast rocks & not appear on ye surface for many pearches unless in great cavities between ye rocks: toward ye mouth, next ye river, ye rocks was of a sandy nature more then generaly higher up, which was more of ye nature of lime stone & some of a cristal grit, but all composed of shells, many of ye cockle kind; but toward ye uper part, very large oisters. We killed a mocasine snake & toward noon it rained & thundred excedingly, but toward night it cleared up.

WILLIAM BARTRAM (1739-1823) was the son of John Bartram and a famous American naturalist in his own right. He was born near Philadelphia, and from his youth, he was in touch with the city's scientific intelligentsia through his father's connections.

The Bartram family had an ancestral home at Ashwood on the banks of the Cape Fear River in Bladen County, North Carolina. William lived there as a young man, working as a merchant for a time and living in the household of his aunt and uncle. He never prospered in business, and he often traveled back and forth between Philadelphia and Ashwood. In the spring of 1773, Bartram began his famous "travels." These travels became the basis for the book which he printed in 1791, *Travels Through North and South Carolina, Georgia, East and West Florida*. The book catapulted him to international fame.

The selection below describes the portion of Bartram's travels from the southern border of eastern North Carolina to the northern border. Not surprisingly, the description of the area in the immediate vicinity of Ashwood is particularly strong. Although he was primarily a botanist, Bartram's description of the various strata of soil on the banks of the Cape Fear River indicate that his interests also included geology.

A definite intellectual tradition informed his work. He was a deist for whom the Linnaean system of classification was the perfect scheme to describe the Creator's orderly universe. The emotional content of his prose, however, marks him as a forerunner of the Romantic movement.

Selection from

TRAVELS THROUGH NORTH AND SOUTH CAROLINA, GEORGIA, AND EAST AND WEST FLORIDA

by William Bartram

Next morning early I sat off again, and soon crossed Little River at the boundary; which is on the line that separates North and South Carolina: in an old field, on the banks of this river, a little distance from the public house, stands a single tree of the Magnolia grandiflora, which is said to be the most northern settlement of that tree. Passed this day over expansive savannas, charmingly decorated with late autumnal flowers, as Helianthus [Sunflower], Rudbeckia [Black-eyed Susan], Silphium [Compass Plant], Solidago [Goldenrod], Helenium [Sneezeweed], Seratula, Cacalia,

Aster, Lilium Martagon [Lily], Gentiana caerulea [Gentian], Chironia, Gentiana saponaria [Soapwort Gentian], Asclepias coccinea [Milkweed], Hypericum [St. John's Wort], Rhexia pulcherrima [Meadow Beauty], &c. &c.

Observed likewise in these Savannas abundance of the ludicrous Dionaea muscipula [Venus's Flytrap] (Dionaea, Ellis epis. ad Linnaeum, miraculum naturae, folia biloba, radicalia, ciliata, conduplicanda, sensibilia, insecta incarcerantia. Syst. vegetab. p.335).

This wonderful plant seems to be distinguished in the creation, by the Author of nature, with faculties eminently superior to every other vegetable production; specimens of it were first communicated to the curious of the old world by John Bartram, the American botanist and traveller, who contributed as much, if not more, than any other man towards enriching the North American botanical nomenclature, as well as its natural history.

After traversing these ample savannas, I gradually ascended sand hills to open Pine forests; at evening got to Old town near Brunswick, where I lodged. Brunswick is a sea-port town on the Clarendon, or Cape Fear river, about thirty miles above the capes; it is about thirty years since this was the seat of government, when Arthur Dobbs, Esq. was governor and commander in chief of the province of North Carolina. Continued up the West side of North West of Cape Fear river, and rested two or three days at the seat of F. Lucas, Esq., a few miles above Livingston's creek, a considerable branch of the North West. This creek heads in vast swamps, in the vicinity of the beautiful lake Wakamaw, which is the source of a fine river of that name, and runs a South course seventy or eighty miles, delivering its waters into Winyaw bay at George-town. The Wakamaw lake is twenty six miles in circuit; the lands on its Eastern shores are fertile, and the situation delightful, gradually ascending from pleasing eminences; bounded on the North-West coast by vast rich swamps, fit for the production of Rice: the lake is twelve miles West from _____ Moore's, Esq., whose villa is on the banks of the North West.

Proceeding again up the North West, crossed Carver's creek, and stopped at Ashwood, the ancient seat of Colonel William Bartram. The house stands on the high banks of the river, near seventy feet in height above the surface of the water; this high bluff continues two or three miles on the river, and commands a magnificent prospect of the low lands opposite, when in their native state, presenting to the view grand forests and expansive Cane meadows: the trees which compose these forests are generally of the following tribes, Quercus tinctoria, Querc. alba [White Oak], Querc. phillos [Willow Oak], Querc. aquatica, Querc. hemispherica, Fraxinus excelsior [Ash], Platanus occidentalis [Sycamore], Liriodendron tulipifera [Yellow Poplar], Liquidambar styraciflua [Sweet Gum], Ulmus [Elm], Tilia [Basswood], Juglans hiccory [Hickory], Juglans cinerea [Butternut], Juglans nigra [Black Walnut], Morus rubra [Red Mulberry], Gleditsia triacanthus [Honey Locust], Hopea tinctoria, Nyssa aquatica [Tupelo Gum], Nyssa sylvatica [Sour Gum], Carpinus [Ironwood], and many more; the Cupressus distichia [Cypress] as stately and beautiful as I have seen any where. When these lands are cleared of their timber and cultivated, they produce abundantly, particularly, Wheat, Zea, Cotton, Hemp, Flax, with variety of excellent vegetables. This perpendicular bank of the river, by which the waters swiftly glide along, discovers at once the various strata of the earth of this low maritime country. For the most part, the upper stratum consists of a light, sandy, pale, yellowish mould or loam, for ten or twelve feet in depth (except the flat level land back from the rivers, where the

clays or marle approach very near the surface, and the ridges of
sand hills, where the clays lie much deeper): this sandy mould or
loam lies upon a deep bed of black or dark slate coloured saline
and sulphureous earth, which is composed of horizontal thin flakes
or laminae, separated by means of very thin, almost imperceptible
veins or strata of fine micaceous particles, which drain or percolate
a clear water, continually exuding, or trickling down, and forming
little rills and diminutive cataracts, being conducted by perpendicular
chinks or fissures: in some places, a portion of this clear water or
transparent vapour, seems to coagulate on the edges of the veins
and fissures, leaving a reddish curd or jelly-like substance sticking
to them, which I should suppose indicates it to spring from a ferruginous source, especially since it discovers a chalybeate scent and
taste: in other places, these fissures show evidently a crystallization
of exceeding fine white salts, which have an aluminous or vitriolic
scent: they are pyrites, marcasites, or sulphureous nodules, shining
like brass, of various sizes and forms, some single and others con-
glomerated: other places present to view, strata of heterogeneous
matter, lying between the upper loamy stratum and the bed of black
saline earth, consisting of various kinds of sea shells, some whole,
others broken to pieces, and even pulverized, which fill up the
cavities of the entire shells, and the interstices betwixt them: at other

places we observe, two or three feet below the surface or virgin mould, a stratum of four, five, or six feet in depth, of brownish marle, on a bed of testaceous rocks; a petrifaction composed apparently of various kinds of sea shells, belemnites, sand, &c., combined or united with a calcareous cement: these masses of rocks are in some places detached by veins and strata of a heterogeneous earth, consisting of sea shells and other marine productions, as well as terrestrial, which seem to be fossile, or in some degree of petrifaction, or otherwise transmuted, particularly those curious productions called birds bills, or sharks teeth (dentes carchariae), belemnites, &c. loosely mixed with a desiccated earth composed of sand, clay, particles of marle, vegetable rubbish, &c. And again we observe shells, marcasites, belemnites, dentes carchariae, with pieces of wood transmuted, black and hard as sea coal, singly interspersed in the black vitriolic strata of earth: when this black earth is exposed to the sun and dry air, the little thin laminae separate, and soon discover a fine, white crystallization, or aluminous powder; but this very soon disappears, being again incorporated with the general mass, which gradually dissolves or falls like quick-lime, and appears then a grayish, extremely fine, dry micaceous powder, which smells like gun-powder.

The North West of Cape Fear, here at Ashwood, is near three hundred yards over (when the stream is low and within its banks), and is eighty or ninety miles above the capes. Observed growing hereabouts a great variety of very curious and beautiful flowering and sweet scented shrubs, particularly Callicarpa, Aesculus pavia [Red Buckeye], floribus coccineis, caule suffruticoso, Aesculus sylvatica, floribus ex albo et carneo eleganter variegatis, caule arboreo, Ptelea trifoliata [Hop Tree], Styrax [Storax], Stewartia, Fothergilla, Amorpha, Myrica, Stillingia fruticosa, foliis lanceolatis, utrinque glabris, fructu triocco, Olea Americana, foliis lanceolato-ellipticis, baccisatro-purpureis (Purple berrie bay), Catesby, Ilex dahoon

[Dahoon Holly], Cassine Yapon [Yaupon], Azalea, varieties, Kalmea [Laurel], Cyrilla, Liquidambar peregrinum, Sideroxylon, Andromeda lucida, &c.

Leaving Ashwood, and continuing up the West side of the river, about forty miles, in the banks of a creek, five or six feet below the sandy surface, are to be seen projecting out many feet in length, trunks of trees petrified to very hard stone; they lie between the upper sandy stratum and the common bed of blackish vitriolic earth; and these stone trees are to be seen in the same situation, sticking out of the perpendicular banks or bluffs of the river in this region: there are several trunks of large trees with their bark, stumps of their limbs and roots, lying petrified on the sand hills and Pine forests, near the road about this creek, not far from the saw-mills.

Crossed Rock-fish, a large branch of the North West, near its mouth or confluence, and at evening arrived at Cross-Creek, another very considerable branch of the river, flowing in through its West banks. This creek gave name to a fine inland trading town, on some heights or swelling hills, from whence the creek descends precipitately, then gently meanders near a mile, through lower level lands, to its confluence with the river, affording most convenient mill-seats: these prospects induced active, enterprising men to avail themselves of such advantages pointed out to them by nature; they built mills, which drew people to the place, and these observing eligible situations for other profitable improvements, bought lots and erected tenements, where they exercised mechanic arts, as smiths, wheelwrights, carpenters, coopers, tanners, &c. And at length merchants were encouraged to adventure and settle: in short, within eight or ten years, from a grist-mill, saw-mill, smith-shop and a tavern, arose a flourishing commercial town, the seat of government of the county of Cumberland. The leading men of the county, seeing plainly the superior advantages of this situation, on the banks of a famous navigable river, petitioned the Assembly for a charter to empower them to purchase a district, sufficient for founding a large town; which being granted, they immediately proceeded to mark out its precincts, and named the new city Cambelton, a compliment to _____ Cambel, Esq., a gentleman of merit, and a citizen of the county. When I was here about twenty years ago, this town was marking out its bounds, and there were then about twenty habitations; and now there are above a thousand houses, many wealthy merchants, and respectable public buildings, a vast resort of inhabitants and travellers, and continual brisk commerce by waggons, from the back settlements, with large trading boats, to and from Wilmington, the seaport and flourishing trading town on the Clarendon, about forty miles above the capes, which is about one hundred miles below this town. The Clarendon or Cape Fear river has its source in the Cherokee mountains, where its numerous confederate streams unite; after leaving the first ridges of the mountains, it assumes the name of Haw river, and coursing the hilly fertile country, above one hundred and fifty miles, receives through its West banks the West branch, called Deep River, and after this union, takes the name of the North-West of Cape Fear, from whence down to Cambelton, about eighty miles, it is navigable for perriauguas of considerable burthen.

Observed near Cambelton a very curious scandent Fern (Pteris scandens) rambling over low bushes, in humid situations; the lower larger fronds were digitated, or rather radiated, but towards the tops or extremities of the branches they became trifid, hastated, and lastly lanceolate: it is a delicate plant, of a yellowish lively green, and would be an ornament in a garden.

Sat off again to Cambelton, continuing yet up the North West about sixty miles; crossed over this branch, and soon after crossed the Roanoke, and then rested a few days at Mr. Lucas's, a worthy old gentleman, a planter on Meherren river. Observed strolling over his fences and stables, a very singular and useful species of the Gourd

(Cucurbita lagenaria); its neck or handle is above two feet in length, and not above an inch in diameter; its belly round, which would contain about a pint; it makes excellent ladles, funnels, &c. At a little distance from Mr. Lucas's, at the head of a swamp near the high road, I observed a very curious species of Prinos, which grows seven or eight feet high, the leaves broad, lanceolate, sharply serrated, nervous, and of a deep green colour; but its striking beauty consists in profuse clusters of fruit, collected about the cases or origin of the last spring's shoots; these berries are nearly round, about the size of middling grapes, of a fine clear scarlet colour, covered or invested with an incarnate mist or nebulae.

Being now arrived on the South border of Virginia . . . I shall pass as speedily as possible from hence to Pennsylvania, my native country; since those. . . regions . . . have been over and over explored, and described by very able men in every branch of natural history.

ANDRÉ MICHAUX (1746–1802) was a French botanist who was commissioned by his government to study trees in America and collect specimens there for the royal gardens. With Charleston, South Carolina, as his base of operations and nursery site, Michaux travelled widely in both the mountains and the coastal plain of North Carolina from 1787 to 1795.

The selection below comes from journals Michaux kept during his expeditions, and it includes accounts from three separate trips to the mountains and one to the coastal plain. Michaux's studies became the basis for two important published works: *The History of North American Oaks* (1801) and *Flora Borealis American* (1803, published posthumously). As the reader will see, Michaux's writing style is sparse and his description is kept to a minimum.

"PORTIONS OF THE JOURNAL OF ANDRÉ MICHAUX, BOTANIST, WRITTEN DURING HIS TRAVELS IN THE UNITED STATES AND CANADA"

by André Michaux

[JUNE 10, 1789]

Saw a Magnolia cordata [Yellow-flowered Magnolia] 18 miles from Charlotte. This Magnolia seems to differ even from the cordata M.[agnolia] discovered a few years earlier; the leaves were of a very distinct blue-green or bluish color on the underside.

Just a little before arriving at the ferry on the Catawba river saw an unknown bush having neither flowers nor fruit; it resembled in some ways the Calycanthus.

Saw near Burke Court house [Morganton] the same bush. . . .

Reprinted from "Portions of the Journal of André Michaux, Botanist, written during his Travels in the United States and Canada, 1785 to 1796. With an Introduction and Expository Notes by C.S. Sargent." *Proceedings of the American Philosophical Society* 26 (January to July, 1889): 1-137. Translated by Assistant Professor Eric Lien, Queens College, Charlotte, North Carolina.

[June 17, 1789]

The 17th left for Black Mountain located . . . Miles from Turkey-Cove.

Our plant collecting on this mountain lasted until the 22nd of
the same [month.] Recognized an Azalea nova species, Andromeda
. . . Vaccinium . . . Viburnum . . . and several other Plants which
the loss of my journals keeps me from describing but my herbarium
is proof that the Plants are new.

Sunday, November 15, 1789 passed by a Plantation located 8
M.[iles] away and 9 Miles before arriving in Charlotte saw the
Triosteum, Clematis erecta; Soil alternately yellow or red clay, grav-
elly; granite rocks and very often rather white and very hard Quartz,
commonly one found ferruginous flint: Red oak with long petioles, Oaks with long petioles and tomentose leaves, and black oak
are the most common; cultivated soil produces Wheat, Oats, and
Corn. On the banks of the Catawba riv.[er] it [the soil] is very
good; the grasses are a bit better than in the lower regions of the
Carolinas but the sheep don't look very good and the other animals
aren't very fat.

Arrived that night in Charlotte in Mecklembourg county in
North Carolina. *26 miles.* Two hundred miles from Charleston.

November 16, 1789 crossed the Catawba river at a place called
Tack-a-segee [Tuckasegee] foard, 14 miles from Charlotte; two Miles
before arriving at this ford we found an unknown bush with opposite leaves and we went to sleep at one Peter Smith's home; two
(one) miles before arriving there, saw near a Creek on the banks of
which were Ilex [holly] and Kalmia [laurel], a Magnolia . . . This
Magnolia is not as tall as the other known species. . . .

November 18, 1789. Very noticeable hoar-frost. Found the country mountainous and the rocks of a Granite composed of shorl [feld-
spar ?], quartz and mica, but more often Quartz or else ferruginous

flint and clay in the softer stones. Arrived at Burke court house. Saw two miles before arriving there the unknown bush from the Catawba river. *29 miles.*

November 19, 1789 left Burke and passed by the home of Colonel Avery who lives on the Catawba river 3 miles from Burke. Found just before arriving there in the Creeks a new Astragalus and a Menispermum [Moonseed] with dark fruit; slept *12 miles* from Burk.

The 20th we lunched further on and saw Magn[olia] cordata [Yellow-flowered Magnolia], Jugl. oblonga [Butternut], and we arrived next at Turkey-cove. En route noticed Epigea procumbens [trailing arbutus ?] and Gautheria procumb [teaberry or wintergreen]. *15 miles* from where we slept to Turkey-Cove.

Turkey Cove is the point from which one can go to various places in the high Mountains.

The 21st visited the northern branch of the Catawba river. Saw an Androm.[eda] arborea 43 inches in circumference.

Sunday the 22nd collected and gathered on the high mountains Acorns from blue-green oak.

The 23rd left for the high Mountains. Saw an Andr.[omeda] arb.[orea] 49 inches in circumference.

November 24, 1789 crossed the Blue Ridges in N. Carolina.

The 25th arrived at the lower region of the Black Mountain and collected Azalea fulva, Azalea nova species &c.

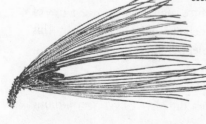

The 26th collected Magnolia cordata, M. acuminata &c. &c.

The 27th Arrived at the southern waterfalls of the Taw [Toe] river and gathered Viburnum nova species. Frost and snow . . .

[November 30, 1789] The 30th I collected Kalm.[ia] latifolia [Mountain Laurel] and Rhododendron.

December 1st through the 5th of the same visited several high Mountains and then packed up my Harvest in the quantity of 2500 trees, Bushes and Plants, in all 7 crates.

Sunday, February 23, 1794 the rain kept me from leaving before 11 o'clock; passed by Hixis ford, little village 28 miles away from Halifax which is the 1st town in North Carolina. The line on this road which separates Virginia from North Carolina is 12 M.[iles] from Hixis ford and 16 miles from Halifax in Carolina. 10 miles from Hixis ford and 2 miles before leaving Virginia territory, saw the Bignonia sempervirens [Trumpet Creeper family] near the Creek called Fontaine Creek. Also saw the Hopea tinctoria one mile before entering Carolina. One mile away from the Line that separates Virginia from Carolina and on Carolina territory saw the Cyrilla racemiflora [He Huckleberry] in a very large swamp, three miles before arriving at the Paterson's Tavern where I slept 16 miles from Hixis ford and 12 M.[iles] from Halifax: 23 Miles.

The 24th. 10 Miles from Halifax and six miles away from the Line between Virginia and Carolina begins the Pinus palustris, fol. longissimis, conis majorib. [Long-leaf Pine]. The Quercus palustris [Pin Oak] with deltoid leaves also begins in this spot. The P.[ine] with 3 long leaves, but cones of average size which begins at Bowling Green is found among [them] as well as the Pine with two and three leaves. The Bignonia crucigera and the Bign[onia] sempervirens, Hopea tinctoria are seen in abundance after having passed to the south of Halifax as well as Nyssa dentata and Cyrilla racemiflora [He Huckleberry] in the Swamps. Slept at Endfield court house at the home of Col. Brandt. 25 Miles.

The 25th dined at the home of Col. Phillips sixteen miles and crossed Tar River 4 M.[iles] away from the place called *Tetts bri[d]ge*:

Saw a Sophora called Yellow Lupin from which, the stems being dried out, & collected the seeds that remained in the pods gathered together in spiles [?] . . .

The 26th soil still sandy, covered by Pine trees called Pinus palustris [Long-leaf Pine]: these trees are cut and the bark stripped, but [only] a part of the wood two feet long by one foot wide.

The bottom of the cut is deeper in order to hold the resin called turpentine. The turpentine is removed once the basin formed by the deep cut is full. Twelve miles before arriving at Peacock bri[d]ge, begins the Laurus borbonica and three miles before Peacock bri[d]ge begins the Andromeda Wilmingtonia; the Stewartia malaccodendron is found in the area surrounding Peacock bri[d]ge. It is about 21 miles from Town creek bri[d]ge to Peacock bri[d]ge. The three species of Myrica in the Carolinas begin in the County as well as the great Carolina Rhexia. . . .

The 28th traveled from Whitefield ferry to Duplaine Court House [Kenansville] or Dixon. *31 Miles*: fifteen miles before arriving at Duplaine Court house begins the Andromeda axillaris, that is 65 miles north of Wilmington. Also saw in abundance the Vaccin. fol sempervirentib. caule repente, fructo nigro: Saw in abundance Andr.[omeda] Wilmingtonia, paniculata, racemosa &c. Bignonia crucigera, sempervirens, radicans et Catalpa.

Sunday March 1st, saw the Andromeda nitida or lucida of the Carolina Swamps, it begins forty-five miles North of Wilmington. Saw in abundance And.[romeda] Wilmingtonia, axillaris, racemosa et nitida: Passed by Washington 8 miles from Duplaine Court house, the Gordonia begins 3 M.[iles] N. of Washington, about 38 M.[iles] north of Wilmington. The Ilex angustifolia . . . begins 26 miles north of Wilmington. It is about 35 M.[iles] from Washington Court house to Wilmington.

Sunday May 2nd, I saw in the dry sand Lupinus perennis and Lupinus pilosus, Atraphaxia [?], bush, spindly limbs, fleshy leaves, green in winter, Vaccinium sempervirens &c. Saw near Bartram on the road to Warmspring, the Chamoerops acaulis begins 15 miles North of Wilmington. Olea americana is found in the area surrounding Wilmington and begins in this area. Stillingia herbacea begins 30 M.[iles] north of Wilmington. . . .

[May] 4th I went to dig up an Andromeda that I had noticed four years earlier as well as the Carolina Ixia and I filled up a Crate of these Plants to send by sea on the Ship of Capit. Mitchell, Sloop . . . in Charleston.

The 5th packed up my collections and put them on board the Ship.

The 6th, the Rain forced me to postpone departure and in the area surrounding Wilmington I saw: Dionoea muscipula [Venus's Flytrap], Olea americana, Andromeda mariana, paniculata, racemosa, axillaris, nitida, Wilmingtonia; Vaccinium arboreum, repens, fructo nigro &c, Bignonia sempervirens, crucigera. . . .

The 8th passed by Charlott bri[d]ge and [by the home of] W. Gauss, Esq. (wooden leg). 13 M.[iles] from Ross Tavern or Lockwood folly.

Sunday 9th left Foster's house. Violent aristocrat. On the coastline saw Pisonia inermis Shrub with berries, opposite branches and leaves. It begins in North Carolina and is found in South Carolina, in Georgia and in Florida &c. . . .

Also saw the Magnolia grandiflora 6 miles north of the Line that separates the two Carolinas.

The 22nd [of July 1794] passed through Charlotte in Mecklenbourg, soil red clay, Quartz stones: Clear water instead of those seen earlier: the Water is the color of dead leaves or dry tobacco: Vegetation, red, black, white Oak, &c. &c. Actea spicata . . .

Slept six miles from Tuck-a-Segee ford.

The 23rd passed by Ben. Smith's located twenty miles from Charlotte. Two and three miles before arriving there saw the Magnolia tomentoso-glanca fol. cordatis longiorib: Stewartia nova? Slept six miles from B. Smith's.

The 24th passed by Lincoln and dined with Reinhart: Calamus aromaticus: slept at the old cobbler's house. . . .

The 30th came back along the regular road that leads to Turkey cove and arrived at the home of one Ainswort.

The 31st collected on the Lineville [Linville] high mountains to the South-East of Ainswort's house and on Rocks and the mountains devoid of trees collected a small shrub Clethra buxifolia.

Friday August 1st collected on the Mountains where the soil is very rich, located to the N.-East: Veratrum viride, album? Convallaria majalis, Convallaria ? umbellata; measured a Tulip tree 23 French inches in circumference. . . .

The 5th postponed departure for lack of provisions.

The 6th left and arrived at a place called Crab tree: Plants noticed Azalea lutea, stylis longissimis; Veratum viride, album.

The 7th on the mountains in the area surrounding Crabtree: Clethra montana; Cassine . . . Rhodod. maximum; Kalmia latifolia; Convallaria bifolia; Trillium cernuum erectum bacca coccinea; Magnolia auriculata, acuminata flore glauca; Frutex Azaliae facies; Vaccinium fol. margine ciliatis, superfice reticulatis, pedunculis axillarib. unifloris corollis revolutis, 4-partitis, staminibus 8, Germine infero bacca pyriforme coccinea quadriloculari: Cypripedium calceolaria duae species, Veratrum viride (on the hills), album; Melanthium . . . Veratrum luteum dans les Ruisseaux; Spiraea (paniculata) trifoliata; Robinia pseudo-acacia, vicosa, hispida: Monarda coccinea, dans les ruiss. fistulosa; Quercus prinus-glauca . . .

ASA GRAY (1810–1888) was born in New York and became one of the greatest botanists of the nineteenth century. Gray received his M.D. at the age of twenty-one, and by that time he was already a dedicated botanist. Author of more than 350 books, monographs, and papers on botany, Gray became professor of natural history at Harvard in 1879. He was a founder of the National Academy of Arts and Sciences and served as president of the American Academy of Arts and Sciences, president of the American Association for the Advancement of Science, and regent of the Smithsonian Institute. Gray travelled widely in the United States and Europe, trained many distinguished botanists, and corresponded with scientists around the world. Charles Darwin wrote Gray his famous letter outlining his theory of evolution on 5 September 1857, and Gray would come to embrace the theory.

Gray's trip to North Carolina in 1841 with John Carey and James Constable came early in a distinguished career. Since the late colonial era, botanists had travelled to the North Carolina mountains to study the incredible diversity in plant life. Gray, however, was the first to explore the mountains in Ashe County.

Selection from
"Notes of a Botanical Excursion to the Mountains of North Carolina"

by Asa Gray

*W*e botanized for several days upon the mountains in the immediate neighborhood of Jefferson, especially the *Negro Mountain*, which rises abruptly on one side of the village, the *Phoenix Mountain*, a sharp ridge on the other side, and the *Bluff*, a few miles distant in a westerly direction. The altitude of the former is probably between four and five thousand feet above the sea; the latter is apparently somewhat higher. They are all composed of mica-slate; and we should remark, that we entered upon a primitive region immediately upon leaving the Valley of Virginia. The mountainsides, though steep or precipitous, are covered with a rich and deep

Reprinted from "Notes of a Botanical Excursion to the Mountains of North Carolina, &c; with some remarks on the Botany of the higher Alleghany Mountains," by Asa Gray. *The American Journal of Science* 42 (1841): 1-48.

vegetable mould, and are heavily timbered, chiefly with chestnut, white oak, the tulip-tree, the cucumber-tree, and sometimes the sugar-maple. Their vegetation presents so little diversity, that it is for the most part unnecessary to distinguish particular localities. Besides many of the plants already mentioned, and a very considerable number of northern species which we have not room to enumerate, we collected or observed on the mountain-sides, *Clematis Viorna* [Leather Flower] in great abundance; *Tradescantia Virginica* [Spiderwort]; *Iris cristata* [Dwarf Iris] in fruit; *Hedyotis (Amphiotis) purpurea* [Bluets], which scarcely deserves the name, since the flowers are commonly almost white; *Phlox paniculata* ? [Garden Phlox] *Aristolochia Sipho* [Birthwort Family], without flowers or fruit; *Ribes Cynosbati, rotundifolium, Michx.*, (R. *triflorum, Willd.*) and *prostatum, L'Her.;* *Allium cernuum* [Wild Onion], and *tricoccum* [Wild Leek]; *Galax aphylla* [Galax]; *Ligusticum actoeifolium* [Lovage], the strong-scented roots of which are eagerly sought and eaten by boys and hogs; the *Ginseng,* here called *sang,* (the roots of which are largely collected, and sold to the country merchants, when fresh for about twelve cents per pound, or when dried for triple that price;) *Menziesia globularis,* mostly in fruit; and the showy *Azalea calendulacea,* which was also out of flower, except in deep shade. . . .

In damp, very shady places high up the *Negro Mountain,* we saw an *Aconitum* [Monkshood] not yet in flower; and on moist rocks near the summit, obtained a few fruiting specimens of a *Saxifraga* [Saxifrage] which was entirely new to us. In a single, very secluded spot on the north side of this mountain, not far from the summit, the rocks were covered with a beautiful small Fern, which proves to be the *Asplenium Adiantum-nigrum* of Michaux, the *A. montanum,* Willd., an extremely rare plant. It is certainly distinct from the *A. Adiantum-nigrum;* being not only a much smaller and more delicate species, (two to four inches high,) but the fronds are narrower, the pinnae ovate and much shorter, 3-5 parted, with the pinnulae toothed or incised at the apex.

The *Veratrum parviflorum, Michx.* [False Hellebore], is of frequent occurrence throughout this region, but was not yet fully in flower, so that our specimens were not collected until near the end of July. . . .

The next day (July 9th) we ascended the *Grandfather*, the highest as well as the most rugged and savage mountain we had yet attempted; although by no means the most elevated in North Carolina, as has generally been supposed. It is a sharp and craggy ridge, lying within Ashe and Burke Counties, very near the northeast corner of Yancey, and cutting across the chain to which it belongs (the *Blue Ridge*) nearly at right angles. It is entirely covered with trees, except where the rocks are absolutely perpendicular; and towards the summit, the Balsam Fir of these mountains, *Abies balsamifera*, partly, of Michaux's Flora (but not of the younger Michaux's Sylva) the *A. Fraseri, Pursh*, [Fraser's Fir] prevails, accompanied by the *Abies nigra* or Black Spruce. The earth, rocks, and prostrate decaying trunks, in the shade of these trees, are carpeted with Mosses and Lichens; and the whole presents the most perfect resemblance to the dark and sombre forests of the northern parts of New York and Vermont, except that the trees are here much smaller. The resemblance extends to the whole vegetation; and a list of the shrubs and herbaceous plants of this mountain would be found to include a large portion of the common plants of the extreme Northern States and Canada. Indeed the vegetation is essentially Canadian, with a considerable number of peculiar species intermixed. Under the guidance of Mr. Levi Moody, we followed the Watauga, here a mere creek, for four or five miles along the base of the Grandfather, until we reached a ridge which promised a comparatively easy ascent. In the rich soil of this ridge, at an elevation of about four hundred feet above the Watauga, we found one of the plants which of all others we were desirous of obtaining, viz., *Carex Fraseriana*. Mr. Curtis had made diligent but ineffectual search for this most singular and rarest of Carices, along the "Catawba near Morganton," and "near Table Mountain. . . ."

Our next excursion was to *Roan Mountain*, a portion of the elevated range which forms the boundary between North Carolina and Tennessee, distant nearly thirty miles southwest from our quarters at the foot of Grandfather by the most direct path, but at least sixty by the nearest carriage road. We travelled for the most part on foot, loading the horses with our portfolios, paper, and some necessary luggage, crossed the *Hanging-rock* Mountain to Elk Creek, and thence over a steep ridge to Cranberry Forge, on the sources of Doe River, where we passed the night. On our way, we cut down a *Service-tree*, (as the *Amelanchier Canadensis* is here called,) and feasted upon the ripe fruit, which throughout this region is highly, and indeed justly prized, being sweet with a very agreeable flavor; while in the Northern States, so far as our experience goes, this fruit, even if it may be said to be edible, is not worth eating. As 'Sarvices' are here greedily sought after, and are generally procured by cutting down the trees, the latter are becoming scarce in the vicinity of the 'plantations,' as the mountain settlements are universally called. . . .

We ascended the north side of the *Roan*, through the heavy timbered woods and rank herbage with which it is covered; but found nothing new to us, excepting *Streplopus lanuginosus*, in fruit; and among the groves of *Rhododendron maximum* towards the summit, we also collected *Diphyscium foliosum*, a moss which we had not before seen in a living state. In more open moist places near the summit, we found the *Hedyotis (Houstonia) serpyllifolia*, still beautifully in flower, and the *Geum geniculatum* [Avens], which we have already noticed. It was just sunset when we reached the bald and grassy summit of this noble mountain, and after enjoying for a moment the magnificent view it affords, had barely time to prepare our encampment between two dense clumps of *Rhododendron Catawbiense*, to collect fuel, and make ready our supper. The night was so fine that our slight shelter of Balsam boughs proved amply sufficient; the thermometer, at this elevation of about six thousand feet above the level of the sea, being 64 Fahr. at midnight, and 60 at sunrise. The temperature of a spring just under the brow of the mountain below our encampment we found to be 47 Fahr.

PAUL BRANDON BARRINGER (1857–1941) was born near Concord in Cabarrus County, North Carolina, to a family of distinguished clergymen, statesmen, and soldiers. As a precocious eight-year-old, Barringer had a remarkable adventure with the great naturalist, John Bachman. Bachman was forced to go into temporary hiding to avoid capture by a Union raiding party in 1865, and Barringer accompanied him. Barringer's recollection of this event, which appeared in a book titled *The Natural Bent*, is a touching portrait of a great naturalist and his young, spellbound pupil.

John Bachman (1790–1874), a Lutheran clergyman, was born in New York but adopted Charleston, South Carolina, as his home. A naturalist since youth, Bachman befriended John J. Audubon during the latter's trip to South Carolina in 1831. Bachman wrote most of the text and edited his collaborative work with Audubon, *The Viviparous Quadrupeds of North America*, which was published in three volumes (1845–1849). Paul Brandon Barringer went on to become an outstanding physician and educator. He was a professor at the University of Virginia School of Medicine and served as president of Virginia A & M (later Virginia Polytechnic Institute).

Selection from
THE NATURAL BENT

by Paul B. Barringer

*A*bout 1865 we had a visit from Dr. John Bachman, the pastor of St. John's Lutheran Church in Charleston, South Carolina. No human life was ever more influential in shaping another's than his was in shaping mine. My Uncle Victor was a philosopher, lawyer, and linguist, but he had no scientific training and did not have much of the scientific method of approach in observation and record. This I love, and old Bachman gave me my first taste of it. He was a philosopher, botanist, zoologist, and astronomer whom chance had condemned to the ministry. Nevertheless, he fitted the functions of the latter ideally, because he was a man of extreme reverence for that great Power that shaped heaven and earth. He was full of the

Reprinted from *The Natural Bent*, by Paul Barringer. Chapel Hill: The University of North Carolina Press, 1937. Used by permission of Anne Barringer Spaeth.

milk of human kindness, but in his life the ministry was submerged.

He was basically a naturalist. He wrote *The Viviparous Quadru-peds of North America* in collaboration with John J. Audubon, the great ornithologist. Two of Bachman's daughters married two of Audubon's sons and contributed their talents and training to the rendering of many of the illustrations in that great work, especially in the drawing and coloring of flowers. The old doctor seems to have been the personal friend of almost every living biologist and had, at the age of sixteen, met Humboldt on his trip to America. Thanks to this acquaintance and to a later friendship with the Earl of Derby, the great patron of science, Dr. Bachman was elected Foreign Correspondent for the Zoological Society of London. When I knew him, he must have been about seventy-five years old, having been born in 1790. I had no fear of old men, so common in children of that day, and as a result I became very intimate with many of them to my lasting benefit.

Like so many Charlestonians, old Bachman went to the mountains of western North Carolina in the summer. There he and his family knew my stepmother in her youth. In the spring of 1865, when visiting the Victor Barringers, he learned by "grapevine" telegraph that the Union General Stoneman, who was then raiding in North Carolina, had heard that he was in Concord and was detaching a scouting party to pick him up.

Dr. Bachman was originally from Rheinbeck, New York, on the Hudson and had come south because of his health. He had an influential and devoted congregation in Charleston and in November of 1860 had delivered a heartily received sermon on Love of Country which was the next duty to Love of God. "If," he said, "our rights had been protected in the Union, we would not desire a political change, but . . . those pledges had been violated and a mightier law than the Constitution substituted. It is better like Abraham and Lot, to separate, when we can no longer live in peace."

I have been told that when the legislative convention was meeting and found themselves by chance without a minister to open the proceedings with prayer, Dr. Bachman, passing on the street, was called in. Whatever the circumstances, when South Carolina passed the Ordinance of Secession, Dr. Bachman gave it God's blessing. For this reason he was a marked man with a price upon his head. To escape the danger from Stoneman's party, my Uncle Victor assigned to him a trusted Negro who was a good cook, a mule, provisions, bedding, and myself, delighted to go as companion and messenger. And we went, so to speak, underground. A small boy would be less suspect than an adult as means of communication, and I was perfectly capable of covering the country on my own. We left in the night, going down into a canebrake on Aunt Lydia Harris's farm, where we stayed for over a week, reports from the outside coming in every other day. The nights are cold in early spring, and the tent was so small that we solved several problems by my sleeping on the foot of his cot.

I had an enchanting companion. He taught me the five thrushes that were common there; the mocking bird, the catbird, the robin, wood thrush, and thrasher. He taught me to recognise [*sic*] six woodpeckers by name: the great woodpecker (now disappeared), the redhead, the yellow-hammer, the sap-sucker, the hairy, and the downy. One day he found a stray garter snake (Utania), and the Negro later dug into a pit of snakes, emerging from their winter torpor. He taught me the difference between the venomous and nonvenomous snakes, showing the marks of the pit vipers, not only the pit between the nostril and eyes of the rattlesnake, copperhead, and water moccasin, but the undivided postanal caudal plate. He explained how this solid plate is necessary for any snake that springs and strikes. They must have a solid grip on the ground with the ventral face of their tails. The nonvenomous do not need this.

At last we heard that a Confederate, General Wheeler, was in

Concord instead of the feared Stoneman and that it was safe to return. That night he gave me a lesson out of his old wisdom that has been one of the greatest pleasures of my later years.

He said, "Son, now I will show you the stars. Look at that sky. That great star is Arcturus, to your right is Spica, and to the left is Ursa Major. The time will come when you cannot chase birds and butterflies, or hunt snakes and rabbits. But, if you will learn the stars, you can sit always at the door of your tent, and they will come to you nightly and return at the same time every year, old friends that will never fail."

JOHN MUIR (1838–1914), naturalist and founder of the modern conservation movement, was born in Scotland and moved to the United States at the age of ten. After attending the University of Wisconsin and studying chemistry, geology, and botany, Muir began trekking through the Midwest and Canada. He worked in a wagon factory in Indianapolis until he received an occupational injury in 1867. In that year, he began walking from Indiana to the Gulf of Mexico. The selection below is from the North Carolina portion of that trip.

Raised by a physically abusive, evangelical Christian father, Muir's own religious beliefs pervaded his understanding of nature. Some have described him as a transcendentalist, but perhaps more accurately, he was an unorthodox Christian who found God revealed in nature.

After marrying in 1880, Muir became a successful fruit grower, raised a family, and made a fortune. From 1891 onward, he increasingly abandoned conventional life to be with nature. Muir was interested in all natural phenomena, but especially forests and glaciers. A gifted writer of numerous books and articles, Muir initiated the conservation movement through his persuasive pen. His writing attracted other progressives, including Theodore Roosevelt, who camped with him in 1903 in Yosemite National Forest. Muir was a fellow of the American Association for the Advancement of Science and a member of the American Academy of Arts and Sciences.

DOCUMENT 9

Selection from
A THOUSAND-MILE WALK
TO THE GULF

by John Muir

*T*his is the most primitive country I have seen, primitive in everything. The remotest hidden parts of Wisconsin are far in advance of the mountain regions of Tennessee and North Carolina. But my host speaks of the "old-fashioned unenlightened times," like a philosopher in the best light of civilization. "I believe in Providence," said he. "Our fathers came into these valleys, got the richest of them, and skimmed off the cream of the soil. The worn-out ground won't yield no roastin' ears now. But the Lord foresaw this state of affairs, and prepared something else for us. And what is it? Why, He meant us to bust open these copper mines and gold mines, so that

Reprinted from *A Thousand-Mile Walk to the Gulf*, by John Muir [1867]. Boston and New York: Houghton Mifflin Company, 1981.

we may have money to buy the corn that we cannot raise." A most profound observation.

September 18. Up the mountain on the state line. The scenery is far grander than any I ever before beheld. The view extends from the Cumberland Mountains on the north far into Georgia and North Carolina to the south, an area of about five thousand square miles. Such an ocean of wooded, waving, swelling mountain beauty and grandeur is not to be described. Countless forest-clad hills, side by side in rows and groups, seemed to be enjoying the rich sunshine and remaining motionless only because they were so eagerly absorbing it. All were united by curves and slopes of inimitable softness and beauty. Oh, these forest gardens of our Father! What perfection, what divinity, in their architecture! What simplicity and mysterious complexity of detail! Who shall read the teaching of these sylvan pages, the glad brotherhood of rills that sing in the valleys, and all the happy creatures that dwell in them under the tender keeping of a Father's care.

September 19. Received another solemn warning of dangers on my way through the mountains. Was told by my worthy entertainer of a wondrous gap in the mountains which he advised me to see. "It is called Track Gap," said he, "from the great number of tracks in the rocks—bird tracks, bar tracks, hoss tracks, men tracks, all in the solid rock as if it had been mud." Bidding farewell to my worthy mountaineer and all his comfortable wonders, I pursued my way to the South. . . . Most of the food in this house was coffee without sugar, corn bread, and sometimes bacon. But the coffee was the greatest luxury which these people knew. The only way of obtaining it was by selling skins, or, in particular, "sang," that is ginseng, which found a market in far-off China.

My path all to-day led me along the leafy banks of the Hiwassee, a most impressive mountain river. Its channel is very rough, as it crosses the edges of upturned rock strata, some of them standing at right angles, or glancing off obliquely to right and left. Thus a multitude of short, resounding cataracts are produced, and the river is restrained from the headlong speed due to its volume and the inclination of its bed.

All the larger streams of uncultivated countries are mysteriously charming and beautiful, whether flowing in mountains or through swamps and plains. Their channels are interestingly sculptured, far more so than the grandest architectural works of man. The finest of the forests are usually found along their banks, and in the multitude of falls and rapids the wilderness finds a voice. Such a river is the Hiwassee, with its surface broken to a thousand sparkling gems, and its forest walls vine-draped and flowery as Eden. And how fine the songs it sings! . . .

September 20. All day among the groves and gorges of Murphy with Mr. Beale. Was shown the site of Camp Butler where General Scott had his headquarters when he removed the Cherokee Indians to a new home in the West. Found a number of rare and strange plants on the rocky banks of the river Hiwassee. In the afternoon, from the summit of a commanding ridge, I obtained a magnificent view of blue, softly curved mountain scenery. Among the trees I saw *Ilex* [Holly] for the first time.

WILLIAM BREWSTER (1851–1919) was born in Wakefield, Massachusetts. He became a leader in Boston's postbellum scientific circles as a founder and president of the American Ornithologists Union and by serving as the curator of ornithology at Harvard University's Museum of Comparative Zoology for nearly forty-five years. By 1881 he was recognized as the leading authority in the country on birds. During his lifetime, he wrote more than 250 scientific papers and many books on birds and related subjects, and he obtained the finest collection of American birds in the United States.

In 1885 Brewster explored the mountains of North Carolina, with a special interest in studying whether northern species nested in the area. As fine as Brewster's notes on bird life were, his descriptions of the virgin forests convey a wonderful, lost world. The following is nearly the complete journal from Brewster's trip.

Selection from

"WILLIAM BREWSTER'S EXPLORATION OF THE SOUTHERN APPALACHIAN MOUNTAINS: THE JOURNAL OF 1885"

by William Brewster

OLD FORT, N.C. TO ASHVILLE, N.C.

[1885,] May 23 At 6 A.M. found ourselves at Old Fort near the head waters of the Catawba River and directly at the foot of the mountains. There we were detained several hours by an accident to a freight train that preceded us. With the Childs Bros. I walked up the track about a mile to the wrecked train and returned on it when it was repaired. The valley was picturesque and beautiful but neither fine nor grand. On the steep, rhododendron-clad hillsides that walled in the stream birds were very numerous and as a dense morning fog rolled away or dissolved under the influence of the

Reprinted from "William Brewster's Exploration of the Southern Appalachian Mountains: The Journal of 1885," by William Brewster. Marcus B. Simpson, Jr., ed. *The North Carolina Historical Review* 57 (January 1980): 43-77. Used by permission.

sun's rays the air rang with their music. I noted thirty-seven species in all, most prominent among which were *Icteria virens* [Yellow-breasted Chat], *Harporhynchus rufus* [Brown Thrasher], and *Myiarchus crinitus* [Great Crested Flycatcher] on the mountains sides and *Empidonax acadicus* [Acadian Flycatcher], *Setophaga ruticilla* [American Redstart], and *Vireo noveboracensis* [White-eyed Vireo] along the stream. Also heard a *Dendroica dominica* [Yellow-throated Warbler] sing a dozen or more times in a belt of pines on a ridge. . . .

We reached Ashville about noon and went to the Swannanoa Hotel. The afternoon was spent in unpacking etc. The country about Ashville is an elevated plateau, broken and rolling more or less cultivated but also sparsely wooded with hard woods & a few pines. The views of the distant mountains are very fine especially at the moment of writing this when the range to the southwest is partially wrapped in a snowy belt of clouds, the remnants of a thunder storm that has just passed. From my window I can hear an Indigo Finch chanting near, a Bewick's Wren has been just singing on the roof of a shed, in the distance a Mockingbird is rolling out a medley of sound, a Bluebird (*Sialia*) is uttering its tender carol and Chimney Swifts are careening about overhead precisely as in Charleston, only their numbers are fewer. The songs of the birds here seem to my ear for the most part normal. Nor are any of them more so than that of a Robin singing a[s] blithely and loudly as if this were Massachusetts instead of North Carolina. . . .

ASHVILLE TO WEBSTER

May 25 Monday Alternately cloudy and clear with three heavy showers during the day. Left Ashville at 9 A.M. on the Webster branch of the Western North Carolina Railroad. At Smather's we found a trestle down and the train was delayed there about five hours. During this time (when it was not raining) I rambled along the railroad for a mile or more and made careful notes of the birds seen and heard. The locality is a fertile valley along Hominey Creek. The steep hillsides that wall it in were heavily timbered with hard-woods with a dense undergrowth of rhododendron. Along the edges of these woods black locust and rum cherries were in full bloom and in places glowing bits of orange, scarlet, and yellow marked the position of the beautiful Azalea (*Rhododendron calendulaceum*), now at its perfection. Near the trestle a hillside rose almost vertically to five hundred feet or more above the valley presenting the appearance of a solid wall of green foliage. On the crest of the ridges were scattered pitch pines (*P. inops*) in the valley fine apple orchards. Birds were fairly numerous, along the stream *Mimus carolinensis* [Grey Catbird] and *Dendroica aestiva* [Yellow Warbler] being the characteristic species, on the hillsides *Vireo olivaceus* [Red-eyed Vireo], *Seiurus aurocapillus* [Ovenbird], *Turdus mustelinus* [Wood Thrush] etc.

After the trestle was repaired we started on but four miles farther were again stopped, a trestle 97 ft. high having been demolished by the recent heavy rains. Here we had to cross on foot to the train on the other side. Passing Pigeon River and Waynesville the cars climbed a steep mountain side to Balsam Gap, descending an equally steep slope beyond. The character of the woods changed but little during this ascent and at the highest point we saw none of the northern Conifers except *Pinus strobus* [White Pine] which was growing sparingly in the woods and a few *Abies nigra* [Red Spruce] set out about the houses. The true fir & spruce belt is much higher—or above 5000 ft.

We left the train at Sylva and were driven to Webster, a distance of four miles. Here we passed the night.

The country about Webster is rolling and varied, ridges, either wooded or under cultivation, sloping steeply down to narrow valleys. The timber is chiefly of deciduous trees with a few scrubby hard pines. The land is rather fertile, the soil clay of a deep blood-red color. There are occasional fields of red clover in full bloom. The familiar village birds are Bluebirds, Purple Martins, Bewick's Wrens, Red-eyed Vireo, Yellow Warbler, Carolina Wrens, Indigo Birds, Great-crested Flycatchers etc.

WEBSTER TO FRANKLIN

1885 Tuesday May 26 . . . Clear with heavy showers in P.M. very hot.

Starting about 8 A.M. we were soon on our way to Franklin. The road for the first ten miles followed the course of a stream, now winding with its many turns, now ascending a steep rise to descend again into a narrow valley where the water sped swiftly between alder fringed banks or fumed and raced over rocky shallows.

The soil was red, sticky clay and our horses labored sadly. At length we reached the foot of the Cowee Mts. and for four miles or more the road zig-zagged upward through noble forests of oak, chestnut, black walnut, and tulip trees until we reached Cowee Gap on the crest of the divide. From here there was an equally steep descent most of the way to Franklin, which was reached about 3 P.M.

There was little change in the bird fauna from the foot of the range to the top. There I heard *Dendroeca aestiva* [Yellow Warbler] to 3000 ft. *H. chrysoptera* [Golden-winged Warbler] to 2800 ft., *Icteria virens* [Yellow-breasted Chat] to 2700 ft. One new bird appeared at 2700 ft., however, and rapidly increased in numbers as we climbed upward. This was *Dendroeca blackburnae* [Blackburnian Warbler]. On the crest of the ridge it fairly swarmed in the oak and chestnut timber (there were few evergreens and these hemlocks) the males in full song. I am satisfied that it was already breeding there for the forests were in nearly full leaf. In the country at the base of the mts. *Helminthophaga chrysoptera* [Golden-winged Warbler] was abundant and generally distributed especially in second growth forests of oak, etc.

Late in the afternoon I took a short walk outside the town and shot . . . birds. . . . They were all killed in a sheltered ravine down which flowed a clear stream fringed with rhododendrons. It was a pretty spot with its cool shade, rushing water, and clusters of orange and scarlet azaleas blazing among the dark rhododendrons. There were no mosquitos or flies to annoy us and the memory of this experience will long linger as a peculiarly happy one.

Franklin is a pleasant town with its broad streets overarched with cottonwoods, its distant mountain views, and its generally quiet, not to say sleepy, effect.

FRANKLIN TO HIGHLANDS
1885 Wednesday May 27 . . .
Cloudy with a steady, pouring rain all day, the mountains wrapped in mist.

We left Franklin at 9:30 A.M. and reached Highlands at about 4 P.M. taking lunch by the way in a little unfinished church where we found a secure shelter from the drenching rain. The road for the first six or eight miles followed a winding stream and was comparatively level. Then began the ascent of a steep mountain where, for hours, the horses plodded on at a snail's pace and our party encased in rubber defied the weather as well as possible. We heard few birds of course but when near the summit the rain ceased and the sun came out for a moment and awakened the dormant woodland life into its maximum activity. Then the interest began and every few moments added some unexpected species to my list. The timber on the mountain sides was chiefly deciduous trees, oaks, chestnuts, beeches, and tulip trees predominating, and many of the trees of large size and grand proportions. The ground beneath was mostly entirely free from undergrowth, being burnt over annually to improve the cattle ranges which extend all over these mountains. It was generally so smooth and free from rocks that a horse could have been ridden anywhere without trouble. The foliage up to 2800 ft. was nearly full, above that half out to 3500 ft., where we entered groves of oaks and chestnuts just starting or were perfectly leafless. After a visit to the beautiful Cullasaja Falls, I spent an hour or so collecting in the woods near by. At the Falls I heard the first *Contopus borealis* [Olive-sided Flycatcher]. In the impenetrable rhododendron bordering the river Canada Flycatchers, Wilson's Thrushes, Wood Thrushes, and Black-throated Blue Warblers were singing. In the open hardwood timber above I found *Dend. blackburnae* [Blackburnian Warbler], *D. pennsylv.* [Chestnut-sided Warbler], *Sphyrapicus varius* [Yellow-bellied Sapsucker] (a pair breeding), *Vireo Solitarius* [Solitary Vireo], *Hydemeles ludoviciana* [Rose-breasted Grosbeak], *Contopus virens* [Wood Pewee], etc.

Upon reaching the top of the plateau on which Highlands is situated we saw the first Juncos. As we whirled rapidly along the smooth road through open park-like oak woods, Tanagers, Grosbeaks, and Solitary Vireos were singing on all sides. In the evening Robins were singing everywhere & Hylas peeping in the woods. The scenery during this day's drive was everywhere wild, picturesque, and exceedingly beautiful but nowhere either fine or grand.

HIGHLANDS

1885 May 28 Thursday . . . A.M. clear with cool and rather high wind.

Waking at day break I heard a glorious burst of bird music through the open window of my bed room. *Turdus migratorius* [Eastern Robin], *T. mustelinus* [Wood Thrush], *T. fuscescens* [Veery], *Thryothorus bewicki* [Bewick's Wren], *Spizella pusilla* [Field Sparrow], *Hydemeles ludoviciana* [Rose-breasted Grosbeak], *Cyanospiza cyanea* [Indigo Bunting], *Contopus borealis* [Olive-sided Flycatcher], *C. virens* [Wood Pewee], *Mimus carolinensis* [Grey Catbird], *Icterus baltimore* [Northern Oriole], and *Pipilo erythrophthalmus* [Rufous-sided To-whee] being the most prominent voices.

Immediately after breakfast we started on horseback for Whitesides, a neighboring mountain of about 5000 ft. elevation. The road after leaving the village plunged down a steep slope and entered a superb rhododendron swamp where many of these shrubs attained a height of 25 ft. They grew in such tangled thickets that it was impossible for anything larger than a cat to get through them and their glossy evergreen foliage presented the appearance of a solid wall of dark green, semi-tropical in aspect. They formed the undergrowth of a forest of superb hemlocks, many of which were three or four feet in diameter and seventy or eighty feet high. The ground beneath was a spongy morass carpeted with green moss (Sphagnum?) and rich in beautiful ferns. In this place the characteristic birds were *Turdus fuscescens* [Veery] (hundreds, making the air ring with their music), *T. mustelinus* [Wood Thrush], *Dendroeca caerulescens* [Black-throated Blue Warbler] (hundreds singing incessantly), *D. pennsylvanica* [Chestnut-sided Warbler], *Myiodioctes canadensis* [Canada Warbler], *Siurus moticilla* [Louisiana Waterthrush] (one singing), *Junco hiemalis* [Dark-eyed Junco], *Certhia f. americana* [Brown Creeper] (one), *Sitta canadensis* [Red-breasted Nuthatch] (two), *Dendroeca blackburniae* [Blackburnian Warbler] (singing everywhere in the tops of the hemlocks), and an occasional Jay screaming overhead or a *Hylotomus* [Pileated Woodpecker] uttering its ringing call in the distance.

Passing through this swamp I rode to the top of an oak ridge beyond, a sightly place where the mountain dropped off a thousand feet on the eastern side. In these woods, I found *Sphyrapicus varius* [Yellow-bellied Sapsucker], *Picus villosus* [Hairy Woodpecker], *Colaptes auratus* [Yellow-shafted Flicker] (numerous), *Cyanocitta cristata* [Blue Jay] (abundant), *Cyanospiza cyanea* [Indigo Bunting], *Vireo Solitarius* [Solitary Vireo] (abundant the only vireo), *Hydemeles ludoviciana* [Rose-breasted Grosbeak] (abundant), *Pyranga rubra* [Scarlet Tanager] (several), *Siurus auricapillus* [Ovenbird], *Bonasa umbella* [Ruffed Grouse] (one).

Returned to dinner, rode up Cistoola in the P.M. getting drenched on our return, and in the evening rode out to Mr. Ravenel's to tea.

The town of Highlands is situated on a nearly level plateau elevation about 4000 ft. Woods chiefly oak & chestnut, the trees of gigantic proportions. Streams invariably bordered by dense rhododendron. Trees often *thickly* hung with *Usnea* moss. Swamps carpeted with Sphagnum mosses. Leucothoe in full bloom bordering the thickets & paths.

HIGHLANDS TO EAST PORTE, TUCKASEEGE RIVER

1885 May 29 . . . Leaving Highlands at 9 A.M. we drove to East La Porte which was reached about sunset. The road was an almost continual descent and for about six miles below Hamburg, steep, rocky, and dangerous, barely six inches from the brink of [a] precipice with the Tuckaseegee River roaring and rushing in white foam over the rapids hundreds of feet below. Throughout this stretch the scenery was simply superb, the picturesque river, the vertical forest-clad walls of the canon, and innumerable picturesque falls, rhododendron-clad banks, and grand old woods multiplying the attractions and giving a never ending variety to the landscape. The forests were the finest we have thus far seen. Many of the oaks and tulip trees exceeded five feet in diameter and with their straight column-like trunks and perfectly open ground beneath recalled the forests of the lower Wabash Valley of Illinois.

The event of the day, ornithologically speaking, was the sight of four Ravens, the only ones seen during the trip. The first winged its way across the road passing through the oak woods and finally alighting in a tree. This was at about 4000 ft. The other three were together in the woods a mile or two above Hamburg at about 3500 ft. One ascended high into the air, then descended with half-closed wings. The other two left their perches as we passed and flapped across the valley uttering their hoarse *cr-r-ruck* as they flew. All looked *enormous*.

There was a marked change in the bird fauna at about 3500 ft. where *Contopus borealis* [Olive-sided Flycatcher], *Junco*, *Hydemeles* [Rose-breasted Grosbeak], Vireo solitarius [Solitary Vireo], *Dend. blackburnae* [Blackburnian Warbler], *Myiodioctes canadensis* [Canada Warbler], *Dend. caerulescens* [Black-throated Blue Warbler], and *Certhia* [Brown Creeper] disappeared and the characteristic valley birds took their places.

We halted for the night at Pott's, a rude little tumble down shanty in a lonely valley where we were entertained to the best of our host's ability. At sunset Brown Thrashers, Chats, Cardinals, Field Sparrows, and Bewick's Wrens were singing. After dark a Whipporwill began.

In the Tuckaseegee Notch I noted the roadside Bass-wood (*Tilea americana*), Dutchman's pipe (trailing over the shrubbery and climbing the taller trees), strawberry plant, hemlocks, cucumber magnolia (in flower), Red maple, sugar maple, etc.

EAST LA PORTE TO ASHVILLE
1885 May 30 . . . Clear and the first day without rain.

Leaving Pott's at 7 A.M. we drove to Sylva and took the 11 A.M. train for Ashville which was reached at 3 P.M. The drive was comparatively uninteresting after what we had previously seen but still the level road following the winding of the Tuckaseegee was far from commonplace. Growing at frequent intervals along the banks of the river was a small tree bearing a cloud of white and extremely fragrant blossoms. Parker, our driver, called it the white ash which, of course, it was not despite the fact that its general appearance, aside from its bloom, *was* ash-like. The river at this point was about sixty yards wide, its banks fringed with alders, black willows, sycamores, Leucothoe, water oaks, and persimmons. In these thickets *Dendroeca aestiva* [Yellow Warbler], *Mimus carolinensis* [Grey Catbird], and *Empidonax acadicus* [Acadian Flycatcher] were the most numerous and characteristic species. There were also many Cardinals and occasional Carolina Wren and I heard two *Siurus motacilla* [Louisiana Waterthrush] (elevation about 2250 ft.) We heard at least 12 *H. chrysoptera* [Golden-winged Warbler].

At Sylva I had a spare hour before the train was due so I took a short walk along the track. On a dead tree top over the river were about twenty Cedar Birds [Cedar Waxwing] and nearly as many *Chrysomitris tristis* [American Goldfinch], the latter in full plumage. Ascending a steep hill-side covered with oaks and interspersed with an occasional hard pine I found only *Vireo olivaceus* [Red-eyed Vireo], *Harporhynchus rufus* [Brown Thrasher], *Lophophanes bicolor* [Tufted Titmouse], *Parus caro.* [Carolina Chickadee], *Cardinalis* [Cardinal], and *Thryothorus carolinensis* [Carolina Wren]. I also shot a single *Dendroeca dominica* [Yellow-throated Warbler] which was sitting in the top of a pine preening itself. I heard what I took to be another chirping but could not find it.

Returning to the river thickets I found them tenanted by *Dendroeca aestiva* [Yellow Warbler], *Setophaga ruticilla* [American Redstart], *Vireo olivaceus* [Red-eyed Vireo], *Vireo noveboracensis* [White-eyed Vireo], *Mimus carolinensis* [Grey Catbird], *Turdus mustelinus* [Wood Thrush], and *Empidonax acadicus* [Acadian Flycatcher]. In the neighboring fields *Cyanospiza cyanea* [Indigo Bunting] & *Spizella socialis* [Chipping Sparrow] were singing.

As the train stopped for a moment near Ashville I distinctly heard *Parula americana* [Northern Parula Warbler] singing in some oak woods.

This ended one of the pleasantest expeditions I have ever undertaken.

ASHVILLE TO BLACK MOUNTAIN
1885 June 1 Monday . . . Cloudless, warm, and a beautiful day. Left Ashville at 8 A.M. in a top buggy drawn by a pair of horses,

my destination being the Black Mountain group. For the first twelve miles the road followed the course of the Swannanoa River, a beautiful stream averaging about thirty yards in width, for the most part shallow and rapid, its banks bordered by fine red birches (4 ft. in diameter), sycamores, red maples, black walnuts, red oaks, water oaks, etc. with an undergrowth of alders. The larger trees grew out over the water, their tops and branches often meeting and interlacing with those on the opposite banks forming an arch of foliage beneath which the river flowed smoothly and silently in places, in others rushed noisily over ledges or rippled musicly down the pebbly shallows. The river valley at large was mostly cleared and under cultivation; hence, with the exception of an occasional Quail whistling in the fields of tall oats or a Cat Bird or Maryland Yellow-throat singing in some fence corner, most of the birds were confined to the timber along the stream. In this cover they were numerous. The most abundant and characteristic species were *Vireo olivaceus* [Red-eyed Vireo], *V. gilvus* [Warbling Vireo] (dozens heard in the tops of the sycamores), *Dendroeca aestiva* [Yellow Warbler], *Vireo noveboracensis* [White-eyed Vireo] (several), *Icteria virens* [Yellow-breasted Chat], *Icterus spurius* [Orchard Oriole] (abundant), *I. baltimore* [Northern Oriole] (a few), *Contopus virens* [Wood Pewee], *Tyrannus carolinensis* [Eastern Kingbird], *Myiarchus* [Great Crested Flycatcher], *Empidonax acadicus* [Acadian Flycatcher] (abundant), *E. minimus* [Least Flycatcher] (one singing on the banks of the river), *Cyanospiza cyanea* [Indigo Bunting], *Cardinalis* [Cardinal], *Setophaga ruticilla* [American Redstart] (one only), *Parus carolinensis* [Carolina Chickadee], *Mimus carolinensis* [Grey Catbird], *Trochilus colubris* [Ruby-throated Hummingbird], *Dendroeca pennsylvanica* [Chestnut-sided Warbler] (one), *Zenaidura* [Mourning Dove], *Stelgidopteryx* [Rough-winged Swallow], *Corvus am.* [Common Crow], *Spizella pusilla et socialis* [Field Sparrow and Chipping Sparrow] and *Turdus mustelinus* [Wood Thrush]. . . .

I reached Glass's at the end of the road and the foot of the mountain at 1 P.M. after a drive of twenty miles.

After dinner at Wm Glass's I started up the mountain with John Glass as guide, a young man, furnished by the stable keeper in Asheville to look after the horses, accompanying us. My companions were on foot while I rode an old mare which was closely followed during the entire trip by her kicking colt, a pretty little creature only a few weeks old, but, of course, a great nuisance.

For the first two miles the path—a smooth and very good trail—ascended very gradually still following the banks of the Swannanoa here, near its source, a rapid mountain stream, cold, as clear as air, and flowing between steep banks fringed with impenetrable rhododendrons, now plunging in a succession of cascades over jagged ledges, now sweeping swiftly but silently between green banks of foliage and anon settling to rest in quiet pools where the water spiders played in the sunshine and speckled trout lurked in every shadow. A few rods back from the stream but within sound of its musical clamor the rhododendrons ceased (they grow only in moist places or near water) and the open hardwood forest stretched away as far as the eye could reach, the ground open, smooth, and perfectly free from undergrowth, with scanty tufts of coarse wild grass or occasional ferns and numerous decaying logs forming the only obstructions. Everywhere it was densely shaded by the canopy of foliage supported, a hundred feet or more overhead, by the sturdy shafts of the oaks, hickories, chestnuts, tulip trees, beeches, sugar maples, and black walnuts. Many of these trees were six or seven feet in diameter at the base and their trunks often rose perfectly smooth and straight to at least fifty feet before reaching the first branch. I saw some that must have been at least 125 ft. high. They stood usually about one hundred feet apart and altogether formed the finest forest I have ever seen east of the Wabash River.

After the path began in earnest to climb the mountain side, we toiled upward for nearly two miles further without noting any change in this superb woods. The first spruces occurred at an altitude of 4050 ft. and a hundred feet higher they became freely intermingled with the hardwoods which rapidly deteriorated in size and entirely ceased or rather gave way to different species at 5050 ft. Long before reaching this elevation there was a marked change in the bird fauna. It began at about 3200 ft. with the admixture of one or two Alleghanian forms and at 4000 ft. became nearly pure Alleghanian, stretching from this altitude to about 5000 ft., when it changed even more markedly and very abruptly to Canadian. The change from Carolinian (the valley fauna) to Alleghanian was not accompanied by any (to me) appreciable floral change but the Canadian fauna began sharply and abruptly with the lower edge of the solid spruce belt or at 5050 ft. Below this a few semi-Canadian species straggled with the straggling spruces down to perhaps 4300; above it I noted only one Carolinian form (*Parus carolinensis*) [Carolina Chickadee]) at about 5100 ft. I saw the first balsams at 5050 ft. the first *Sciurus hudsonicus* [Red Squirrel] at 4200 ft. Altogether the faunal belts on this mountain were more sharply & clearly defined than I have ever seen them elsewhere.

We reached our camping ground about an hour before sunset after a terribly steep, hard pull for the last two miles. In one place the trail crossed a narrow ledge with a sheer fall of several hundred feet on one side and a vertical wall on the other. At the very worst point my mare slipped and fell but fortunately lay still until I disentangled myself and got her by the head. For much of this distance the path had been scooped out by water and was nothing but [a] narrow trench filled with loose, rolling stones. On the whole, however, it was better and smoother than most bridle paths among our New England hills.

After unsaddling my horse and turning her loose to graze, I started to explore the vicinity of our camp. It proved [to be] a long narrow plateau about one hundred yards wide at one end, narrowing at the other to less than ten yards, where it became a ridge that stretched for half a mile or more to the southward. On the eastern side it broke off abruptly sloping nearly as steeply as the roof of a house down to the valley of the Swannanoa blue and misty in the distance below; on the western the land rose more gradually but still sharply to the highest regular ridge of "the Black." Below the forest of hardwoods already described lay spread out like a carpet only a few scattering spruces rearing their dark spires amid the sea of light green foliage. Above them was simply one solid continuous belt of black growth, chiefly *Abies nigra* [Red Spruce], with only occasional patches of lighter green marking the presence of Yellow birches. This plateau was for the most part clear (there had once been a sort of half-way station there and a rude house, now in ruins, was a favorite summer resort before the war) and down its center stretched a broad strip of emerald turf sprinkled with the blossoms of the white clover but everywhere about the edges black spruces & balsams grew in dense clusters with sunny opening between precisely as they grow on elevated pasture edges in northern Maine and New Hampshire. Among them were scattered a few stunted hawthorns, tupelos, buckeyes, and an occasional small oak. They would have doubtless occupied the whole of the neglected opening years ago had it not been for the half-wild mountain cattle whose bells tingled musically as they sought shelter in the forest at the first noise of our approach.

About the edges of this lovely spot Ruffed Grouse were drumming and Quail whistling on all sides. I shot three Quail among the spruces killing all on the ground and a pair at one shot, a sad piece of vandalism [?] but I wanted their skins as well as their bodies, which we cooked for supper. Robins and Wilson's Thrushes were also exceedingly numerous and I heard several *Dendroeca virens* [Black-throated Green Warbler] and *Sitta canadensis* [Red-breasted

Nuthatch] both for the first time in this region. Juncos literally swarmed about the clearing and a *Chrysomitris tristis* [American Goldfinch] was singing in the top of a yellow birch. From the hardwood forest below came faintly the song of *Turdus mustelinus* [Wood Thrush], *Pyranga rubra* [Scarlet Tanager], *Siurus auricapillus* [Ovenbird], & *Vireo solitarius* [Solitary Vireo]. Finally the sun set and as the twilight gathered in the valley below and gradually enveloped the higher slopes and ridges there was a grand chorus of Robins, Wilson's Thrushes, and Snowbirds for a brief space. Then the stars began to glimmer and twinkle in the steel blue vault above, a wolf howled dismally on the ridge above and night closed over the scene as we wrapped ourselves in our blankets and made our preparations for the night.

BLACK MOUNTAINS
1885 Tuesday June 2 . . . Clear and a perfect day.
4 to 5 A.M. Awakening at 4 A.M. I found that the eastern horizon was beginning to flush while overhead the moon gleamed like a piece of silver in the clear but still dusky heaven. A Robin piped a few notes sleepily and doubtfully, another joined in more boldly; then came a grand burst of song from the Robins with next the trilling of a Junco and finally a full chorus of Robins and Juncos lasting for the next half hour. During this time the western slopes of the mountains continued dusky, the great gulf below wrapped in mist, only the crest of the ridge to the eastward being touched by the morning light. At 4:30 the first Wilson's Thrush joined the chorus then another lower down the mountain began its song. The keen, almost frosty wind swept past over the mountain side chilling me as I listened, drowning some of the bird voices, bringing others from ridges far away.

5 A.M. Up to this time only the three species just mentioned were heard. The light over the eastern ridge had gradually become

stronger bringing out details of trees, rocks, and the outline of neighboring ridges, but the great gulf or "cove" below was still wrapped in gloom, the distant low country and mountains in pale bluish haze. A Quail now joined its cheery voice to the general chorus from the edges of the neighboring spruces, *Dendroeca virens* [Black-throated Green Warbler] began singing on all sides and the commonplace but sweet notes of *Chrysomitris tristis* [American Goldfinch] swelled the general volume of sound. These were all the species constituting this simple but effective choir. Doubtless there would have been others had the morning been less cold and windy. (Notes taken while lying wrapped in my blanket before arising.)

Leaving the camp at 5 A.M. I spent the following two hours in the immediate neighborhood. Birds were fairly numerous but exceedingly shy while the density of the evergreens rendered it most difficult to get shots at them. Moreover nearly every bird shot in the spruces lodged where it could be obtained only at the cost of a hard climb.

Upon exploring the mountain side for about half a mile above the camp I found the woods mainly composed of *Abies nigra* [Red Spruce] with a few *A. fraseri* [Fraser Fir] and a plentiful sprinkling of yellow birches. The mountain side was steep, the ground densely carpeted with yellowish-green sphagnum mosses. In these woods, *Dendroeca virens* [Black-throated Green Warbler], *Sitta canadensis* [Red-breasted Nuthatch], & *Junco hiemalis* [Dark-eyed Junco] were abundant; *Myiodioctes canadensis* [Canada Warbler], *Parus atricapillus* [Black-capped Chickadee], and *Bonasa umbella* [Ruffed Grouse], common; I also heard one *Anorthura hiemalis* [Winter Wren], several *Chrysomitris tristis* [American Goldfinch], two *Ch. pinus* [Pine Siskin], and three flocks of crossbills (*Loxia americana*) [Red Crossbill]. Near the clearing I saw *Trochilus colubris* [Ruby-throated Hummingbird] (one), *Vireo solitarius* [Solitary Vireo] (one), and several Chimney Swifts scaling over the woods. Red Squirrels were here abundant,

snickering on all sides precisely as in our northern wood. *Tamias striata* [Eastern Chipmunk] was also present but much less numerous than in the hardwood timber lower down. There were many butterflies chiefly *Papilio turnus* [Tiger Swallowtail] and *P. asterius* (?) [Black Swallowtail], but all belonging to familiar Massachusetts species. I half expected to find the white banded species so common in the White Mts. but it was apparently absent.

Returning to camp and eating a hurried breakfast, I saddled my mare and was soon on the way to the summit. For about a mile and a half the path wound its way upward usually in zig-zags after the usual fashion of trails in this region. It was walled in by young firs and spruces while the larger trees of the same species cast a dense, gloomy shade rarely penetrated by a shaft of sunlight. The air was cool, damp and bracing, the woods somber and for the most part silent, for birds as a rule were few and far between here. The characteristic species proved to be *Junco hiemalis* [Dark-eyed Junco], *Sitta canadensis* [Red-breasted Nuthatch], *Anorthura hiemalis* [Winter Wren], all abundant; *Parus atricapillus* [Black-capped Chickadee], *Certhia americana* [Brown Creeper], and *Dendroeca virens* [Black-throated Green Warbler], common; *Myiodioctes canadensis* [Canada Warbler], two males; *Turdus migratorius* [Robin], one at 5700 ft; Picus villosus [Hairy Woodpecker], one at 5600 ft.

Upon reaching the summit I found myself on a long narrow ridge stretching miles away on a nearly perfect level and rarely more than twenty yards in width. On this ridge rise several peaks elevated from four to six hundred feet above the general elevation of the ridge, which is close on 6000 ft. (my barometer made it 5950 ft.) For the last half mile I noticed a gradual deterioration in the size of the firs and spruces and on the summit of the ridge they were very appreciably stunted, none being over forty feet high and twelve inches in diameter. Black spruces predominated with however a larger admixture of balsams than was seen elsewhere. There were also many yellow birches and an occasional rhododendron. Many of the trees were dead and bleached, in places standing in grim groups, in others prostrate and heaped on one another in tangled masses, with vigorous young saplings growing up to conceal the ruin beneath. The ground was rough and rocky but rocks, boulders, logs, and crevices were alike carpeted with the yellowish-green sphagnum soaked with water by the recent rains. Save for the presence of an occasional rhododendron these woods were precisely similar in appearance to those opposite the Half-way House on Mt. Washington. They were inhabited by similar birds also although bird life was less abundant here and the species found represented by but few individuals. There on the crest of the ridge I noted only a few Juncos, three *Parus atricapillus* [Black-capped Chickadee], one *Anorthura* [Winter Wren], one *Myiodioctes canadensis* [Canada Warbler], one Certhia [Brown Creeper], and a number of *Sitta canadensis* [Red-breasted Nuthatch]. A small *Buteo* which I identified as *Buteo pennsylvanicus* [Broad-winged Hawk] was also seen sailing overhead. At this altitude there was but one bird which would not be met with in northern New England viz *Cathartes aura* [Turkey Vulture] which was often in sight sweeping on easy wing high over the crowning peaks of the range. Both the Wild Turkey and Quail are also said to occur numerously over the entire range.

Of mammals we saw nothing besides the two Squirrels but I found the track of a large buck in the moss on the ridge and my guide pointed out the foot print of a small bear (probably a cub only a few days old) in the mud of the path. The Canada Lynx (called Catamount here) is said to be found sparingly on the higher mountains where it replaces *Lynx rufus* [Bobcat] of the valleys. The Puma also ranges over all the mountains but is rare.

At about 10 A.M. we started down the mountain. . . . We reached Wm Glass's at noon and after dining started for Asheville where we arrived about six o'clock. The return drive down the valley of the

Swannanoa was charming for the river was at its loveliest in the clear afternoon light and long shadows from the mountains stretched over the fields of grain and the emerald meadows bordering the stream. The birds were singing freely and there was a delicious ripe, mellow quality in the air such as we occasionally notice in New England in October. Altogether it was a fair picture—such a picture in fact as no one fond of nature could look on without a keen sense of enjoyment. It was a fitting close of a delightful and successful trip for with this day ended my season in North Carolina.

BRADFORD TORREY (1843–1912), ornithologist and nature writer, was born in Weymouth, Massachusetts. Torrey was not trained as a scientist, but as an adult in Boston, he became interested in bird watching. He published his first article on the subject in 1883. Altogether he published ten books of nature writing intended for a popular audience, mostly consisting of essays that described his nature travels.

The following excerpts appeared in Torrey's book, *A World of Green Hills: Observation of Nature and Human Nature in the Blue Ridge*. As these excerpts suggest, Torrey was interested in plants as well as birds. The setting is Highlands, North Carolina, and the surrounding environs just before the turn of the century. The text shows that Torrey was well aware of the earlier visit of William Brewster to the same region.

Selection from
A WORLD OF GREEN HILLS:
OBSERVATION OF NATURE AND HUMAN
NATURE IN THE BLUE RIDGE

by Bradford Torrey

*A*t Highlands the birds were a mixed lot, Southerners and Northerners delightfully jumbled: a few Carolina wrens (one was heard whistling from the summit of Whiteside [Mountain]!); a single Bewick wren, singing and dodging along a fence in the heart of the village; tufted titmice; Carolina chickadees; Louisiana water thrushes and turkey buzzards: and on the other side of the account, brown creepers, red-bellied nuthatches, black-throated blues, Canada warblers, Blackburnians, snow-birds, and olive-sided flycatchers.

An unexpected thing was the commonness of blue golden-

Reprinted from *A World of Green Hills: Observations of Nature and Human Nature in the Blue Ridge*, by Bradford Torrey. Boston and New York: Houghton, Mifflin and Company, 1898.

winged warblers, chats, and brown thrashers (the chats less common than the other two) at an elevation of 3800 feet. Still more numerous, in song continually, even on the summit of Satulah, were the chestnut-sided warblers, although Mr. Brewster, in his tour through the region, "rarely saw more than one or two in any single day:" a third instance, as seemed likely, of a species that had taken advantage of new local conditions,—an increase of shrubby clearings, in the present case—within the last ten years. Here, as everywhere, the presence of some birds and the absence of others were provocative of questions. Why should the Kentucky warbler sing from rhododendron thickets halfway up the slope at the head of Horse Cove, and never be tempted into other thickets, in all respects like them, just over the brow of the cliff, 500 feet higher? Why should the summer yellow-bird, which pushes its hardy spring flight beyond the Arctic circle, restrict itself here in the Carolinas to the low valley lands (I saw it at Walhalla and in the Cullowhee Valley), and never once choose a nesting-site in appropriate surroundings at a little higher level? Why should the chat and the blue golden-wing find life agreeable at Highlands, and their regular neighbors, the prairie warbler and the white-eyed vireo, so persistently refuse to follow them? And why, in the first half of May, was there so strange a dearth of migrants in these attractive mountain woods?—a few blackpoll warblers (last seen of the 18th), a single myrtle-bird (on the 7th), and a crowd of rose-breasted grosbeaks and Blackburnian warblers (on the 8th and 9th, especially) being almost the only ones to fall under my notice. After all, one of the best birds I saw, not forgetting the Wilson's phalarope,—my adventure with which has been detailed in a previous chapter,—was a song sparrow singing from a dense swampy thicket on the 25th of May. So far as I am aware, no bird of his kind has ever before been reported in summer from a point so far south. He looked natural, but not in the least commonplace, as, after a long wait on my part,—for absolute certainty's sake,—he hopped out into sight. I was proud to have made one discovery!

In such a place, so limited in the range of its physical conditions,—a village surrounded by forest—the birds, however numerous they might be, counted as individuals, were sure to be of comparatively few species. Omitting such as were certainly, or almost certainly, migrants or strays,—the blackpoll, the myrtle-bird, the barn swallow, the king-bird, the solitary sandpiper, and the phalarope,—and such as were found only at a lower level, in Horse Cove and elsewhere; omitting, too, all birds of prey,—few, and for the most part but imperfectly identified; restricting myself to birds fully made out and believed to be summering in the immediate neighborhood of Highlands; omitting the raven, of course,—I counted but fifty-nine species.

All things considered, I was not inconsolable at finding my ornithological activities in some measure abridged. I had the more time, though still much too little, for other pursuits. It would have been good to spend the whole of it upon the plants, or in admiring the beauties of the country itself. As it was, I plucked a blossom here and there, stored up a few of the more striking of them in the memory, and enjoyed many an hour in gazing upon the new wild world, where, no matter how far I climbed, there was nothing to be seen on all sides but a sea of hills, wave rising beyond wave to the horizon's rim.

The horizon was never far off. I was twice on Satulah and twice on Whiteside, from which latter point, by all accounts, I should have had one of the most extensive and beautiful prospects to be obtained in North Carolina; but I had fallen upon one of those "spells of weather," common in mountainous places, which make a visitor feel as if nothing were so rare as a transparent atmosphere. . . .

But even as things were, I was not so badly used. There was more beauty in sight than I could begin to see, and, notwithstanding the comparative narrowness of the outlook,—partly because of it,—one of my most enjoyable forenoons was spent on the broad, open, slightly rounded summit of Satulah. . . . The date was May 12. I had been in Highlands less than a week, and my thoughts still ran upon ravens, the birds which, more even than the southern snow-bird and the mountain vireo, I had come hither to seek. They were said often to fly over, and this surely should be a place to see them. They could not escape me, if they passed within a mile. But though I kept an eye out, as we say, and an ear open, it was a vigil thrown away. Buzzards, swifts, and a bunch of twittering goldfinches were all the birds that "flew over." A chestnut-sided warbler sang so persistently from the mountain side just below that his sharp voice became almost a trouble. From the same quarter rose the songs of an oven-bird, a rose-breasted grosbeak, and a scar-let tanager. On the summit itself were snow-birds and chewinks: and once, to my delight, a field sparrow gave out a measure or two. After all, go where you will, you will hear few voices that wear better than his,—clear, smooth, most agreeably modulated, and temperately sweet.

The only trees I remember at the very top of the mountain were a few dwarfed and distorted pines and white oaks,—enough to remind a Yankee that he was not in New Hampshire. On the other hand, here grew our Massachusetts huckleberry (*Gaylussacia resinosa*), which I had seen nowhere below, where a great abundance of the buckberry,—so I think I heard it called (*G.*

90

ursina),—taller bushes, more comfortable to pick from, with larger blossoms—seemed to have taken its place. I should have been glad to try the fruit, which was described as of excellent quality. On that point, with no thought of boasting, I could have spoken as an expert. With the huckleberry was chokeberry, another New England acquaintance, fair to look upon, but a hypocrite,—"by their fruits ye shall know them;" and underneath, among the stones, were common yellow five-fingers, bird-foot violets, and leaves of trailing arbutus, three-toothed potentilla (a true mountain-lover), checkerberry, and galax. With them, but deserving a sentence by themselves, were the exquisite vernal iris and the scarlet-painted cup, otherwise known as the Indian's paintbrush and prairie fire, splendid for color, and in these parts, to my astonishment, a frequenter of the forest. I should have looked for it only in grassy meadows. Here and there grew close patches of the pretty, alpine looking sand myrtle (*Leiophyllum buxifolium*), thickly covered with small white flowers,—a plant which I had seen for the first time the day before on the summit of Whiteside. Mountain heather I called it, finding no English name in Chapman's Flora. Stunted laurel bushes in small bud were scattered over the summit. A little later they would make the place a flower garden. A single rose-acacia tree had already done its best in that direction, with a full crop of gorgeous rose-purple clusters. The winds had twisted it and kept it down, but could not hinder its fruitfulness.

These things, and others like them, I noticed between times. For the most part, my eyes were upon the grand panorama, a wilderness of hazy, forest-covered mountains, as far as the eye could go; nameless to me, all of them, with the exception of the two most conspicuous,—Whiteside on the one hand, and Rabun Bald on the other. For my comfort a delicious light breeze was stirring, and the sky, as it should be when one climbs for distant prospects, was sprinkled with small cumulus clouds, which in turn dappled the hills with moving shadows. One thing brought home to me a truth which in our dullness we ordinarily forget: that the earth itself is but a shadow, a something that appeareth, changeth, and passeth away. The rocks at my feet were full of pot-holes, such as I had seen a day or two before, the water still swirling in them, at Cullasaja Falls. As universal time is reckoned,—if it *is* reckoned,— old Satulah and all that forest-covered world which I saw, or thought I saw, from it, were but of yesterday, a "divine improvisation," and would be gone to-morrow.

More beautiful than the round prospect from Satulah, though perhaps less stimulating to the imagination, was the view from the edge of the mountain wall at the head of Horse Cove. Here, under a chestnut tree, I spent the greater part of a half a day, the valley with its road and its four or five houses straight at my feet. A dark precipice of bare rock bounded it on the right, a green mountain on the left, and in the distance southward were ridges and peaks without number. A few of the nearer hills I knew the names of by this time: Fodderstack, Bearpen, Hogback, Chimneytop, Terrapin, Shortoff, Scaly, and Whiteside. Satulah was the only *fine* name in the lot; and that, for a guess, is aboriginal. The North American Indians had a genius for names, as the Greeks had for sculpture and poetry, and will be remembered for it.

I had come to the brow of the cliffs, at a place called Lover's Leap, in search of a particular kind of rhododendron. It bore a small flower, my informant had said, and grew hereabout only in this one spot. It proved to be *R. punctatum*, new to me, and now (May 23) in early blossom. Four days afterward, in the Cullowhee and Tuckaseegee valleys, I saw riverbanks and roadsides lined with it; very pretty, of course, being a rhododendron, but not to be compared in that respect with the purple rhododendron or mountain rose-bay (*R. Catawbiense*). That, also, was to be found here, but very sparingly, as far as I could discover. I felicitated myself on having seen it in its glory on the mountains of southeastern Tennessee. The common large rhododendron (*R. maximum*) stood in thickets along all the brooks. I must have walked and driven past a hundred miles of it, on the present trip, it seemed to me; but I have never been at the South late enough to see it in flower.

What I shall remember longest about the flora of Highlands—and there is no part of eastern North America that is botanically richer, I suppose—is the azaleas. When I drove up from Walhalla, on the 6th of May, the woods were bright, mile after mile, with the common pink species (*A. nudiflora*); and at Highlands, in some of the dooryards, I found in full bloom a much lovelier kind,—also pink, and also leafless,—*A. Vaseyi*, as it turned out: a rare and lately discovered plant, of which the village people are justly proud. I could not visit its wild habitat without a guide, they told me. Within a week or so after my arrival the real glory of the spring was upon us: the woods were lighted up everywhere with the flame-colored azalea; and before it was gone,—while it was still at its height, in-deed,—the familiar sweet-scented white azalea (*A. viscosa*), the "swamp pink" of my boyhood, came forward to keep it company and lend it contrast. By that time I had seen all the rhododendrons and azaleas mentioned in Chapman's Flora, including *A. arborescens*, a tardy bloomer, which a botanical collector, with whom I was favored to spend a day on the road, pointed out to me in the bud.

The splendor of *A. calendulacea*, as displayed here, is never to be forgotten; nor is it to be in the least imagined by those who have seen a few stunted specimens of the plant in northern gardens. The color ranges from light straw-color to the brightest and deepest orange, and the bushes, thousands on thousands, no two of them alike, stand, not in rows or clusters, but broadly spaced, each by itself, throughout the hillside woods.

They were never out of sight, and I never could have enough of them. Wherever I went, I was always stopping short before one bush and another; admiring this one for the brilliancy or delicacy of its floral tints, and that one for its bold and pleasing habit. For as the plants do not grow in close ranks, so they do not put forth their flowers in a mass. They know a trick better than that. Thousands of shrubs, but every one in its own place, to be separately looked at; and on every shrub a few sprays of bloom, each well apart from all the others; one twig bearing nothing but leaves, another full of blossoms; a short branch here, a longer one there; and again, a smooth straight stem shooting far aloft, holding at the tip a bunch of leaves and flowers; everything free, unstudied, and most irregularly graceful, as if the bushes had each an individuality as well as a tint of its own. Often it was not a bush that I stood still to take my fill of, but a single branch,—as beautiful, I thought, as if it had been the only one in the world.

One walk on Satulah—not to the summit, but by a roundabout course through the woods to a bold cliff on the southern side (all the mountains, as a rule, are rounded on the north, and break off sharply on the south)—was literally a walk through an azalea show; first the flame-colored bushes beyond count and variety beyond description; and then, a little higher, a plentiful display of the white viscosa, more familiar and less showy, but hardly less attractive.

Better even than this wild Satulah garden was a smaller one nearer home: a triangular hillside, broad at the base and pointed at the top, as if it were one face of a pyramid; covered loosely with grand old trees,—oaks, chestnuts, and maples; the ground densely matted with freshly grown ferns, largely the cinnamon osmunda, clusters of lively green and warm brown intermixed; and everywhere, under the trees and above the ferns, mountain laurel and flame-colored azalea,—the laurel blooms pale pink, almost white, and the azalea clusters yellow of every conceivable degree of depth and brightness. A zigzag fence bounded the wood below, and the land rose at a steep angle, so that the whole was held aloft, as it were, for the beholder's convenience. It was a wonder of beauty, with nothing in the least to mar its perfection,—the fairest piece of earth my eye ever rested upon. The human owner of it, Mr. Selleck, (why should I not please myself by naming him, a land-owner who knew the worth of his possession!), had asked me to go and see it; and for his sake and its own, as well as for my own sake and the reader's, I wish I could show it as it was. It rises before me at this moment, like the rhododendron cliffs on Walden's Ridge, and will do so, I hope, to my dying day.

*D*ONALD CULROSS PEATTIE (1898–1964), botanist and author of numerous highly acclaimed nature books, grew up in Chicago. Peattie acquired his fine prose style honestly. His father was a journalist and his mother was an essayist, novelist, and literary critic for the *Chicago Tribune*.

Peattie was a rare combination of poet and scientist. At Harvard, he was awarded the Witter Bynner Poetry prize. As an adult, the scientific method became his core belief, but his writing remained lyrical. For all of his praise of things scientific, his relationship with nature seems to have never lost the child's sense of wonder.

The following selection, from Peattie's book, *The Road of the Naturalist*, reveals the context and history behind his vocation as naturalist. That sense of calling sprang from a special attachment and affection for the region around Tryon, North Carolina, where he spent much of his youth and young adulthood. Peattie wrote another book, *A Natural History of Pearson's Falls and Some of Its Human Associations*, about the Tryon area.

Selection from
THE ROAD OF A NATURALIST

by Donald Culross Peattie

My mother . . . would reach into the grimy midwinter misery of my city life, and pluck me out of it, and take me to that far-off country where winter was no more than long frost crystals making forests under the red mud. A land where a hidden bird called 'Peet-o, peet-o,' and another flashed into sight red as a banner, over a brook that chuckled to its stones. In our cottage, where the fat-pine kindled her fire, my mother's typewriter went clickety-clack. I came in out of the beginning of spring, bringing her pine-saps, a fistful. I had found them under leaves, and they smelled of carnations, inside their dead brown husks, and were cold as fungi to my fingers.

Another year (I think it was my eighth), I had the luck to catch the measles, and got earlier into my chosen life, for the longest stay there. I was still shaky, and wore dark glasses to protect my eyes, when I got on the south-bound train. The station porter as he went hurrying along the boards was calling the magic words, 'Big Fo' Train! Big Fo'! Pullmans in the reah!' Pullmans in the reah!' I knew those smoky, poky old green and varnished Pullmans now, and the three times you had to change trains on the journey. And I knew that, come the second morning, I would tear off the blue glasses and see in all their shining clarity the swinging hills, and hear the rivers' roar rise under the trestles as we crossed them and come right through the double windows. Then the wheels curve into the giant horseshoe that lets you see the waggling tail of your own train; the engine gives a long call to the echo in the passes, and you are there.

But we went farther, up and up the mucky red clay road that sucked at the horses' hoofs and the rocking wheels of the yellow surrey. Between the boles of tulip trees and armored pine I saw the world of people fall away, grow small, grow hazy blue, forgotten. In several months upon that isolated summit of the Appalachians I began to discover a world older and greater. It is the world now of my established habitation, my working days and holidays, and it lies open to all men, in valleys as on mountains, by any road you choose to enter it.

Each day, up on that mountain-top, I saw nobody, and each day again there was no one to see. I was lonely, and complained of it, and knew at last that I did not care. For I had a brook that to me was as alive as an animal; it slipped with an alert silence over sands where glinted what was gold or only fool's gold; either was as bright. Red tritons nimbly got away again out of my hand. The turtles let me hold them, but they went inside themselves and so got away too, after all. Squatting with my chin between my knees, I built dams in the brook until my hands were cold as the running water; I built some stone cities on the ledgy shore.

The brook said nothing about where it was going, but when I followed it I heard the shouting and the singing even before I got there and beheld the foamy plunge of the great fall down the mountain-side. That most eternal movement, wind of a waterfall, stirred the glistening laurel leaves all down the sheer steep even on a still day, and I had a sense of hallelujah and rejoicing as far back into the woods as I could hear the cataract.

Somewhere up here there was a cave with bats in it; I could not find the way to it again. I often went, though, to the springhouse that held an odor, under its odor of moss, of cold essential granite, a core smell of deep down. I would go back to the log cabin where my mother wrote all day, but I did not linger indoors, for she had not let me bring any books but *Alice*. . . .

And now I knew the mayflower and trillium by name, and the Carolina wren and the cardinal, all the singing birds except the one who sang alone in the rain, lifting his voice and letting it fall in a long silver whistle. I knew the smell of plants I could not name; I had a small hatchet and made trails in the woods, hacking sweetgum and spice bush and sassafras, sheering their pungent bark so they bled odors that I got by heart. There amid the glittering leaves I stood a long time listening for the thrush to sing again. Slowly the notes came ringing through the woods, a mile away and bell-clear. . . .

From this high vantage point, this mountain holding me up to the sky in its sure back, I could look out and discern the foreground of a continent. Northward from the Narrows rose Sugarloaf, higher than I, and beyond lay the Chimney Rock country, bright green and dark green with forests, all the way to the Black Mountains, highest of all; there, I knew, the thinner air was heady with balsam and spruce. I had none here but the dried needles in my little pillow. Southward lay the Valley view. Far down there stretched

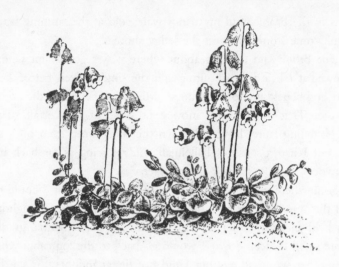

the fields where people lived; I could make out the small white dome of the county courthouse set amid them. Away rolled the red clay land, hazy pink turning to blue, toward unseen ocean and a city by the sea called Charleston, inhabited by Confederates in gray. Standing on a rock above all this I heard a silence deep as any sea, and saw the turkey vultures trim their sailing wings upon it. Once in a week there was a sound from that land fathoms down below, the sound of church bells. One trail led east, out to the mountain's rim. From what I called my sunrise rock I could see morning, and the reaches of Rutherford County. And sometimes I could catch the labor of a train down there when it struck high country, and the wail of its whistle as it plowed its lonely course through blue distance.

My sunset rock, lying out to the west, gave on the uptossed crests of near-by mountains that as the color faded took on the tints and insubstantial quality of bubbles. Sometimes the clouds rolled in below and hid even these heights, and on my loftier mountain-top I rejoiced that, while men put up umbrellas down below, my world was lifted higher, into the sun. Sometimes I saw the storm coming straight at me, in a slant banking threat across the sky, to break in pattering tumult on the cottage roof. At night I slept, resting between the mountain's shoulders, waking only if the men were out after 'coon or possum; far away I heard the yells, the shots, the dogs baying, and I imagined the light of the torches licking up the pine trunks and how they caught the treed thing's eyes in a sudden furious glitter. . . .

Nature at home is just as filled with beauty and wonder as the places where bronze-limbed girls wear red flowers over their ears. I was once, while working for the Government, told off to entertain a visiting English naturalist. I asked him what he wanted most to see, and he said, 'A rattlesnake, a poison-ivy bush, a milkweed flower, and an opossum.' Exploration begins at the back fence, and the limits of the field are the ends of the world.

But in a world so wide and so new, a naturalist, if he would seriously learn, must stake out for himself some province to define and master. It was upon one of my frequent visits to the Bronx Botanical Garden that I discovered, twenty years ago, how much earlier I had all unconsciously laid claim to one such province as my own.

The day was late in winter; I was turning over the sheets in the herbarium; the specimen I lifted next from out its neat manila folder looked back at me familiarly. I had seen this plant before, long, long ago with the eyes of love and only a child's understanding. Now I saw it, in the first glimmerings of my comprehension of the great plant system, as science sees it. And I knew before I looked at the label what would be written on the spot where the place of collection is entered. For though there are many kinds of trillium in the world, there is no other place where this kind springs.

Therefore the label bore the name of the mountain where I had heard the thrush when I was eight, and watched dawn and sunset from the rocks. The word was like a secret between myself and Nature. Deeply it had lain buried with that other life closed years ago, which now opened suddenly beyond this flower. There the white fall plunged and the mountain-tops rolled misty blue away, and all at once I could remember how this trillium smelled, a dark honey perfume. I lifted the specimen closer; the flower rose serene out of its three great rhombic leaves, solitary and symmetrical; under my hand lens it spoke to me in the tongue I was beginning to understand.

I took my specimen in to Doctor Barnhart. I said—most casually remarking it—the place name which was passport to me. Doctor Barnhart reached for his atlas, and turned to the page that mapped the Carolinas. Historian of botany that he is, he began to trace out the routes of the collectors who had gone that way. First went old John Bartram, Philadelphia Quaker, Botanist to George Third. But he had passed a hundred miles to the north, collecting seeds for his garden. Alexander Garden, Charleston physician, correspondent of Linnaeus, dapper godfather of gardenia his namesake, had gone north in 1755 with Governor Glen when the treaty with the Cherokees was made at the foot of 'the Saluda Mountains.' But he had missed my country by forty miles to the southwest. My mountains must have been sighted, a smoky penciled line upon the west, by André Michaux, emerging from the wilderness with new plants commanded by his king for Marly and Marie Antoinette's Versailles.

Somebody, Doctor Barnhart remarked, closing the atlas, ought to get down in that country again. He might find Michaux's mysterious magnolia. Or even his shortia, the flower once lost for a century. . . .

I was following [the great tradition of science] when I started

102

south not after shortia alone but for my remembered trillium and any and all good things that might fall to me as a collector. For now I had a vasculum to sling across my shoulder, and two plant presses, each a double lattice of stout ashwood with straps to bind it. I had stocked up, too, on the specimen driers that go in a plant press—extra thick blotting paper, cut like herbaria sheets to the same standard size, of a highly bibulous stock. One of my two suitcases was crammed with nothing but these. At Biltmore I changed trains; and when, arrived in Tryon, I threw up the suitcase lid to get my driers out, I found instead a stranger's clothes tenderly wrapping a revolver and two quarts of snake-bite whiskey. My dismay must have been slight compared to that of the Southern gentleman who reached for his liquor and found the thirstiest blotting paper that the Cambridge Botanical Supply Company could offer.

Margaret Morley lent me driers. She was leaving the field forever, and she gave me her microscope, all her scientific library, and her blessing. She it was who told me where to find the walking fern, and the seven kinds of trillium. (Even the Carolina wrens whistled 'Trillium, trillium, trillium!' all day beside the brooks.) And where I should look for the seven wild gingers hiding their flowers close to the earth under their leaves, and sweet pinesaps, and shortia itself. After tramping sixty miles, sleeping on the ground by my campfire or in the cabins of mountaineers, my fingers, too, touched it at last. There on Horsepasture Creek, in the Blue Ridge near Toxaway, I gathered a few plants to colonize nearer home.

In that wild place, the loam-bound roots in my two hands, I felt at the center of things. I had simply walked off that map which shows New York City as the axis of America. No one had detained me; my parents, who asked nothing better of their children than some sound conviction, had seemed relieved when I announced that I was quitting. Only years later did I learn that they suspected those mixed fevers and languors which New York gave me to be what is called the malady of poets. The truth of it was that I was quite healthily beginning at last to go about my business.

I climbed Mount Mitchell to breathe its balsams and spruces. I learned the six pines and the two hemlocks of my province, and mastered one by one the azaleas, the early pink, the kind with leaves fragrant in drying, the flame azalea, the late white one. And the trilliums and the laurels and the magnolias. There was no saxifrage I had not scaled a cliff to pick.

Not that it was this detail that mattered, any of it, nor even the sum of all the details (which a decade later came out as a two-hundred-page publication, describing the more than a thousand species of flowering plants here native). The gain which counted, made in that summer when I came of age, lay behind and beyond mere systematics. It does not matter what class of organisms—plants, birds, insects, or strange sea plunder—first stirs the understanding to a grasp at the structure and function of living things, and their relationships, at evolution and geographic distribution and ecology. The principles will carry over to any other group. They leave an impress on the mind, which cannot be erased. Graved deep enough, these given laws are tablet of a faith.

This I know now; then I was simply happy, alone with Nature every day and all day long. No one knew in what glen or on what ridge I wandered; no one was there to watch me as I changed identity, tramping and climbing and sleeping noons or nights whenever I fell weary. Confusion and uncertainty ran out of the soles of my boots. Conviction slowly came.

The new vision added dimension to a world that had been flat. Everything in it now had atmosphere behind; far-off ranges came at a stride miles nearer in this clearer air. I saw newly; I knew at last what it was that I wanted to know. I understood how I wanted to think. I found that for me the natural world, seen with the eyes of science, was—and is—reality.

I did not know much, but what I had learned I had to believe. As art (which had been the preoccupation of my youth) *feels* its way intuitively toward reality, through emotion and sympathy, so science *knows* its way, step by hard-won step. And Nature was what I wanted thus to know; it came to me with the exaltation of a conversion.

WHEN WILLIAM SEEMAN (circa 1921–?) was a ten-year-old boy, he chronicled a lengthy canoe trip he took with his father and another companion, Shady, through eastern North Carolina. The group started down Goose Creek in Durham County and followed it into the Neuse River. They then continued down the Neuse River all the way to the Atlantic Ocean. This talented young writer eventually published an account of this journey in a book titled *Down Goose Creek*. What follows is a selection from that book called "Through the 'Let-'Lones'." It describes a particularly remote section of the Neuse River just east of Smithfield in Johnston County.

"THROUGH THE 'LET-'LONES' "

from

DOWN GOOSE CREEK

by William Seeman

A few days after we met up with the hunters, we came to a place in the river the superstitious negroes call the "let-'lones." This is a wild, swampy country lasting for about ten miles—as the crow flies—but it takes a couple of days to get through.

The river seems to go crazy here. Instead of going on straight, it curves and twists back in a regular labyrinth of horseshoe bends. Some of these bends are miles long, and bring you back—after you have been paddling for hours—to within a stone's throw of where you started. . . .

As we got into the swampy wilderness, it looked like we might

Reprinted from *Down Goose Creek*, by William Seeman. New York: Fleming H. Revell Company, 1931.

really be approaching the devil's stamping-ground after all—the cane grass was so high and snaky, and the vines so thick. Great spreading elms and ash trees shaded the river. Now and then we saw a cypress tree, too, and wild pecan trees. Very often we saw or heard squirrels in the pecan trees. The river became narrow and sluggish, like it might have been shrunk up and paralyzed by the evil spirits that lived there. But we soon began to find many bright and interesting sights about us. So we forgot the frightful stories we had heard, and paddled along as merrily as ever.

Dad—who had been studying up on the geology of the region—said that ages ago, when those huge land-icebergs came sliding across the country, they had plowed up great ditches in the ground. One of them had stopped here and melted. Along with its miles of ice, this glacier had also brought many thousands of tons of rock. When the ice melted, great boulders—some as big as houses—were left lying high and dry. So the real reason the Neuse River now twisted about so much here was because it had found it easier to cut its channel along those glacial ditches than through the rocks.

In a pool beside one of these large boulders, Shady and I tried our hands at a little fishing. He yanked out a beauty of a black bass, but all the luck I had was to lose my only minnow. . . .

We saw our first venomous snake that morning. It was a cotton-mouth moccasin that was sunning on a shoal at the mouth of a small creek. It went sliding off into the water as we came near. But

so slowly that Shady had time to shoot at it twice. He missed both shots though.

As we were now coming into a section where we knew venomous snakes of several kinds were common,

Shady and I decided to have a daily rifle practice, to improve our aim. And we began practicing that very day.

It is easy to catch snakes alive . . . but it is important to be sure they are harmless snakes. Most snakes *are* harmless, but a good deep bite from a venomous kind—such as a rattlesnake or moccasin—will usually bring death to the strongest man or other animal in an hour's time unless medical treatment is given quickly.

The difference in a venomous snake is that its two long hollow upper teeth—or fangs—are filled with venom from a poison sac in the gums. When the snake's mouth is closed, the fangs lie folded back against the roof of his mouth. But when he strikes, he opens his mouth wide and the fangs stand out straight in front of his mouth—piercing the flesh of his victim and shooting in the poison liquid like a vaccination needle. This venom is so deadly that even a baby snake a few hours old can kill a man just as well as an old grandpa rattler with seventeen rings on his tail.

We also passed an otter slide that day. This was just a slick, worn place on the muddy bank which was used by a family of otters for sliding into the water.

I saw a tortoise swimming. He was very clumsy and could not swim near as good as a turtle. When we came near, he ducked his head in the water. But that was all he knew about diving, and he looked very comical with his head stuck under water and his body in plain view on top.

Late in the afternoon we saw a flock of young blue herons flying towards the swamps to roost. They flew in single file—one behind the other. They were pure white, and made a beautiful picture against the dark woods.

We camped for the night in a piney woods that stretched down to the river lowgrounds. There were a lot of doves there, and Shady shot one. There was also a crow's roost a little back of where we camped. The crows were flying about over the pines with their young ones, and cawing all kinds of crow talk to each other. We lay still and watched them for quite awhile.

Crows have lookouts the same as soldiers, and you can't get anywhere near a flock without them seeing you and warning the others. Early the next morning I got up and walked off with the gun towards the roost. I eased along as quiet as a mink, and was just about to crack down on a crow about seventy-five feet away. But just then I heard the quick "caw-caw" of a sentry right over my head and they all flew off.

Under the roosting trees I found a lot of hard, crumbly balls about half-an-inch thick. They looked like putty, but when I broke one of them open I found hair and bones inside. When I showed them to Dad, he said they were crow "pellets." He explained how they are formed. A crow swallows his food whole, and when he eats anything too tough to digest—say, a whole mouse or a very tough beetle—his stomach rolls up the indigestible pieces into a ball while he sleeps. Then the next time he opens his beak for a yawn, out the pellet rolls. With such up-to-date stomachs, I guess the young crows can eat all they want and never have a pain. So if I am ever turned into a bird I hope it will be a crow!

There were a lot of curious noises in the "let-'lones." . . . One of these noises sounded just like a man driving down a stake. Dad said it was made by a bittern—a kind of bird of the heron family. We heard a barred owl hooting loudly in the middle of the day. It sounded as if he was really saying what the negroes say he says— which is: "Who—who—who cooks for you-all?"

Of course many of the clucking sounds came from frogs of different kinds. Some of the noises didn't seem to come from either frogs or insects, though, and we decided that these might possibly be made by snakes. I have read in a book by Mr. Hudson—the British naturalist—that some snakes do have voices and can make quite a few sounds. . . .

It would be a hard job to describe the many beautiful flowers that grew in the "let-'lones." There were whole beds of red horsemint, jewel weed, rose mallow, and many other kinds that we knew. But there were also many beautiful kinds of swamp flowers that none of us had ever seen before. The water hemlock—from the roots of which was made the poison that Socrates drank—grew here taller than a horse. The giant mint, or "Joe Pye weed," was even taller than the hemlock, and some of the ferns grew way above my head.

Sometimes we got into swarms of black gnats, eyeflies, and gadflies, too. When they got very bad, I put on a cap I made out of a large paper bag. This bag pulled down clear to my shoulders, and was a fine protector. I cut a small peephole in it and a breathing hole. We were never bothered much by mosquitoes till about sundown—which is their regular feeding time. And by that time we were generally in camp, with a fire going to drive them away.

On our second afternoon in the "let-'lones" we saw a big flock of buzzards "playing baseball." That is what the country people say they are doing when a lot of them are flying round and round in wide circles high up in the sky. What they were really doing, though, was climbing up above the black thunderclouds so the coming rain wouldn't wet their feathers. There was a pretty hard shower for a little while, but the sun came right back out again.

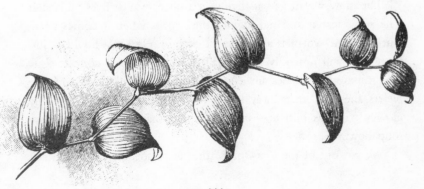

We flushed a wild turkey hen and seven or eight half-grown young ones up out of a thicket of reeds. They flew up so suddenly that we all just sat gaping at them. I didn't have any idea turkeys could fly so swiftly—the tame ones are so clumsy. But those wild ones sailed off to the woods like bullets and never flapped their wings but once or twice.

Shady succeeded in killing a small heron, though, and since we couldn't have turkey for supper, we tried that. Herons aren't considered a food bird nowadays, but as we had read that they used to be a favorite dish with the French kings, we thought we might eat it if they could. It tasted a good deal like wild duck—only stronger—and had a very fishy flavor.

I also picked about a quart of fine big blueberries for supper—which went fine with the beef and bird.

That night I found a curious thing I had never seen before. After supper—when I went outside the tent to bring in my "diddy-bag" with my sketch book and things in it—I was surprised to see a streak of fire on the ground about four inches long. When I looked at it closer I saw that it was moving. I called Dad, and he said I had found a glow worm. We took the creature inside to examine it. It was thick, creamy colored worm about the size of a tobacco worm. But when we turned the lantern off, it shone with a beautiful purple and green light.

The glow worm gets its living in a queer way. It lives on snails. The snails fear it and retreat into their shells when it comes near. But the glow worm is a wonderful chemist. He has a liquid in his body that will not only kill a snail instantly, but will cook it also. The minute he touches any exposed part of a snail's body with his feelers, the snail melts away into a thick liquid like soup. Then the glow worm sips him up—using the poor snail's own shell for his soup bowl.

We got out of the "let-'lones" the next morning. Nothing had happened to us any worse than running out of bread and being slightly chewed up by mosquitoes. We were sorry not to have found any signs of either bears or ghosts.

The river now straightened out through a flat, sandy country.

H ERBERT HUTCHINSON BRIMLEY (1861–1946) was born in Wellington, Bedfordshire, England, and moved to North Carolina as a young man. He was the founder and director of the North Carolina State Museum, and during his fifty years of service, the museum became a model institution which housed an outstanding collection of animal, plant, and geological specimens from the southeastern United States. Brimley was also a writer. He wrote *Fishes of North Carolina* (1907) with coauthor H.M. Smith, and *Birds of North Carolina* (1919 and 1942) with coauthors T.G. Pearson and C.S. Brimley, his brother. Through his work at the museum and as an author, Brimley made lasting contributions to science and the study of nature.

Brimley's wife "Pal," who accompanied him on the following outings, was Bettie Moore Love. The New River is located in central Onslow County about a dozen miles from the Atlantic. Cowhead Creek empties into French's Creek, and Duck Creek is slightly down river. Both of these creeks come into the New River at Farnell Bay. The following essay, "Flapper Frolics," was originally unpublished.

"FLAPPER FROLICS"

by H. H. Brimley

The Flapper is a skeleton-framed, canvas-covered canoe, four-teen feet long by thirty-six inches beam. She is decked fore and aft and has a seven foot cockpit amidships surrounded by a two-inch coaming. The fresh, brackish, and salt-water reaches of tidewater North Carolina are her stamping ground, and her coaming would be like a fine-tooth saw were it notched for all the fish and game the little ship has brought in.

For a number of years past my wife and I have spent a mid-summer vacation of two or three weeks on, in, and around the broad waters of New River. One morning last August we decided

Reprinted from "Flapper Frolics," by H.H. Brimley. In *A North Carolina Naturalist, H.H. Brimley: Selections From His Writings*, edited by Eugene P. Odum. Chapel Hill: The University of North Carolina Press, 1949.

to paddle the Flapper along the river shore—the so-called "river" being about two and a half miles wide at this point—down to Goose Creek, a small tributary of which the fishing qualities seemed to be but little known. "Paddle" is incorrect, however; "shove" would be better, as I kept the boat close to the sandy shore-line and used my long single-blade for poling.

We were silently enjoying the beauties of the early morning, some mullets jumping out in the river having my attention at the time, when Pal, sitting in her canoe chair towards the bow, turned her head slightly and whispered back, "Look, what are those animals?"

I glanced inshore and there, almost abreast of the boat and not more than thirty yards away, were a pair of gray foxes sitting on their haunches on the bare sand and close to the water's edge. My paddle was over the starboard quarter on the offshore side and I pressed the blade down on the hard sand bottom to lessen our headway.

The foxes seemed quite unconcerned, glancing at us or up and down the river without any sign of fear or restlessness. A slight air from the river drifted us slowly in towards them, and I do not think I ever enjoyed a more beautiful and entrancing eye-feast than was presented by that picture in the book of Nature.

The foxes were adults—presumably a pair—and immaculate from nose pad to tail tip. As we drifted to within perhaps twenty-five yards one of them came to a standing position, looked us over rather carefully, then turned tail and gracefully trotted into some scattering dead bushes that fringed a deeper thicket behind. Then it stopped, turned, and looked back.

When the distance between the canoe and the remaining fox had been reduced to about twenty yards, that, too, came to its feet and rejoined its mate, and both silently faded away into the thicket without hurry and without showing anything more than a degree of caution in their movements. And Pal and I agreed that we had been highly favored in being allowed a slight glimpse into the home life of one of the most secretive of the denizens of the wild places.

Goose Creek turned out to be a stinking mudhole, fine for alligators but no good for bass, so we came out on to the river flats, took off shoes and stockings and set about catching a mess of crabs for bait. As soon as we had enough we waded ashore and turned the crabs into bait by removing the shells and cutting up the meat into suitable sized pieces for still-fishing for spotted weakfish, the water being brackish enough even at this distance from the ocean—about a dozen miles—for many species of salt-water fish to frequent.

We had only our five foot casting rods that we had been using for black bass, but we rigged our lines with 2/0 snelled hooks and half-ounce sinkers. Paddling out to windward of the "Iron Mine," an area of river bottom rocky in character, we cast our lines out on either side of the canoe and allowed the boat to drift. It was not long before Pal had a strike and hooked some kind of a fighting varmint that tested her tackle to the limit. I soon realized that she was fast to a big gaff-topsail (sea) cat, and I know of no other fish of equal weight that puts up so stubborn a fight. Encouragement was in order, but suddenly I noticed a definite angle between the handle of her rod and the rod itself, and it then dawned on me that water had been in that handle before to the extent of softening the glue. I yelled to her to give him slack and let him shake the hook, or her rod would be a goner. And the hook was shook!

Then, one got mine, and I'm here to say that I was more than tired when I got him into the boat—after hammering his head with the back of my hunting hatchet. This fish turned out to be about the largest sea cat that had ever been caught from the Club. I soon got another—smaller—and then we paddled in, as the gaff-topsails seemed to have taken the Iron Mine for the day, and we had enough.

It was well before sunrise that July morning, in another year, when we started up Cowhead Creek to try for a big 'gator that seemed to have an attraction for a certain section of marsh along the creek bank. As I was to do the shooting, the bow seat in the Flapper was mine for the trip, Pal handling the boat from my usual position in the stern. We both paddled until within two or three hundred yards of our objective, when I shifted paddle for rifle, threw off the safety, and stood by for the next move. Pal is a skilled canoe-handler, and the little ship seemed almost to drift of her own accord under the influence of her deft, noiseless strokes.

Slowly the marsh came in sight around a sharp bend, and slowly the canoe glided along, but no sign of 'gator, big or little, greeted our anxious eyes. Without a spoken word, without a sound of any kind, we slowly worked along between the swamp-lined banks until opposite an old log-landing on our left, where the high ground came down to the water's edge and where the bushes had been cleared away for bringing the logs down for rafting. The movement of the boat ceased, and the faintest of whispers came from Pal— "Look!"

I looked, and just back of the landing was a wild turkey hen with young ones. She had seen us—trust a wild turkey for that— and was clucking to her brood as she herded them for cover. But for nearly a minute—or so it seemed—she and several of her chicks were in full sight, a streak of light from the rising sun reflected resplendently from her smooth bronze plumage. And I know of nothing in Nature more beautiful.

"My, but that was worth coming for," said Pal. "We're repaid— and I don't want an old alligator skin traveling bag, anyway. Let's go back to breakfast!" And back to breakfast we went.

At the opposite end of another long summer day we were working down Jumping Run casting for bass as we drifted, with an occasional dip or two of the double paddle to retain our headway and to hold the boat straight. Pal is one of those satisfactory companions who instinctively take in the beauties of these wild swamp streams and who know that gentle movements and absence of noise often afford some opportunity for a little insight into the lives of the wood-folk.

A sudden roar of powerful wings and a crash of branches from a group of trees on the creek bank almost abreast of the canoe—and seven great turkey gobblers left their roosting place and winged their way back into the depths of the swamp. A wild turkey is always grand, but that fact is never impressed on me more strongly than when a big gobbler unexpectedly takes wing from a tree near at hand. Multiply that by seven—and you have a real thrill!

Pal and I were casting for bass up Duck Creek one summer morning when we heard a 'gator bellowing, and the full power of his voice indicated a big bull. I was beginning to despair of ever getting one of these big fellows with my rifle as their shyness and cunning seemed almost uncanny, so this summer I had rigged a couple of lines with the idea of fishing for them. Apart from the use I could make of one or two good hides, I had in mind the fact that we had lost two of our best deer dogs down the throats of these monsters not very long before.

"There's your traveling bag," I remarked to Pal, "let's catch something we can use to bait the hook!" But this turned out to be one of those days when nothing would strike. We worked both sides of the creek for a mile and a half without success, the nearest approach to alligator bait being a jack (pickerel) that struck Pal's bait and only broke loose as I was slipping the landing net under him.

On our way back to the mouth of the creek, where the gas boat was to pick us up about one o'clock, we heard dogs running on the Weil Place. "Suppose we drift along this stretch for awhile and see if they put the deer to water," I suggested to Pal. "That suits me, I've never seen a swimming deer and I'd love to!"

But the sound of the dogs began to fade away towards French's Creek, so we started over to the shady side to resume our fishing—when I saw the deer. "Look! There he is. I'll paddle down and give you a sight at short range!"

The deer's head showed smaller in the water and we soon realized that it was a fawn, but, rather stupidly as I thought at the time, it tried to land on the side it had come from. Thinking this poor judgment on the part of the fawn, I headed it off, not wanting to put it ashore on the side the dogs were. They were evidently someone's deer hounds that had got loose, but, fortunately, such dogs do little if any harm to the deer in a country intersected by as many broad, twisting creeks as this is.

I got the little fellow turned, and put him ashore on the Foster side of the creek. We had a clear view of his shining, spotted body as he climbed the bank and dashed into the bushes, and you can believe me that he wasted no time in leaving! "That was the most beautiful thing I ever saw in my life," was Pal's comment, and I came pretty near to agreeing with her. Evidently the fawn's mother had given the dogs her scent and had taken them directly away from where she had left her offspring. I feel sure that they got together again that night.

While eating dinner a little later at the Club House we learned that one of a litter of small setter puppies had died during the preceding night—which sounded like alligator bait to me! So, after the meal was over I hunted up the deceased—and that puppy surely was good and dead! He was a fluffy little thing and about the shape of a basket ball when I found him, the weather being hot.

When the sun was getting low that afternoon, I took one of the 'gator lines and fixed the puppy on the hook, tying the body to the leader both back of the fore-legs and forward of the hind-legs, with the hook stuck through the cartilage of one ear. But I would not care for baiting 'gator hooks with ripe puppies as a steady job!

In fact, we could not stand it in the boat and had to tow it astern while paddling back to Duck Creek.

Half a mile or so from the mouth of the creek we turned into a twisting gut running back through the marsh from which we had heard the old bull singing earlier in the day. This gut was well known to us as a regular alligator den, and it was here that we had planned to set the baited line. Passing the first bend, I made fast the end of the line to the limber part of a live cedar limb overhanging the water. Then, carrying the line to a dead, partly submerged cedar, I lightly hung the baited hook from the extreme point of one of the snaggy branches, with the bait just above the surface. We backed the canoe a few strokes and looked the outfit over. The setting was perfect—or so it seemed—and as we came into the creek and started back for camp Pal remarked, "I feel sure we will have him in the morning!"

"I think so, too," I replied, "unless some little five or six footer gets to the puppy first 'cause that's the very choicest thing in baits that was ever placed before an expectant 'gator!"

Early next morning, before the cook had even started a fire, Pal and I were on our way to Duck Creek. All the rest of the bunch in camp were too skeptical to care to go with us—but *we* had expectations! Foolishly, perhaps, I left my rifle at the house and only took along my long-barrelled nine-millimeter Luger pistol.

As we entered the gut we could hear the splashing and before we rounded the bend we were fully advised that we had a bite. Tight as a fiddle-string stretched the line from the elastic cedar limb; a few yards farther and the dead cedar came into sight; another stroke—and there came into view the big bull we wanted so much, tearing the water apart in his struggles to get free. One last drive against the straining line, one last lift of his great, rough head, and he went down in a flurry of water that sent the swells surging against the muddy borders of the marsh.

He looked so imposing—in a rough-neck way—that I didn't care to put the frail canoe too close to where he might next rise, so I laid her off a little and stood by with the Luger. Minutes passed, and no sign. More minutes ticked off until half an hour had gone by and still no sign that an alligator had ever been within a mile of the place.

Knowing that no 'gator could remain below for this length of time in water of summer warmth, following the physical exertion this one had just been through, I realized that the mighty effort we had witnessed had resulted in his freedom. But to make sure, we stayed out the hour—and then sadly returned to camp, but only after ascertaining that the 'gator had tied the bight of the line in such a series of turns and twists around the under-water part of the dead cedar limbs as to give him a dead pull against a solid resistance in place of playing on the lively spring of the branch to which the line was attached. And when we took up the line later on we found that the mighty struggles of the big bull had pulled down the hard-twisted wire of the swivel until the eye had been so contracted in diameter as to cut the gang of linen surf lines used as a leader.

One cold winter's day I had been on a deer stand on Cowhead Neck that was most easily reached by taking the canoe to the upper log-landing on Jumping Run. After the unsuccessful hunt was over I was quietly paddling back to camp, with a rather flawy little breeze astern.

When within a hundred or two yards of the main body of French's Creek I noticed a disturbance in the water ahead that I could not at first identify, but it finally dawned on me that it was caused by a pair of otters at play. And that was the winter when fur was at the highest point ever known! And here before me lay an opportunity to secure a valuable piece of fur for Pal that would have a far greater value than its market price by reason of the sentiment attached. So I let the Flapper drift down before the wind, only using the paddle to keep the animals over the port bow.

This was my second experience only of seeing otters undisturbed in their natural surroundings and it was a joy to watch them—and perhaps a sin to attempt to kill! But man is a conglomeration of contradictions and I did not go deeply into the ethics of the situation then.

They were large otters, and the time of the year indicated that their fur was prime. Plunging, rolling, and wallowing, they reminded me much of porpoises in some of their stunts—and the canoe continued to drift closer! But the little choppy waves and the flawy breeze made it difficult to hold her in position and lessened her stability as a gun platform. Finally, when both were down at the same time, I laid in my paddle and took up my rifle. Then one appeared, swimming rapidly, with only the top of the head visible. The rifle cracked, and the spout of spray showed that the bullet had gone too high. Then the second otter came up and the bullet intended for him struck short of the mark, and he went down.

That was the last of them, of course, and I haven't seen a live wild otter since.

Digging out a bass was a method Pal and I employed in securing a nice one last summer in Duck Creek. This fish hit my bait pretty near where it fell and before I could stop him he was fast in a tangle of sunken brush and tree-tops near shore, and hung up for keeps. So, while I kept a tight line by taking up the slack, Pal worked the Flapper inshore until the line was up and down. Then I held on to a projecting snag while my partner performed the digging act. But the point where the line was fast was five feet under water and it didn't dig well, so I joined the excavating brigade. Every now and then I managed to get a few inches of line on the reel, but there was no sign of the fish and I was convinced that he had pulled loose. It finally became a question of saving as much line as I could, together with a brand new Shimmy Wiggler with a gorgeous Parmachenee Belle trailer.

It was rather rough digging with a six foot spruce paddle for a spade, the light blade showing a strong tendency to come to the surface, and only one hand being available. Matters were really getting desperate.

"Oh, there he is, close alongside the canoe!" said Pal, as he suddenly appeared among some sunken branches she had stirred up from the coffee-colored depths—and a few moments later he was flopping on the floor-boards between us, a three-and-a-quarter-pound big-mouth.

"Well," remarked Pal, with a sigh of relief, "I knew it couldn't be done—but there he is!"

*E*DWIN WAY TEALE (1899–1980), naturalist, author, photographer, and illustrator, was born in Joliet, Illinois. Teale was a staff writer for *Popular Science* magazine and the author of nearly thirty books. His most famous books chronicled the changing of the seasons in America. Teale won nature writing's highest award in 1943, the John Burroughs Medal, and in 1966 he received the Pulitzer Prize for general nonfiction.

The selection below, and the two selections which follow, are taken from *North With Spring*, an account of Teale's journey from Florida to New England to study the unfolding of spring. Like Donald Culross Peattie's essay, this selection, titled "Trillium Glen," also describes the area around Pearson's Falls near Tryon, North Carolina.

"TRILLIUM GLEN"

from

NORTH WITH SPRING

by Edwin Way Teale

*W*e had driven down a dusty road that afternoon and walked past silvery trunked beeches and among robin's plantain and violets and star chickweed, into the soft, leaf-filtered light of a mountain glen. . . . The coolness of a grotto surrounded us. The air of the glen was perfumed with the scent of thousands of woodland flowers. It was murmurous with the music of falling water. We were at Pearson's Falls, near Tryon, North Carolina, at the southern end of the Blue Ridge Mountains.

Like the leaves of a partly opened book, the walls of the narrow glen rose steeply on either side. They were tilted flower fields, starred from top to bottom with the great waxy pink and white blooms of immense trilliums. Changing colors as they grow older, some wake-robins range from snowy white through pink to deep purple-pink before their petals wither. Our first and most lasting impression of the ravine was this trillium tapestry that ascended on either hand.

But there were other flowers too: hepatica, columbine, Dutchman's-breeches, bloodroot, lady-slipper, spring beauty, wood anemone—just to name them over is to bring to mind the sight and smell and feel of woodland loam. Nowhere else along the way did we find so glorious a wild flower garden as in this hidden nook among the North Carolina mountains.

Half a century ago John Muir tried to buy a section of prairie land at his boyhood farm in Wisconsin, hoping to turn it into a sanctuary where the pasque-flower would bloom in the spring and conditions that existed in pioneer times would be maintained for future generations to see. He was unable to acquire the land. But, more and more, local groups are carrying out Muir's idea. They are performing invaluable service by preserving representative areas in different parts of the country. Habitat areas, as well as species of birds and wildflowers, can become extinct. Conservationists have grown increasingly conscious of the importance of these small, "type-specimen" sanctuaries. There is no finer example in the country of the value of such a preserve than the glen at Pearson's Fall. Since 1931 it has been a sanctuary maintained by the Garden Club of Tryon.

Our lives touched it at this one point, at this one time in spring when its magical beauty was unrivaled. Along the path to the falls we hardly advanced a foot without pausing to delight in some new wildflower. White violets blooming among hepaticas; the umbrella leaves of the mandrake sheltering the forming May apples; the massed plants of the false Solomon's seal crowding together on a rocky ledge; the white Dutchman's-breeches and the red columbine—the

Jack-in-trousers—these, each in turn, attracted our attention. We bent close to see foam flowers that enveloped their upright stems in little clouds of white. The tip of each tiny floret seemed dipped in wax of a delicate apricot hue.

Up the slopes the striped flowers of the jack-in-the-pulpit rose among the trilliums. Like the skunk cabbage, the jack-in-the-pulpit blooms before its leaves appear. It also is a plant that changes its sex, becoming female after storing up food for three or four or even five years. Another oddity among the familiar woodland flowers around us was the bloodroot. Each year it consumes the rear portion of its root and adds a new section to the front part, thus continually renewing its root-stock. Theoretically a bloodroot should be immortal. However, it requires special conditions for its existence. It dies, for instance, if the trees around it are felled.

It is no accident that most of the spring's earliest flowers bloom on the woodland floor. This is the time, before the leaves of the trees are completely unfolded and the shadows have grown dense, that the maximum amount of light for the growing season reaches the plants. It is then that they complete their most important vegetative and reproductive functions. Just as there is a direct relationship between the amount of light reaching the interior of a forest and the character of the vegetation growing there, so there is a direct relationship between the amount of light at different seasons and the time of blooming of these woodland plants. Of necessity, wildflowers of the woods bloom early.

In several places the sides of the glen were dripping like the walls of a grotto. Where a continual trickle of water ran down saturated wicks of moss on one little ledge beside the path, a half-circle of maidenhair ferns clung to the disintegrating rock. In *A Natural History of Pearson's Falls*, an early book by Donald Culross Peattie that did much to arouse interest in preserving the glen, thirteen different ferns are listed as native to the ravine. They include the walking fern, the rattlesnake fern, the sensitive fern, and the ebony fern. Nine species of violets also grow in the glen. We saw—below the troops of trilliums, the trout lilies, and the lady-slippers—violets of many kinds: white violets, yellow violets, blue violets. During almost the whole length of our trip we found violets, like the multitudinous footprints of spring, scattered over the map before us.

At the head of the glen the path brought us to the white lace of Pearson's Falls. It is lace formed of water by gravity on a loom of granite. In a thin, foaming layer the water of Pacolet River slides down the face of successive shelves of rock. The sound of this falling water is murmurous, calming, companionable. Here is no mighty, roaring Niagara, no deep-tongued bellow. This was a sound for a glen to enclose.

Red-gold sand forms a little bar at an edge of the pool into which the cascade falls. On this bar I picked up one perfect wing of a yellow swallowtail butterfly. Perhaps it had fallen into the ravine when some bird stripped it from the body of a captured insect. Lying there in the full brilliance of its colors, it recalled the Guiana Indians, in the South American jungles, who cling to the poetic belief that the most beautiful butterflies contain the souls of their ancestors.

Night and day the falling water of Pearson's Falls generates a cool, moist breeze. It stirred the ferns and the lady-slippers and the pendant white flowers along the underside of branches of the silver-bell tree that leaned out over the pool. It blended together the perfumes of many wildflowers. Sometimes, as we slowly walked back along the trail, we came to areas where one scent predominated, as when we passed strawberry bushes and caught the overwhelming spilled-wine fragrance of their dark red flowers.

The perfume of the wildflower is never a product of the nectaries. It comes from special cells holding the essential oils that produce the fragrance. When you break open the skin of an orange you see similar cells near the surface. Oftentimes the essential oils are waste products of the plant. They are occasionally stored in scentless chemical compounds within cells in the flower buds. When the flowers unfold, the compounds are chemically changed so that they produce fragrance. The cells that contain the essential oils may be in the leaves, the petals, or even the stamens of a plant.

It is the petals of the yellow jessamine, for example, that is the source of that flower's famous perfume. Thyme, equally famous, has its oils stored on the surface of its leaves in flask-shaped cells that are easily broken. It gives off its perfume at a touch or under the hot sun. The cells of rue lie just beneath the surface of the leaf and are roofed over with a thin layer that is pierced in the middle by a narrow slit. These lids on the cells swell, bend down at the edges, and thus—at the same time—enlarge the opening and press the fragrant oil out onto the surface of the leaf.

Writing more than three hundred years ago, an English herbalist noted the earlier observation that the seat of the perfume of the musk rose was in its stamens. "Some there be," he declared in the quaint wording of his day, "that have avouched that the chiefest scent of these roses consisteth not in the leaves but in the threads of the flower." This observation has since been verified by scientific tests.

Students of orchids have discovered a curious fact about their perfume. The elaborate specialization of some of these flowers includes giving off different scents by day and by night. *Pilumna fragrans*, for instance, is said to have a vanilla smell in the morning and a narcissus smell in the evening. *Dendrobium glumaceum* suggests heliotrope during the day and lilac at night. *Cattleya bogotensis* resembles in its scent a carnation in the morning and a primrose in the evening. It is the lily-of-the-valley in the daytime and the rose in the nighttime that is suggested by *Phaloenopsis schilleriana*.

So powerful are the perfume oils of flowers that $^1/120,000$th of a grain of oil of rose is all that is required to affect our sense of smell. That sense, incidentally, can be cultivated. After World War I a number of blinded French veterans were trained by Paris perfumers and became experts at analyzing scents by nose alone.

At one time, in France, it was believed that the smell of mint was the basic scent from which all others were derived. Psychologists today divide smells into six elementary odors: spicy, flowery, fruity, resinous, foul, and scorched. Because each perfume produces its own peculiar effect upon the olfactory cells, just as each musical note has its own characteristic effect upon the ear, a European scientist, several generations ago, sought to arrange all the odors of the world in a scale corresponding to a musical scale. He actually worked out such a scheme, assigning low notes to the heavy perfumes, such as vanilla, and high notes to the sharp odors, such as peppermint and citronella.

Below the pool where I had found the butterfly wing and where the breeze from the falls swayed the silver-bell flowers[,] Pacolet River plunges down a rocky bed along one side of the glen. The foaming stream is broken and rebroken; it swerves, slides over tilted slabs of granite, batters huge brown boulders; it is hurtling, tumbling all the way. If, instead of turbulence, calm had marked its flow, with quiet pools along its path, they would have reflected the beauty of flowering trees. For down all the course of the river through the glen redbud and dogwood and silver-bell trees lean out over the water. The white of the bellflowers and the dogwood matches the white of the foam. Rhododendrons are there too, laden with their 5-petaled white flowers with golden dots spattering the top two petals. We noticed that over and over again bees that came to the flowers alighted on the top two petals. We wondered if the insects were led there through mistaking the golden spots for pollen.

As we accompanied the river back to the mouth of the glen, with the perfume of innumerable wildflowers sweet in the air, I recalled an old inscription engraved on the tombstone of an early American naturalist:

"Lord, 'tis a pleasant thing to stand in gardens planted by Thy hand."

It was already past sunset when we walked under the beeches and among the star chickweed once more. The coolness of evening was increasing in the glen. From somewhere ahead, on a forested slope, came the bell music of a wood thrush. The memory of this rare and beautiful place we were leaving—its water music, its flower perfume and flower color—was one that often, in later recollection, brought us special pleasure.

ONE NORMALLY thinks of destruction of habitat or, perhaps, overhunting as responsible for loss of species. However, that is not always the case. Some wild plants have been gathered for market by folks in the mountains of North Carolina to a point that endangers the plant's survival.

The following selection, titled "Kite Hollow," appeared in Edwin Way Teale's *North With Spring*. It is the account of Teale's meeting with an old-time "herb gatherer" from near Lenoir, North Carolina. The native genius of Mrs. Toy Miller revealed itself in her enormous accumulation of plant lore.

"Kite Hollow"

from

North With Spring

by Edwin Way Teale

"Mrs. Toy Miller. Kite Hollow. Off Happy Valley. On the road to Blowing Rock."

I wrote it down in a spiral-ring pocket notebook.

We were in a huge rambling wooden building at Lenoir, North Carolina. Around us rose the smell of drying plants and roots and barks. The building was the headquarters of the Greer Drug Company, one of the country's largest dealers in medicinal herbs. Mountainfolk in hundreds of lonely spots were out in the spring weather gathering herbs, grubbing out roots, making a wild harvest to sell the Greer Company. One of the most active of the Blue

Ridge plant hunters is Mrs. Toy Miller. She ranges through Kite Hollow, along a mountain stream north of Happy Valley, and over the ridges beyond. I noted the directions for reaching her; for we hoped to go along on a hunt for mountain herbs.

The Greer Company, we found in looking over a price list, is in the market for such odd items as elder flowers, catnip leaves, balm of Gilead buds, skunk cabbage roots, wild strawberry vines, mistletoe twigs, horse nettle berries, haircap moss, shonny haw bark, and maypop pops. In the United States there are more than 250 species of roots, herbs, and barks of value in the manufacture of drugs. A bulletin put out by the U.S. Department of Agriculture, *American Medicinal Plants of Commercial Importance*, is a Who's Who of these salable herbs. It is also a dictionary of curious botanical folk names. The harvest of an American plant hunter may include badman's-oatmeal, truelove, tread-softly, simpler's joy, lords-and-ladies, shoofly, nature's mistake, or mad-dog skullcap. He may bring home Aaron's-rod, Noah's ark, Jacob's-ladder, or Devil's bones. Or he may return with juglans, kinnikinnic, hackmatack, missey-moosey, daffydowndilly, hurr-burr or robins-runs-away.

In the cavernous loft of the building at Lenoir we walked among piles of white pine and wild cherry bark, mounds of mullein leaves and blackberry roots, and rows of burlap bags filled with fragrant sassafras bark—the first product of the New World shipped back to Europe by the Pilgrims. Wooden barrels held Adam and Eve roots. Star grass roots, like small onions, were drying near adjoining mounds of yellow jessamine bark and pokeweed roots. And extending across a wide carpet of cloth lay bushels of balsam poplar, or balm of Gilead, buds. More buds were coming in every day. This was spring, the harvest-time of the budpickers. A waxy substance extracted from these buds is used in salves. For the dried buds, the Greer Company pays 60 cents a pound. Other prices range from 3 cents a pound for birch bark and 4 cents a pound for sumac berries to $1 a pound for star grass roots and $5 a pound for golden seal roots.

The highest price of all is paid for ginseng, from $8 to $10 a pound for the dried roots. Although there is no evidence that ginseng possesses any therapeutic or pharmacological properties, it has been in constant demand in China for centuries. The superstition that it has magic ability to restore virility to the aged has resulted in as much as $700 a pound being paid for especially fine roots in Manchuria. Most American ginseng grows far back in the mountains. The roots are at their best, shrinking least and bringing the highest prices, during a few weeks in autumn. André Michaux records that, in 1793, ginseng was the only product of Kentucky that could be transported profitably overland to Philadelphia.

Mailtime at the Greer Company brings a varied assortment of letters, penciled in unregimented spelling on odd scraps of paper by mountain plant hunters. The morning we were there, a note was deciphered suggesting that the writer should get twice the regular price for his roots because they were dug at a place "where the most dangerous snakes in the world live."

Not all the wild products handled at the Lenoir warehouse go into making drugs. Leaves of deer's-tongue are in demand for flavoring smoking tobacco. Another wild herb is necessary in the manufacture of silver polish. Sassafrass bark goes into making perfumes as well as medicines. A recent development has been the collection of pollens for the treatment of allergies. One year, in less than a month, the Greer Company shipped $40,000 worth of ragweed pollen to northern pharmaceutical laboratories. In a kind of nightmare chamber for hay fever sufferers, we saw row on row of glass vials and jars filled with brightly colored dust—pollen from more than a hundred different plants.

Some of the first pollen handled by the Greer Company came from Kite Hollow. The red dirt road that leads into this side valley eluded us that day and it was afternoon before we came to the beginning of the hollow. A mile or so away we had asked directions for finding Toy Miller's house.

"Anybody down there can tell you," we were assured. "They're all kinfolk in the hollow."

The house we were hunting, gray from long weathering, clung to the foot of a steep descent. A dozen rows of peas and a small patch of catnip for the cat occupied a cleared space in the weeds at the back of the house. Chickens, dogs, cats, and children swarmed over the porch and unfenced yard. The herbwoman came to the door—thin, tired looking, her left cheek and lower lip bulging with snuff used "for the toothache." She was, she said, going up the creek that afternoon—the balm of Gilead buds were right for picking— and we were welcome to come along. . . .

We started down the hollow. The herbwoman was alert, pleasant, friendly. She had been born near Blowing Rock and was, she said, "a mountain girl from the beginning." She had a kind of natural dignity and her mountain dialect was interspersed with words of an older and better diction. She had been collecting wild plants, roots and barks for fifteen years. Once, when lumbering operations felled a stand of white pines near Kite Hollow, she and her husband skinned the bark from the logs and, in seven hours, earned $41. Another time, in two days, they earned $61—piling up more than 800 pounds of bark at [seven-and-a-half] cents a pound. Those were long-remembered bonanza days.

Where a decaying rail fence staggered along under a load of honeysuckle vines we stopped amid wild strawberries. The ground was white with their blossoms over an area of a hundred square yards. The herbwoman comes here to pick strawberry leaves sometimes. They sell for 20 cents a pound. But she never comes to pick strawberries. By the time they are ripe the rattlers and copperheads that live in the honeysuckle tangle are out and active.

"There's a heap of berries here," she told us, "but you can't get near 'em for snakes."

Once, back in the mountains, she was standing in thick bushes when she heard a buzzing sound and looked down in time to see the brownish body and V-shaped crossbands of a timber rattlesnake slide almost across her foot. The snake, apparently, did not see her. What did she do?

"I made tracks out of there in a hurry!"

In the main, however, when she is hunting herbs in the mountains she gives little thought to snakes.

"Hits a wonder," she observed, "I ain't all eat up."

We followed the creek, swollen with spring rains, until we came to the first of the balm of Gilead trees. Under favorable conditions these balsam poplars reach a height of 100 feet. The young twigs are hairy and the cigar-shaped leaf buds are fragrant and shining with yellow wax. Indians used this wax for sealing the seams of their birchbark canoes. Honeybees collect it to stop up cracks in the hives. Pioneers valued the wax so highly as a healing salve that they planted balm of Gileads near their cabins. It was a medicine tree. Today these "balm buds" still form the source of an important ingredient in many manufactured salves.

We pulled down branches and picked off the buds. They rattled into the basket. We went from tree to tree. The sun was warm, the air filled with fragrance. Above the roar of the swollen stream, tumbling over the boulders of its bed, the calling of a cardinal carried far from his perch in the top of a willow tree. The ringing "What cheer! What cheer! What cheer!" was repeated over and over again.

"Hits got a big enough mouth," said the herbwoman succinctly.

The farthest she goes into the mountains in her plant collecting is about four miles. This is for the rarer herbs. The most sought-after of the roots grow scarcer every year. There is only one place now in the mountains where she is sure of finding ginseng. Also rapidly disappearing in the region is the "Noah's ark," the yellow lady-slipper. Its roots, collected in autumn, sell for $1 a pound, dried. The mountains of western North Carolina supply a large part of the nation's medicinal plants. Yet even here, where at one time the supply seemed unlimited, uncontrolled collecting is having its effect. Herb hunters have to roam farther and farther into remote regions to make their harvest. Near settled communities, many species have been completely extirpated.

As we walked along, the herbwoman pointed out plants that she would visit later. Horse nettle—apple of Sodom or treadsoftly—grew in a sandy place. Its berries, split and dried in autumn, bring 36 cents a pound. The dried roots bring 25 cents. The spindle-shaped roots of the yellow dock sell for only 9 cents a pound. Mullein, that plant of many names—candle-wick, blanket leaf, Adam's-flannel, old-man's-flannel, hare's-beard, velvet plant, clown's lungwort—was beginning the production of the thick, felty leaves of a new year. The leaves and tender tops of the mullein, picked and dried, have a market value of 10 cents a pound. Once we passed a mound of pokeweed. This was a wild garden the herbwoman visited annually. Pokeberries bring 15 cents a pound; the roots, which unfortunately "dry up to next to nothing," bring only 10. Nearer the stream, in a boggy stretch, skunk cabbage massed its sappy green leaves. Here harvest days come in early spring. The roots and rootstocks are dug up and dried, after being split to hasten the process. The split, dried roots sell for 20 cents a pound.

One of the few things the herbwoman never collects is mistletoe. These clumps usually grow too high in trees. However, much of the mistletoe that reaches northern states during the holiday season comes from North Carolina, tons being shipped from one county alone. Some modern Daniel Boones, expert with a squirrel rifle, are said to harvest the topmost bunches in their own peculiar way, snipping off the branches with well-directed lead.

Along the creek, as we walked back, willow trees leaned, in clouds of new, pale-green leaves, far out over the rush of the mountain stream.

"I've skinned more willow bark in this place than most people think," the herbwoman volunteered.

In recent years the streamside willows have become a new source of revenue. The catkins have assumed special importance. For willow pollen has gone to market. Each spring Mrs. Miller collects bushels of the staminate catkins, shifting their floral dust through a fine cloth into a dishpan. The best time for harvesting pollen, she has found, is in the morning just after the dawn mist has evaporated.

The fluffy, greenish catkins of the black willows are as long as a little finger. Sometimes the tassels are more than three inches in length. They represent the largest pollen source with which the herbwoman deals. The smallest is the white flower of the plantain.

On one of the hottest days of June, the previous year, she had followed the black-top road through Happy Valley, picking plantain flowers on either side. A score of times cars pulled up and people who thought she must be crazy wanted to know what she was doing.

When R.T. Greer, head of the Lenoir company, needs a new kind of pollen, he frequently puts Mrs. Toy Miller on its trail. Her knowledge of local plants is widely respected. Will Rogers once observed that we are all ignorant; we are just ignorant about different things. Our companion that day had had little schooling; she had never been beyond sight of one small part of the Blue Ridge Mountains. Her knowledge was narrow—but it was deep. She was an expert, an authority in her field.

A century and a half before, when André Michaux was wandering through the wilderness of the New World, collecting plants for Old World herbariums, he had recorded in his journal, in the spring of 1795, that he was "herborising in the Bleue Ridges." We too, that day, had been "herborising" in those same mountains.

As we drove away down the red dirt road heading for Statesville, we reflected on how humbling such a trip as ours eventually becomes. I remembered a famous explorer once saying to me: "The main thing I learn on every expedition is my ignorance." Everywhere we went we met new and unfamiliar things. Everywhere we went we encountered people who had spent their lives reading from one particular shelf in nature's library. They knew more about it—more about their area and their particular field—than we could ever hope to know. We could but sample the books they had time to read in detail.

We were near Hickory, North Carolina, in the sunset that evening when we caught the perfume of the first lilacs of our trip. They bloomed in a farmyard close to the road. A little farther on we ran through a great swirl of apple petals carried from a hillside orchard. And all along the way mockingbirds and cardinals sang in the failing light. It was dusk when we reached Statesville.

IN 1920, the young Bertram Whittier Wells, a man who would later become one of North Carolina's most distinguished ecologists, saw the Big Savannah, near Burgaw, North Carolina, from his railroad car window. Nearly fifty years later, he wrote about the impression Big Savannah made on him: "I saw a vast flat area literally covered with wild flowers. I immediately made up my mind to see it again. . . . I became convinced there was no such area of equal size and perfection with over a hundred species of herbaceous wild flowers blooming in profusion from late February to middle December. . . . As my memory goes back . . . the two summers of day after day on the Big Savannah continually surrounded in floral beauty . . . stand out beyond everything else."

Despite more than twenty years of effort by Bertram Whittier Wells and others to preserve it, the Big Savannah is gone. In the late 1950s, it was drained and put into cultivation. The loss is irreparable and should rend the heart of any North Carolinian who loves nature. Edwin Way Teale's description of Big Savannah in 1951 remains to haunt us. The essay is titled "Prehistoric Trapline," and is from *North With Spring*.

"PREHISTORIC TRAPLINE"

from

NORTH WITH SPRING

by Edwin Way Teale

*A*ll through that moonlit night, while fireflies shimmered in the white ground mist, a mockingbird spun out the brilliant thread of its song behind our cabin a mile from Wilmington. Whenever we awoke, the passion of its melody filled the night. Moving northward through the South, we had been in advance of the main singing season of these birds. Only here did we experience the full virtuoso performance of a mockingbird in the spring. The memory is indelible: the low-lying mist luminous in the moonlight; the scented air; the trees dark in their shadows; the flashing, greenish pin points of innumerable fireflies; and, unseen in the shadows, the singer, with passion unwearied, pouring forth his tumbling melody hour after hour through the night.

This was our introduction to a region of special attraction. The next morning, at six, we were breakfasting with Mrs. Cecil Appleberry, one of the most enthusiastic and capable amateur naturalists we met on our trip. During the following days she guided us down the byways of the Cape Fear region, the original home of the Venus's-flytrap, an area of pine woods and bays and true savannas.

Twenty-five miles north of Wilmington, near Burgaw, we came out upon the vast wildflower garden of one savanna that stretched away for 1,500 acres, flat as a Western prairie, lush as a bottom land. A wash of yellow ran across the whole expanse. Thousands upon thousands of the biscuit-shaped flowers of the pitcher plant, *Sarracenia flava*, were nodding above the grass on their slender stems. As spring advances, a kaleidoscope shifting of tints, a sequence of colors, sweeps over the savanna. At their appointed time, in the procession of the wildflowers, different blooms become dominant.

First come the bog dandelions of March, then the violets, the blue butterworts, the white fleabane, and the great iris show of May when the expanse of the savanna, from end to end, is one wide lake of blue. No wonder foreign botanists come from far parts of the world to see the Burgaw savanna! We envied those who lived close enough to watch the whole rainbow sequence from the beginning to the end. Like Pearson's Falls and the Great Smokies, the Burgaw savanna is a fragment of this nation's heritage that is infinitely valuable and that should be permanently preserved.

Our visit came when pitcher plants dominated the scene. And all over the flat coastal plain of the Cape Fear region, during those days, pitcher plants bloomed everywhere. They were the most obvious of a host of carnivorous plants—sundews, butterworts and those most astonishing of botanical inventions, the Venus's-flytrap—that prey upon insects. Probably nowhere else on the continent are there such concentrations of insectivorous plants as on the coastal plain of North Carolina. For untold millions of years they have been reversing the normal procedure: everywhere, animals eat plants; here, plants were consuming animals. They were trapping them with glue, with slippery surfaces, with mazes of spines, with bending leaves and with leaves hinged at the middle and set to snap shut on the body of the victim. Here, as we wandered over savannas and open pine flats, we were following nature's trapline, a prehistoric trapline, infinitely older than man.

Bats swooping low, have sometimes been caught and held prisoner by burdock burs. In Oregon, some years ago, a young short-eared owl was discovered held fast by the sticky leaves of the tarweed, *Asio flammus*. These instances, and others of their kind, were accidents. The plants derived no benefits from them. But here the trapping of small victims was no accident. Here it was being accomplished by means of some of the most amazing ruses and stratagems of the botanical world. And here the plants benefited directly. They were plants that ate meat. They secreted juices. They digested their victims. They functioned almost like animal stomachs. In this way they supplemented a diet deficient in needed elements.

One whole morning, with Mrs. Appleberry leading the way, we wandered down floral traplines that extended for miles across flatland among scattered pines. Often the ground was spongy with spagnum moss. We would walk fifty yards at a time on carpets that were thick, moist, and soft. In some places the top of this layer of spagnum had changed from gray-green to a yellowish hue that made the area seem coated with sulphur. A pair of indigo buntings dashed about, the male brilliant blue, the female brown and sparrowish. And singing somewhere in a pine ahead of us, a Bachman's pine-woods sparrow repeated over and over again its song of one long note and then a trill on a lower pitch.

The slender upright trumpets of *flava* rose in clusters, in rows, all around us. Three of different heights stood side by side, their tops descending like a trio of notes on a sheet of music. I split open one trumpet and found nearly five inches of insects packed in the lower part of the slender tube. All except a few at the top were dead. The fluid in the pitcher, largely secreted by the plant, has been found to drown insects more quickly than ordinary water. It is also thought to stupefy the victims. Physicians who have experimented with an extract taken from *Sarracenia* pitcher plants, have reported that, in some ways, the drug is superior to novocain as a local anesthetic for human beings. Enzymes also are present in the secreted fluid. They assist in digesting the captured insects. Young trumpets, not yet open, are sometimes half full of liquid.

The flow of this fluid within the pitchers is stimulated—like the flow of saliva—by food. Bits of raw meat, beef broth, and milk produce an increase; but cheese, casein, and raw whites of egg do not. In one series of experiments, two scientists, Frank Morton Jones and J.S. Hepburn, found that the introduction of small fragments of raw meat increased the fluid volume within a pitcher plant by as much as 157 per cent. In five days after beef broth was introduced, the fluid content increased 387 per cent. And when milk was used, the fluid increased by one-fifth in a single day and in seven days it gained by as much as 1,242 per cent. The experimenters also introduced dilute solutions of various acids and alkalis. No noticeable change in fluid volume resulted. But the tests revealed an interesting fact. No matter whether the introduced liquid was alkali or acid, the fluid in the pitcher-plant—as within the human stomach—soon returned to neutrality. The common idea that the liquid within these pitchers is nothing more than rain water is far from true.

In fact, all the thousands of slender trumpets of *flava* rising around us had a kind of awning or roof above their open mouths. Another pitcher plant of the area, *Sarracenia minor*, is equipped with a peaked

roof or rain hat that shelters its opening. In both instances, these extensions, resembling the top of a jack-in-the-pulpit, prevent most of the rain from entering the pitchers. Except for such a provision, heavy downpours would fill the pitchers until they overflowed and thus lost some of the captured insects. This is what happens in the commonest of sphangum-bog pitcher plants, *Sarracenia purpurea*, a plant found as far north as Labrador. We saw its wine-red flowers scattered among the yellow blooms of *flava*. Extending spokewise out from the center of the plant, its curved pitchers lift their wide, unprotected mouths to the sky. Every heavy rain overflows them. In spite of this, the plant thrives for 2,000 miles along the Atlantic coast from Florida northward.

One factor in its success is hundreds of downcurving hairs, massed together like quills on a porcupine's back along the inside of the top of the pitcher. We ran our fingers over them. Going down, they slid in a smooth toboggan; coming up, they met the resistance of the forest of downcurving spines. The insect that slips down this chute-the-chutes finds it impossible to crawl out again. Its descent is a one-way trip. And slipping is made easy by the smooth, rounded lip of the pitcher. I watched one ant come up on the rim of a *flava* trumpet. It ran along for a dozen steps, then suddenly skidded sidewise and shot downward out of sight. I slid a forefinger over the spot where it had lost its hold. The rim of the plant was polished and waxy.

Even the possibility that some of the winged insects might fly upward and out of the trap has been take care of in two of the American pitcher plants, *Sarracenia minor* and *Darlingtonia californica*.

Each has a thin, translucent spot in the hood that extends over the mouth of the pitcher. The insect, which might otherwise escape, is attracted to the light of this window and flying against it is knocked back down into the pitcher again.

Each pitcher is a leaf, a leaf with its edges grown together. Many are veined with purple, delicately tinted with shadings of yellow and green. They have the beauty of flowers even when the real flowers of the plant are absent. Like flowers, these leaf traps attract insects by means of nectar and perfume. Some pitcher plants are scented like violets, others have a rich fruity odor. One, *Sarracenia minor*, leads ground insects such as ants up the side of the tube and over the rim by means of a path of sweet nectar.

The ant that most often loses its life in pitcher plants is *Cremastogaster pilosa*. Yet, strangely enough, this species sometimes nests in the dry tubes of the very plants whose green pitchers are bringing death to large numbers of its kind. Other small insects live even more dangerously. They dwell within the active traps themselves. The scientific name of one small carrion fly, *Sarcophaga sarracenia*, indicates its close association with pitcher plants. It lays its eggs on the mass of decaying insects in the tubes. The larva, apparently immune to the digestive acids and enzymes of the fluid, feeds and grows and when it reaches full size bores through the side of the tube and pupates in the ground. The larva of a minute gnat has a somewhat similar history. And in the North the mosquito, *Wyeomyia smithii*, spends its larval life in the fluid within *purpurea* pitchers, hibernating frozen in ice during the winter. Remaining frozen in solid ice for months on end and surviving in the vegetable stomach of a pitcher plant are both commonplace events in its remarkable life cycle.

Predatory creatures also haunt these predatory plants. Spiders lurk near their open mouths, catching insects attracted by the perfume and nectar, before the plant can trap them. A tiny tree toad

and a small lizard not infrequently make their home in the carnivorous plants. And minute parasitic wasps descend within the tubes to
lay their eggs on moth larvae that feed on the inner tissues and spin
their cocoons within the dangerous confines of the pitchers. Each
hollow leaf, so cunningly fashioned for entrapping its prey, is a little
world in itself.

We wandered through a universe of these worlds. As far as we
could see, the damp, flat land was studded with the "huntsman's
horns" of the tubes and the "sidesaddle flowers" of the *flava* blooms.
Once, as I looked down at a cluster of trumpets, a movement beyond caught my eye. In an opening below a dark decaying log, a
scaly head thrust out and drew back like the quick flicking of a
tongue. I stood motionless. The head appeared again. Every perfect
green-tinted scale caught the sunshine. The lizard, a blue-tailed skink,
seemed newly formed of polished metal. It was close to its curious
breeding season in which the female lays three or four eggs and
then solicitously curls about them, protecting them for weeks, only
to ignore the young completely as soon as they appear from the
egg. Her further attention is unneeded. The baby lizards can care
for themselves from birth.

All over the Cape Fear region the soil is deficient in nitrogen.
By absorbing the soluble nitrogenous material from the bodies of
captured insects, the carnivorous plants of the coastal plain make up
for this lack. L.G. Willis, a soil chemist we visited near Wilmington,
believes that the insect diet also contributes needed copper. This
metal, almost entirely absent in the soil, is present in small quantities in the blood of insects.

The following day, in different places, we saw other traplines
running across wide expanses of open land or beside hardpan ba-
sins. I remember one stretch where the ground had been burned
over late in winter. Wiry grass blades were pushing up through soil
that was dark and wet and glistening. Here, for yards on end, the

earth was covered with a rich red mat, a carpet formed of the close-packed rosettes of the sundew. Each coglike plant lay flat on the ground. At the end of the stems, the round leaves, about the size of shirt buttons, supported a maze of purple-tinted tentacles. A hundred fifty or more grow on a single leaf. Those at the center were stubby; those at the edges of the leaf were longest. Each ended in an oval swelling. Within this swelling, a gland produces drops of glistening glue. Where the sun struck the droplets, all the leaves sparkled as though covered with dew.

For gnats and mosquitoes and other winged minutiae we saw drifting above the red rosettes, the droplets represent a deadly dew. If they touched no more than two or three of the maze of tentacles they were caught fast as though on Tanglefoot. The pitcher plants were vegetable pitfalls. Their traps were passive. But the snare of the sundew is combined with action.

As soon as an insect is caught, the tentacles move, almost like the fingers of a closing hand, to carry the victim to the center of the leaf. Other tentacles touch it. Other drops of glue increase the plant's hold upon it. Thus it is enfolded by a curious rolling motion. And all the time the tentacles are pouring out additional fluid. The struggles of the victim rapidly cease. Wrapped in the leaf, surrounded by the mucilage of the sundew, it drowns, usually in less than a quarter of an hour.

Now the leaf of the plant becomes the counterpart of the animal stomach. Digestive juices begin dissolving the insect; the leaf begins absorbing the nutriment. The sundews we saw closing that morning would remain closed for several days. Then when all the nutriment had been obtained from the victim, the tentacles would disengage themselves, fan slowly outward, and the leaf would assume its original position. With droplets of glue glistening in the sun, it would lie in wait for another victim.

The stimulus that sets in motion this chain of actions is apparently both mechanical and chemical. A tentacle will begin to move at a pressure of less than $1/70,000$ of a grain. Darwin found that a sundew would react to $1/20,000,000$ of a grain of phosphate in aqueous solution. To close entirely, the plant needs chemical as well as mechanical stimulus. Thus if you drop water on the leaf or put a small pebble on it, it may begin bending its tentacles but soon returns them to their original position. But substitute a drop of milk for water or a bit of meat for the pebble, and you see the leaf close over it as it would enfold an alighting insect. Thus it demonstrates its amazing ability to differentiate between edible and inedible substances.

At the time he was making his classic experiments with insectivorous plants, Charles Darwin noted an interesting thing about the mucilage of the sundew. It is a powerful antiseptic. It halts almost completely the action of bacteria. In one test, Darwin placed a bit of meat on a sundew and a second piece on moss. Later he examined them both under a microscope. The meat taken from the sundew was free of bacteria while that which had lain on the moss was "swarming with infusoria."

Also antiseptic is the glue of another carnivorous trap. This is the "butter" of the butterwort. Shepherds in the Alps have used it for generations as a healing salve. During the days we wandered among the rooted traps of Cape Fear, the blue spring flowers of the butterworts were rising among the yellow of the sidesaddle flowers and the red of the sundew. Each nodded at the top of a slender stalk which rose from the center of a rosette of pale-green fleshy leaves. The sides of these long and narrow leaves curl inward, forming troughs in which the glue of the trap is secreted. The upper surface of each leaf is shot through with an infinite number of tiny glands, as many as 25,000 to the square centimeter. From these glands comes the thick glue that traps small insects and the digestive juices that dissolve all except the hard chitin shells of the victims. Like the sundew, the butterwort combines adhesion and action. Once a small insect alights and is trapped, the curled sides of the leaf roll slowly inward, squeezing out more glue from the hundreds of thousands of glands on its surface.

In all the plant traps that we encountered, it is the leaf that is modified to capture prey. In the pitchers, the leaf is rolled into a tube with the edges joined; in the sundew, the leaf bears moving, glue-studded tentacles; in the butterwort, the leaf curls inward and its upper surface is equipped with immense numbers of small glands. But the most remarkable leaf of all is found in the plant we had come to Wilmington especially to see, the celebrated Venus's-flytrap. Sundews range around the globe. There are more than a hundred different species, the greatest variety being found in Australia. But in all the world there is only one species of flytrap. And nowhere else on earth is it found except on the Carolina coast.

Before the American Revolution, John Bartram sent living flytraps to England. They caused a sensation among botanists. In 1768, Carl Linnaeus wrote to John Ellis, who had sent him pressed specimens from London: "Though I have doubtless seen and examined no small number of plants, I must confess I never met with so wonderful a phenomenon." Darwin rightly called the flytrap "the most wonderful plant in the world."

Its wonder lies in its leaf. The two halves have been compared to upper eyelids with lashes along the edge. They are hinged at the stem so that they open and close in the manner of the jaws of a steel trap. Normally the two segments lie open. Stubby hairs, usually three on each side, form the trigger of the botanical trap. When a hapless insect brushes against these hairs, the jaws snap shut.

Although we saw pitchers plants by the thousands, sundews in vast numbers, butterworts and their blue spring flowers scattered over miles of flatland, we sought the hinged leaves of the flytrap for hours in vain. Immense numbers have been dug and sold to nurseries and 10-cent stores. Around Wilmington, where the original plants were found, the Venus's-flytrap has become scarce. On the afternoon of our second day, somewhere along the Old Shell Road on the way to Wrightsville Beach, we drew up at a filling station. A farmer was just climbing into a Ford truck. Yes, he told Mrs. Appleberry, he knew where we could find flytraps. One of the few places in the county where they still grew in numbers was along the edge of a "bay" on his farm. We followed his truck. And as we did so, the sky darkened. Hardly had we reached the spot when pelting rain began. It continued hour after hour, all the rest of the day, far into the night—the driving deluge of a long spring rain.

The following morning, under cloudless skies, we returned to the bay. This shallow basin underlaid by hardpan, a kind of swamp without standing water, stretched away into a tangle of low bushes, ferns, and scattered pines. Where natural drainage descended the slight dip at its edge, the flytraps grew. It is in such places, where white soil drains down into dark, that they are most often found. Such plants as hound's-tongue, round-leaved boneset, blazing star, and running blueberry are frequently associated with them. But Venus's-flytrap is never found where ragweed grows. Wire grass sometimes invades flytrap areas, pushing back or eliminating the insectivorous plants. And when bushes grow too tall, reducing the sunlight, the flytraps disappear.

Around us the green rosettes of the extended leaves spread away amid low vegetation. Some were small, hardly three inches across; others were half a foot in diameter. Each suggested a circle of spoons extending outward from a common center. Most of the traps were held open at an angle of 40 or 50 degrees. A few were opened as far as 80 degrees. The shiny upper surface of each hinged leaf was flushed with red. There a vast number of minute tinted glands were massed together. From them pours the fluid that digests the victims of the flytrap.

I squatted beside one trap in which this fluid had completed its work. The leaf had opened again, revealing the husk of a large dark fly. Everything except the legs, the wings, the chitin shell of the insect had been digested. Half a dozen minute ants were investigating the remains of the fly. They found no nourishment in it. The plant had sucked it dry. It had dissolved and absorbed everything edible before the jaws of the trap had opened.

In this case the victim of the flytrap was a fly. In most instances, however, it is likely to be some crawling ground insect, an ant or a beetle. I watched one dark beetle, about three-eighths of an inch long, wander over the jaws of another trap later that day. It may have been attracted by the sweetish fluid exuded on the leaf. It plodded this way and that, stopping often. Minutes passed before it blundered against the trigger hairs of the trap. With a quick movement like the swift closing of a hand, the halves of the leaf came together. The trap was sprung; the beetle was caught.

The speed with which the jaws of the trap snap shut depends upon the temperature. The movement is speeded up by heat, slowed down by chill, just as the activity of the insects is increased by hot days and lessened by cool ones. Under a midsummer sun, a flytrap will close from wide-open position in a single second. That movement comprises a complex series of events.

When the beetle touched the trigger hairs, minute electrical disturbances resulted. The stimulus ran through the living cells of the upper side of the leaf. These cells are swollen with water under pressure, pressure that holds the trap open against the tension of the spring. Now this force suddenly gives way. The water escapes into spaces between the cells. The spring mechanism, formed of the woody substances in the veins, snaps shut the trap.

As the jaws close, the trigger hairs, hinged at their bases, fold against the surface of the leaf like the retractable landing gear of an airplane. The long spines, extending out from the edges of the jaws, meet and intermesh. At first the two halves of the leaf remain slightly concave like clamshells. They do not press tightly together. The imprisoned insect finds itself in a barred cage. If it is small enough it still can slip between the bars of the interlacing spines. Darwin thought this provision kept the plant from wasting its time on tiny creatures relatively valueless as food.

Studies made by Frank Morton Jones near Wilmington have shown that this is so in practice. He collected fifty Venus's-flytraps containing insects and measured the victims. Only one of the fifty was less than five millimeters—about one-fifth of an inch—long. Only seven were less than six millimeters. The rest were ten millimeters or more, with the largest having a length of thirty millimeters—almost one-and-one-fifth inches. Grasshoppers and millipedes have been found captured by flytraps. I placed a dark angleworm, which came to the surface of the ground beside me, on one trap. Its writhing touched the triggers and the jaws closed upon it. But it was too long, too slender, too slippery for the plant to hold. Jones concluded that the flytrap victims ranged from those as large as the leaf could imprison down to those about a quarter of an inch long. Smaller insects are able to creep between the bars of the cage.

Several times I ran a grass blade across the leaf of a plant to watch the action of the trap. A single contact with the trigger hairs is not enough. They have to be touched twice or two have to be touched in quick succession. This also aids the plant. It prevents it from needlessly closing on every fragment of a falling leaf or other inanimate object that touches it. The traps that I sprung with my grass blade would remain closed for from twenty-four to thirty-six hours. Those containing insects often stay shut for a week while the assimilation of the food takes place.

After the first swift movement of the trap closing on its prey, the two halves begin a gradual flattening out, pressing together in a deliberate squeeze that continues from a half to twelve hours. At the same time the red-tinted glands begin pouring out their digestive secretions. The trap becomes a stomach absorbing the edible part of its prey. Formic acid is present in the fluid secreted by the glands. It inhibits the action of bacteria and prevents decay within the plant. If a slender piece of meat is placed in a flytrap, part inside and part out, the protruding portion will decay while the part inside will be entirely free of bacteria. If the rotted portion is placed within a fresh leaf, the odor disappears.

As the days pass and the trapped insect is reduced to nothing more than a hollow chitin shell, pressure begins building up in the surface cells of the leaf. Slowly the spines, interlaced like the fingers of two hands, disengage. The twin jaws of the trap fall gradually apart. The meal is over. The plant is "hungry" again. With trap reset, it awaits the coming of a new victim.

How many times in succession does a single trap capture and digest its prey? In 1923, in an almost-forgotten chest in an attic at another Wilmington—Wilmington, Delaware—that question was discovered in a letter that had crossed the ocean half a century before. Charles Darwin had asked it of his American correspondent, the Delaware botanist, William M. Canby. So far as Canby could discover, a leaf caught insects as many as three times but never more.

Watching these flytraps attracting insects with bait and color, closing over their prey like pouncing animals, digesting them, opening their trap leaves to repeat the performance—watching them with wonder that remained unwearied—we saw them as things apart from the stolid unconsciousness of ordinary plants around them. A special cunning had been wrought into these creations of sap and tissue and chlorophyll. They were geniuses of the plant world.

In all that prehistoric trapline where we wandered among prototypes of pit and Tanglefoot and steel-jawed trap, these plants were the ones we had most wanted to see. One other thing Mrs.

Appleberry had promised us. So far it had eluded us. This was the painted bunting, that little avian rainbow, the nonpareil.

On the afternoon of our last day in the Cape Fear region, after we had eaten hamburgers at a roadside restaurant known as "Jess James" and were driving slowly down a byway off the Old Shell Road, even this came to us. Mrs. Appleberry had described its song and we all were listening as we rode along. Nellie heard it first. It came from the top of a high pine at our left, a sweet warble that was broken off only to begin again. We scanned the upper branches through our glasses. Flashes of movement appeared and disappeared among the topmost needles. The interrupted strains of a tantalizing song continued. Five minutes went by. Then into a sunlit opening surrounded by shining needles darted a bird of breath-taking beauty. As it flitted and turned in its feeding, we saw the soft red-rose breast, the indigo blue of its head, the brilliant green of its back. No other bird native to North America is so colorfully beautiful. It is well named the nonpareil.

Thus our stay in the Cape Fear region, amid the strangeness and wonder of botanical traplines, was bounded by the beauty of birds—by beauty of birdsong at the beginning, by the beauty of bird form and color at the end.

JOHN K. TERRES (1905–), field naturalist and author, was born in Philadelphia, Pennsylvania. He served as managing editor and editor of *Audubon Magazine* from 1949 to 1960, and he has written and edited numerous books on birds, mammals, insects, and plants. In the early 1960s, Terres moved to Chapel Hill to write an encyclopedia of bird life. During his stay, he began regularly visiting the Mason Farm, a remarkably wild tract belonging to, and located near, the University of North Carolina. From those outings, Terres wrote *From Laurel Hill To Siler's Bog: The Walking Adventures of a Naturalist*, a book that contains the selection below, titled "Cottontail," and other essays that beautifully detail the creatures and wild things on the Mason property.

The book is a treasure. One reviewer wrote: "Because this book is a work of art we are held in its spell in a timeless world. . . . It is not poetry, but poetry (exact observation, deeply felt) breathes through the lines. Mr. Terres manages to distill pages of notes into a single vivid phrase, and hours of close watching over a period of years into a rich tale." In 1971, *From Laurel Hill To Siler's Bog* received the John Burroughs Medal for the outstanding nature book.

"COTTONTAIL"

from

FROM LAUREL HILL TO SILER'S BOG: THE WALKING ADVENTURES OF A NATURALIST

by John K. Terres

I saw the fourth week of March, windless and gentle, begin to crowd April. Starring the slopes of Laurel Hill and carpeting the floor of Big Oak Swamp, pink-white spring beauties sent their warm fragrance across the drying Carolina fields. In a tuft of grasses, dead and brown, under a tall stalk of last year's horseweed, the pregnant cottontail rabbit crouched in her bed.

Last fall I had caught her in a box trap I had set in Big Oak Woods. While I held her warm body close, with one hand restraining her slashing, sharp-clawed hind feet, I had marked her with a small, harmless identifying tag that I attached to her right ear. She

Reprinted from *From Laurel Hill To Siler's Bog: The Walking Adventures of a Naturalist*, by John K. Terres. New York: Alfred A. Knopf, 1969. Used by permission of the author.

was only a few months old then and had already made the bed, or "form," in which she now sat, brown and still, twenty feet from the edge of the woods. It was one of several of her resting places I had found in which she might hide during the day. For a cottontail rabbit is a creature of dawn and dusk, and of the night. Watching her from the place where I stood on the old farm road, I could see the white tag in her right ear. Although I had seen other rabbits use her form briefly, the present occupant was Cottontail herself.

From my calculations, I knew that she would soon give birth to her second litter of the year. The first, born in February, had not done well. Barely hidden by the thin ground cover of late winter, crows had discovered it. From a distance I saw three of them at the nest, but I arrived too late to frighten them away. I suspected that two of them were the pair of crows that had nested for six successive years in a tall pine in nearby Finley Tract. The third may have been one of the pair that built a nest of sticks, lined with finely shredded bark and mosses, in a cedar tree a quarter of a mile away on Laurel Hill. While Cottontail ran at one crow, causing it to fly, the other two reached into the nest, and each flew off with a squealing young. By the next day, the three baby cottontails that were left had disappeared. The crows may have returned for them, or possibly Cottontail herself had moved them to another place.

From her bed in which she sat quietly on this March day, Cottontail could see straight ahead into leafless Big Oak Woods. And she could see even in back of her, through the spaces in the tuft of dead grasses that the winds had twisted around her three-pound body. Enemies come to a cottontail from all sides. Upward she could see the brown speck that hung two thousand feet away in the vast dome of blue above Laurel Hill. With her I watched the red-tailed hawk swing in circles, its head bent earthward, searching the North

Carolina farm for the movement of any animal that might be suitable prey.

Cottontail tightened her body, as though preparing for a sudden leap and swift flight. Perhaps she was waiting for my sweeping glance to rest on her still form, but I ran my gaze over and beyond her, as swiftly as the running breeze that touched the grasses around her and then was gone. Had I looked too long, she would have known that I had discovered her and would have left her form in a swift dash across the field and into Big Oak Woods. She may have feared the red-tailed hawk more than she feared me. She kept her place.

Cottontail's large brown eyes—high in her head, just below the long, sensitive ears—gave her almost periscopic, or "around and around," vision. She could see, microscopically, the stink beetle that crawled up the grass past her moist, wobbling nose. Seconds later, she may have seen it snatched out of the air by a buzzing robber fly that sank its beak into the beetle and drained its life juices. I saw and marveled at the swiftness of the predatory fly's strike.

Cottontail's dark eyes remained fixed in a watchful stare. She may have seen the hurrying Tapinoma ant that ran from under her feet, but she gave no sign. A yard away, the ant tumbled into a conical pit made by an ant lion in the sand. Instantly the sicklelike jaws of the fiercely predatory insect reached up at the bottom of the pit to pull the ant under. Death by violence, even in miniature, was the cottontail's world. She herself might be struck down before she could bear the six young that had gradually swollen her double uterus these last twenty-seven days. At their places of attachment, the blood of her young now mingled with her own. Perhaps their stirrings warned her of the new venture for which she must now prepare. Within twenty-four hours, her litter would be born. One more task remained. . . .

One of the miracles of the cottontail's world is its unusual breeding cycle. No wild mammal of North America, except some of the field mice, is more prolific. In the South, from February to July or August, the cottontail may have six or seven litters with an average of five young in each. In one summer, she can produce thirty-four young rabbits, and some of these may breed and have young before the long summer has ended. After five years, if Cottontail and all her progeny still lived, 3,779,136 rabbits would be swarming over the Mason Farm.

Of course, no such thing happens. The red-tailed hawks of Boothe Hill, the gray foxes of nearby Willow Oak Swamp, the bobcat of Edwards Mountain, the half-wild dogs, and the snakes, weasels, and hunters that move over the Mason Farm sweep most of them away. Only a remnant of the cottontail population lives through winter and into spring. These are the sustainers of the cottontail race. . . .

The past winter I had seen the first of the wild "jump sequences" of the cottontail courtship that lead, in twenty-one days, to the first mating of the year. It began early in January in the dusk of a snowless field by Big Oak Woods near the place where I sat hidden in a tree. During the fall, Cottontail had abandoned her open-field bed for the security of a brush pile at the wood's edge. She was warmer there, protected from the north winds and touched for a few hours each day by winter sunlight. To be near Cottontail's winter bed, I had built a wooden platform above the ground. I had fastened it securely between the close-growing trunks of several trees and had wrapped it around with burlap. Hidden as in a wildlife photographer's blind, I could watch the brown field and the wood's edge below without being seen.

Late that mild January day, I heard a barred owl hoot from Willow Oak Swamp and saw a last cardinal flutter to its roost in a nearby cedar tree. Through an opening in the burlap, I saw Cottontail's brown shape leap from the brush pile. She moved out into the field, her white eartag showing in the dying light. This time she did not stop to groom her fur or to browse on sumac bark as she usually did on leaving her bed. Another cottontail had suddenly appeared, and I saw it follow her. From what I learned later, this was a male. He came toward her slowly from the rear. When he was ten feet away, Cottontail turned quietly to face him. She crouched and laid back her ears in the threat pose. She would accept courtship up to a point, but that was all at this time.

The male, facing her five feet away, stood high on all fours, his ears straight up. Suddenly he rushed at her and Cottontail leaped high in the air. The action was so fast in the dusk that I could not see all, but while she is in the air, Cottontail is said to throw a jet of urine at the male as he passes under her. It is part of the premating behavior that works both animals a little closer to the time of mating.

At the end of his rush the male turned, and both faced each other again. Now Cottontail dashed at him and he leaped over her, apparently throwing a jet of urine at her as he passed. Some of these jumps were tremendously long for such a small animal. In the winter snow I had measured the ordinary leaps of an undisturbed cottontail at from three to five feet and the wild bounds of a cottontail chased by a fox at from eight to nine feet; but some of these courtship jumps were twelve to fifteen feet long.

In the pale light of the gathering dusk, I saw the jump sequence suddenly end. The two brown forms moved away from each other and toward Big Oak Woods. There Cottontail began to nibble the bark from a young red maple along the wood's border; the male moved into the woodland and disappeared. Bark makes up most of the winter food of a wild rabbit, and not until April, with new grasses and fresh herbs, would Cottontail change gradually to the green foods of summer. . . .

My luck ran out that January in my observations of Cottontail's courtship sequence. I became seriously ill and for weeks was unable to hide in my blind and watch her. At the time, while I was recuperating from a severe respiratory infection, I worried over the fate of the small brown rabbit. However, I did not need to watch her to know what would follow, if she lived. Scientists had studied the breeding period of the cottontail rabbit so intensively that it had become one of the most thoroughly explored of any small wild animal.

Twice more in January Cottontail would join the male in the jump sequences. The jump periods would come at seven-day intervals, with Cottontail's increasing rhythmic urge, and that of the male, for close contact with each other. Each time the sequences would be longer and more fevered as the female approached her estrus, or "heat." The longer days of midwinter would bring more light; passing directly through a rabbit's eyes, or through its orbital tissues, the increasing light would stimulate the hypothalamus of Cottontail's brain, which in turn would cause her pituitary gland to give off increased sex hormones. This would start her breeding cycle.

In Cottontail the interaction of two ovarian hormones would bring cellular changes in her uterus and vagina and the ripening of her egg follicles. In the male it would lead to the forming of sperms in the testes.

If my calculations for Cottontail's courtship sequences that January had been correct, on the twenty-second day—seven days after the third and last jump sequence of the year—the male in the dusk would come after Cottontail, chasing her closely. One would barely be able to see them in the gathering gloom, but there would be no jump period at the time, for Cottontail would have reached her first heat, or estrous cycle, of the year. Thereafter, there would be no preparation by the jump sequences and her heat would come regularly every twenty-eight days until the spring and summer breeding season ended.

The male chasing Cottontail in the dusk would finally catch up with her. Cottontail, no longer resistant, would crouch in the submissive posture. He would mount her, and from that union probably would have come Cottontail's first unfortunate litter, which had been killed by crows.

Now in March, long after my illness and long after I had discovered that Cottontail was still alive, I was to see her complete her preparation for the birth of her second litter and to watch the surprising spectacle that immediately followed the birth of her young. . . .

For an hour I had been watching Cottontail crouched in her form. The mild March day was ending, and she would soon emerge from her bed to start her long night. I heard the sweet, piping cries of chorus frogs from the roadside ditch as I moved quietly toward my observation tree. A red-shouldered hawk began its musical wailing along Morgan Creek. Its cries must have startled the pileated woodpecker of Big Oak Woods. The big, red-crested bird cackled loudly and flew up to its roosting hole in the top of a giant oak. As I passed the frogs, they fell silent. Quietly as I had walked, they must have seen or heard me. By the time I had settled in my tree platform, their cries had started again.

At 6:00 P.M., Cottontail leaped out of her bed and sat for a moment in the low green grass. She reached down to lick her sides and, catlike, began to groom her fur. She sat up on her haunches and washed her forepaws with her tongue, then ran her paws down over her long ears. For a time she was busy with them, then she turned suddenly away and began to nibble at the March grasses and chickweed whose tender green was sweeping across the field.

Now Cottontail seemed nervous and she often stopped feeding to sit high on her haunches and look around. I saw that she was gradually moving to the center of the field. When almost at midfield, she stopped, sat up to look again, then dropped all fours and began to dig with her front feet. She was digging her nest cavity, and I thought she had chosen the place wisely, or with inherited cotton-tail caution. Most of the foxes, raccoons, opossums, and other animals that hunt over the Mason Farm travel the farm roads or along the ditches, stream banks, and woodland trails. Out in the center of the old weedy field, a rabbit's nest with its young would be less likely to be discovered by hungry four-footed predators.

She did not dig long. Later, I discovered that she must have excavated most of the four-and-a-half-inch-deep cavity during the last few days because she now turned to the next operation to complete it. She ran away from the nest cavity to a clump of foxtail grass. Quickly she bit off the dried grasses and, with them cross-wise in her mouth, returned to the cavity. I could see her put her head down and arrange the grass stems with her mouth and fore-feet. Back and forth between grasses and her nest she traveled, stopping occasionally to browse the green stems of dandelion or to sit up and look cautiously around.

Suddenly, in the evening gloom of the March day, I saw another cottontail hop toward the nest. From what followed, I learned that this was the dominant male, perhaps the one that had sired Cottontail's first litter—and the second, for which she was now preparing. Behind him came four other rabbits that I could see were following Cottontail's tracks, their noses to the ground like trailing hounds.

Through my powerful binocular I watched the dominant male vigorously chase them away, then return to the nest. He nosed over it carefully and was so preoccupied with it that when Cottontail returned, she had to hop around him to deliver another mouthful of dried grasses to her nest. He seemed to be inspecting her work, but he quickly left the nest to again drive away the four rabbits that had boldly returned to within a few feet of Cottontail. Obviously these were all her suitors, and the dominant male intended to keep them from her. But why were they all interested in a pregnant cottontail about to give birth to her young? Their behavior seemed curiously untimely, but I was soon to see the reason for it.

Very quickly Cottontail stopped carrying grasses to her nest and began pulling loose the molting hair from her shoulders and flanks. She had begun a new pattern of behavior. She had completed her grassy nest lining next to the raw earth. Now she was beginning the final inner nest lining of her own fur which would cradle her young and blanket them over from above. Their birth was imminent; her uterine contractions might even have begun.

As she pulled hair from her rump, I saw her fall. Her hind quarters seemed paralyzed as she sprawled helpless on the ground. She fell several times before she was able to stand again and go on with her hair pulling. Apparently the uterine convulsions that now periodically seized her caused her to lose temporary control over her hind legs.

While the male watched, Cottontail made several trips to the nest and worked the fur into the inner lining. She moved a little way from the nest and again began to pull at her fur. The male came close, smelled of her, then touched her with his forefeet. Cottontail leaped on him and rode him to the ground. He squealed as she held him down by pressing one of her hind feet on his neck, and she bit him on the rump. He squealed again, and she released him and went back to her hair pulling. The other males drew closer and one of them ran around in impatient circles. The dominant male came close to her and smelled of her, but he did not touch her. Apparently, he was checking something about Cottontail, but what it was mystified me.

Cottontail gave birth to her young quickly. I was watching her steadily through my binocular as she continued to pull at her fur while near the nest. Suddenly she stopped, turned, and squatted over the nest. Then she whirled about several times and ended up facing in the opposite direction. She straightened her back and jerked her pelvis downward. With this action I believe that she forcefully delivered one or more young into the nest chamber. Then she sprawled over the nest for about five minutes, looking straight ahead. From her position I think she nursed her newly born cottontails for the first time. The nursing over, she scratched dead grasses over the young, then dashed away.

I had suspected what was to come, but was not prepared for the strange behavior of the males that now began in the March dusk. Cottontail had moved to the edge of Big Oak Woods where the five attending males were waiting for her. She ran aggressively at them and drove them away, but when she turned from them, they followed her closely like hounds on a hot trail. All moved with ridiculous exaggeration, standing unusually high on their hind feet, deeply sniffing the air, and rapidly rotating their ears. They moved jerkily and often collided as they hopped wildly about.

Cottontail had slowed down, and the dominant male dashed at the others to keep them away. Then he turned and caught up with her. Now, instead of repelling him, she crouched submissively and he mounted. He made four swift pelvic thrusts and it was over. Cottontail broke away and moved into the darkening Big Oak Woods. I saw her cottony white tail disappear in the darkness with the five males in pursuit.

With her loss of interest in the males, Cottontail would begin another behavior pattern in which she would closely guard her helpless young. She would remain somewhere not far from them, and to nurse them, for a day or two after they were born, she would crouch over the nest—belly down—with the young ones nuzzling her breasts from their hiding place in the nesting cavity in the ground.

Each nursing time, before Cottontail left, she would rearrange the furry blanket and then scratch grasses over the nest to cover it.

Despite a rabbit's care in hiding her nest and young, dogs, foxes, skunks, cats, and large snakes find the helpless young ones and eat them. Sometimes shrews and field mice attack and kill the young in the nest. One day, along a logging road on Laurel Hill, I watched a weasel carry a young rabbit from a cottontail's nest and enter a pile of rocks in which the weasel had a family of its own. The rabbit's nest was empty and I suspected that the weasel had carried away every one of the cottontail young to feed them to her own litter.

One morning, in a grassy field above a pond, I saw a collie swallowing a young rabbit. Three dead ones, about ten days old, lay at the dog's feet. It had dug the young rabbits from the nest and killed all of them just before I arrived.

A rabbit's devotion to its young can be pathetic when its efforts to protect them are futile. But it can be a splendid thing when a mother cottontail willingly confronts a relatively enormous foe to save her young from destruction.

One day a young North Carolina farmer told me a remarkable story of an adult rabbit, one that not only illustrated the animal's courage, but a kind of rabbit wisdom which required exquisite timing. It was an act of which I was sure Cottontail herself would have been capable. One spring morning, while he was plowing a field, the roar of his tractor frightened a rabbit from her hiding place in a patch of grass. When he walked to the place he found the rabbit's nest. It held four young ones about a week old, their eyes just opened. The farmer covered them again with the mother's protective blanket of grass and fur, drove a stick into the ground to mark the place, and continued his work. When he got to that part of the field, he plowed around the nest, leaving a small island of undisturbed land with the young rabbits in the center of it.

The next morning, when the farmer drove to the field to continue his plowing, he heard a sharp yelp in the distance. Then he saw a long-legged black dog and a smaller beagle gallop out of the woods and start across the plowed field. The stray dogs were roving aimlessly but with their noses to the ground and moving in the general direction of the rabbit's nest in the center of the field. The dogs were too far away to head them off. He shouted at them, but they came on, and within seconds would reach the cottontail's nest. Then, out of a blackberry patch at the field's edge flashed the brown form of an adult rabbit. Presumably it was the female cottontail that the young farmer had seen leave the nest the day before.

The rabbit crossed the field in tremendous bounds and reached the nest just ahead of the dogs. She ran to meet them, then swerved sharply and cut across the field in front of their noses. Surprised by the rabbit's boldness, the dogs stood like statues, their heads up, mouths open. Then with a roar they were after her.

The black dog was much swifter than the beagle. Within seconds he had overtaken the cottontail and was stretching, open-jawed, to catch her. Just as his mouth was closing on her rump, the rabbit jerked away in another direction. The black dog rushed past the cottontail, but the beagle changed direction with her and was very close to her bobbing white tail. Again the rabbit turned, but the black dog was there and about to seize her. She swerved once more and, with the dog's slavering jaws at her tail, dived into an open, grassy ditch that drained water from a nearby woodland across the field. The beagle plunged into the ditch after her.

The rabbit raced up the ditch bottom, a brown streak. The black dog, now running on the bank above the cottontail—his back arched, his long legs reaching far ahead—was closing rapidly. It seemed to the farmer that it was impossible for her to escape. He was sure then that the rabbit could not reach the woods ahead of the dogs. With the black muzzle almost touching her bobbing tail, the cottontail gained the edge of the road on which the farmer stood. But instead of trying to cross it as he had expected her to do, she suddenly disappeared. She had run inside a drainage pipe buried under the road.

The dogs, brought up short, howled and shoved their noses into the opening, but it was too small for them to enter. The rabbit, knowing her territory and all its escape routes and hiding places, had calculated her race to the last split second, and had won.

During the few hours of each March day that I tried to trace the survival of Cottontail and her growing litter, only once did I see her threatened by dogs, although the stray animals that ran about over the Mason Farm must have chased her many times. The miracle was that she, and her litter in the field, had survived at all, with the constant threat of death from so many natural enemies. But she proved to me that a cottontail might live for a relatively long time and that she has stratagems which protect her quite as effectively as her strong hind legs and her wisdom in keeping close to the woodlands with its hollow logs into which a rabbit can escape if pursued too hotly by dogs, foxes, hawks, or owls. One March morning, Cottontail showed me a special ruse that I think she uses to outmaneuver an enemy when her litter is threatened.

At dawn I walked the east border of Big Oak Woods, hoping that I might glimpse Cottontail before she had retired for the day to her bed. I had arrived at my tree-platform blind too late to watch for her in the early morning dark.

Suddenly, from the edge of the leafless woods ahead, I heard a loud bawling, then a chorus of frenzied yelps. Then I saw two tan-and-white dogs streaking westward under the leafless trees, hot on the trail of either a rabbit or a fox. From their starting point near the wood's edge, I was sure that they had frightened Cottontail from her bed under a brush pile, and when I arrived there I found that she was gone. I left the woods and stood on the road, listening.

The rabbit, if it were Cottontail, was doing a surprising thing. From the wild cries of the dogs, fading rapidly westward, it was apparent that she was leading them quickly and directly out of her territory. Usually a rabbit will run only a few hundred yards before circling and finally coming back almost to the bed from which the dogs started it. If, by that time, the rabbit's side jumps and back-tracking have not shaken the dogs from its trail, it will usually turn away and circle in another direction, laying down another maze of scent trails to confuse the dogs, but staying inside its home area.

Within ten minutes I heard the hounds baying faintly from far-away [*sic*] Laurel Hill, just south of Muskrat Pond. Then they fell silent. I stood quietly for five minutes, then I heard one of the dogs howl long and dolefully. The animal's voice held a note of despair, and I knew that it had lost the trail.

I stood without moving for another ten minutes. There was no sound from the dogs and I heard only the lisping notes of a pair of Carolina chickadees in Big Oak Woods. Then came a light patter of feet, a mere whisper of sound from the woods. Some animal was coming toward me, but it was not a squirrel which moves with a rush of sound and a scattering of leaves on the forest floor. This sound was light as the drumming of first raindrops. It ceased, and I stood still, holding my breath. The sound came again, and suddenly, at the woods' edge I saw Cottontail. She leaped out on the road, stopped, and sat up. We were squarely in view of each other, not more than one hundred feet apart. Her brown body was twisted toward me, her ears high. I noted that her two front feet hung down over her narrow chest. I kept very still, scarcely breathing.

For a moment Cottontail held her pose. Apparently reassured, she dropped her front feet to the ground and leaped ahead into the grassy depths of the roadside ditch. She was hidden by the weeds and grass, but I heard her coming toward me. When opposite the place where I stood, she leaped out of the ditch to a grassy road that leads eastward across the open fields to Finley Tract Woods. Hopping slowly away, she did not travel far. When she reached a lone multiflora rosebush, she quietly disappeared under its protective, downcurving canes. There, as I discovered the next day, she had settled herself in another grassy bed in which I was to see her, off and on, all that spring. Her "form" under the rose bush was only a few hundred yards from her March litter in the old field, and I wondered if she might have chosen it to keep closer watch over her family. . . .

When Cottontail's young were about fourteen days old, they left the nest not to return. Each weighed about one quarter of a pound and began its first nibbling of green plant food in the April grasses and clover. Sometimes, in the day's-end gloom of the old field, I saw Cottontail sit up, I am sure, before a young one which had crept out of its grassy hiding place to nurse.

In three weeks the cottontails were weaned. As far as I know, some of them lived for a while within Cottontail's own four to six acres before they left to establish nearby territories of their own.

One April evening, I saw three of the young rabbits playing. They chased each other in small circles through the lengthening green grasses and over the dusty farm road. Early one morning, Cottontail herself joined one in a game in which the young one dashed at her and she leaped over its head. The small one turned and ran at her again, and Cottontail jumped high as it passed. Twice more they played their little game before it ended. The last that I saw of them, Cottontail's white tail was bobbing like a beacon ahead of the youngster as she led it under a thorny rose hedge.

P

ᴀᴜʟ Kᴏᴇᴘᴋᴇ (1918–), naturalist, was born in Cleveland, Ohio, and was a professor of music theory and composition at North Carolina Central University in Durham from 1954 to 1979. He wrote his book, *Two-Moon Pond*, to relate "the experiences of a pair of northern city dwellers who settled on five rural acres in North Carolina piedmont. The five acres included a one-acre pond where surface, one night, reflected a rising full moon." The following selection is "Big Turkle!" from *Two-Moon Pond*.

"BIG TURKLE!"

from

TWO-MOON POND

by Paul Koepke

*T*urtles are plentiful in and around Two-Moon Pond: mud turtles, box turtles, cooters, pond sliders, the smelly little stinkpots, and the spotted turtles that my Ocracoke friends call "highland hicketies." But by far the most plentiful are those tough, formidable holdovers from the Pleistocene like the one . . . I had just dispatched.

Chelydra serpentina [snapping turtle] is a pretty fancy name for a grim old U-boat of a beast that spends its winter in some muddy burrow and the warmer seasons lying in wait on the pond bottom or cruising below the surface seeking anything those merciless jaws can crunch. But having little Latin and less Greek, it remains

Reprinted from *Two-Moon Pond*, by Paul Koepke. Winston-Salem, N.C.: John F. Blair, 1983. Used by permission of the author.

unperturbed by polysyllabic niceties and continues its ceaseless predatory rounds.

This year, after a particularly severe winter, I saw a snapper's
conning tower rise for the first time on a blustery first of March.
It apparently liked what it saw, and with plenty of food available, it appeared more and more frequently as the weather warmed,
and it was soon joined by others.

The snapper's tastes are catholic, to say the least. Newts, fish,
crayfish, snakes, muskrats, smaller members of its own species—
anything, in short, that lives and moves in the pond of a size worth
the trouble is considered fair game. Fishermen must look sharp to
their stringers, particularly if any fish they catch are bleeding, and
waterfowl are in great danger of being seized from below, never to
rise again. This spring, for example, a female red-breasted mergan-
ser disappeared below the surface with flaps of protest before our
eyes. When we reached the spot, a subaqueous old meat-grinder of
a snapping turtle was already tearing it to shreds. But despite the
fabled voracity of these turtles, their depredations have had only a
minor impact on our pond life. We keep no domestic waterfowl,
and I feel certain that they are no more of a threat to the fish
population than the kingfishers, herons, and ospreys who are regular visitors. And since they are a definite asset where muskrat con-

trol is concerned, I bid them Godspeed, and . . . allow them to cruise unvexed.

With the coming of April and the warming of the water, the snappers are moved to participate in what passes with them for the process of reproduction. The encounter usually takes place in the northeast quadrant of the pond and always on the surface. A thrashing tumult in the water is the signal that an amatory engagement is under way, and year after year I play the voyeur, fascinated by what seems to be one of the most brutal copulative procedures in nature.

It is clear at the outset that neither of the pair can stand the sight of the other. The male is the aggressor who will not be denied, while the female is equally determined that she will see him sliced to ribbons before she will submit. And so they face off like two Civil War rams, maneuvering slowly for an advantage, edging into striking position so that their sharp, hooked beaks can be brought into play. After forty-five minutes or an hour of this cut-and-slash, the raw, pink flesh of their gashed heads and necks is plainly visible, and it is only then that the male finds the opportunity he seeks. Although he initially mounts from the rear, a flattish plastron fits poorly on a rounded carapace, and soon they are plastron to plastron, locked in a love-hate embrace which sets them slowly barrel-rolling until their union is consummated. The rolling procedure is quite necessary, as it turns out, since, because of the overhang of the carapace and the leeway afforded by the plastron, only the bottom turtle, upside down, can get its head out of the water to breathe.

When at last they part, the impregnated female swims slowly off to the shallow, muddy end of the pond while the male, his stint in the lists of love complete, lies puffing and wheezing on the surface until he gets his wind back and can resume his interminable search for something else to snap at.

A Hindu mystic was once asked about his concept of the earth, and he replied that the earth was an island floating on water in a huge bowl resting on the back of an enormous elephant, which was supported by a colossal turtle. When asked what held the turtle up, he indicated that it rested on yet another even greater turtle. When pressed further he finally replied, "Let's face it: there's always another turtle." And so it is at Two-Moon Pond. Catch them as we will, there is a seemingly endless supply of snappers, for there are ten ponds of an acre or more within a half-mile of ours, and when the wanderlust is on them, they may well leave the old homestead and move off to more congenial waters. On a number of occasions, by day or night, I have come upon them, lumbering across the lawn like miniature Sherman tanks and headed for my pond. One moonlit night, in fact, I went to investigate a hitherto unnoticed hump in the lawn and found myself standing near the water's edge in the immediate rear of a large snapper. As I bent over for a closer look, it suddenly wheeled 180 degrees with remarkable agility for a creature so cumbersome and made for the protection of the water. I was in the way, of course, but not for long. I bounded into the air like a springbok, and when I landed, the turtle had vanished into the dark pond. From that time forth, I did my nighttime hummock checking from a respectful distance with a flashlight.

Perhaps the greatest problem in playing host to these big, surly brutes is that occasionally one will swim too close to the vertical run-off pipe during overflow and find itself firmly pasted in place by suction. The protective shield around the mouth of the pipe has long since turned to ferrous oxide, and only a stub of cedar post which once supported it remains above water. As a result, whenever a snapper gets hung up it must be removed, either manually from a boat or by trying to snag a flange of its shell with a large Hopkins lure and a surf rod from the shore. Manual removal from a boat is not bad if the turtle is in headfirst and half strangled, but if it has made contact plastron down, it is usually in a towering rage and firmly stuck. To get it free without benefit of a stable platform and adequate leverage is dangerous and almost impossible. I therefore prefer to cast twenty feet with the treble-hooked lure until a purchase is secured and heave. The turtle usually comes loose with a mighty slurp, and the overflow continues. As for the Hopkins lure, that always winds up somewhere in the big winged elm immediately behind me. I loose a lot of Hopkins lures that way.

And so the wheeling seasons come and go, and in and around our little watery world the snappers lurk in some secluded hideaways or slip effortlessly like gray-green shadows through the dark water, pausing now and then to up snorkel without a ripple and as quietly disappear. . . .

*P*AUL KOEPKE's observations from *Two-Moon Pond* include this essay on the grim work of predators. For those who entertain a rosy, romantic view of nature, this piece is a jarring reminder of a more savage reality. Decapitated rabbits, skewered voles, and impaled songbirds are unfortunate victims of the drama of survival at Two-Moon Pond. The essay is titled "The Dead of Winter."

"THE DEAD OF WINTER"

from

TWO-MOON POND

by Paul Koepke

There was another low, irregular series of hoots from the female great horned owl in the post oak a hundred feet to the east and a higher-pitched reply from the male nearby, but . . . the ominous signals from the owl seemed [not] to disturb the blasé rabbit. It had long since accepted me as a harmless domestic biped and went on nibbling whatever it had found in the rime-stiff grass under the bright mercury-vapor night light.

Suppressing a shiver in that biting January dawn, I hunched my warm coat collar closer to the nape of my neck and resumed my stiff-legged stumping down the causeway to retrieve the morning

Reprinted from *Two-Moon Pond*, by Paul Koepke. Winston-Salem: John F. Blair, 1983. Used by permission of the author.

paper. Seeing me move, the rabbit decided to call it quits for the night and loped leisurely off to disappear in a patch of ivy near the big juniper. The owls, their quarry gone, fell silent.

The rabbit was the last of three who had cavorted and lollygagged around our place during the past summer and autumn. One had fallen victim to a passing vehicle, and I had found the other dead by a pyracantha with a dime-sized warble fly hole in its left flank. As for the survivor, it appeared that its number was up as well, particularly if it persisted in feeding in a brightly illuminated patch of open lawn with great horned owls in the offing.

But the owls never got a second chance. I found the rabbit under a chestnut tree the following morning, neatly decapitated, the top of its skull trepanned with surgical precision, and the brains consumed. This was weasel work. That savage but meticulous killer goes straight for the neck, drinks the blood, eats the brains, and, unlike owls or other predators, leaves not so much as an unattached tuft of fur or a spot of gore behind.

The heart of winter is a bitter, bleak, uncharitable place for warm-blooded wild creatures. Most of the seeds and green growth are gone, the ponds are frozen, the earth iron-hard. Now, under the lash of necessity, predators are forced to even greater efforts and their victims to hunger-driven heedlessness. The kingfisher, barred from the pond surface by a sheet of ice, must now seek out the shallow, spring-fed rills of moving water and make do with what little it can find. The great blue heron, on the other hand, is more resourceful. I was dumbfounded one cold winter day to see a big, gawky spindleshanks attempt a landing thirty feet outside our front window on our ice-locked pond. "No, no! It's slippery, you fool. Come down on land or you'll crash in flames," I muttered to myself, only to have the heron come to rest on the glassy surface as gently as a wisp of thistledown and begin its stately promenade along the dam.

I considered this an exercise in utter futility, for the heron did not have a prayer of catching a fish through two inches of ice. But once again I was wrong, for it was eyeballing the ivy-covered dam face with close attention. Suddenly it stopped and slowly extended its neck until, with a sudden thrust and withdrawal, it extracted a small, dark, struggling form, which was vigorously shaken before it began its last dark journey down that long gullet. It was then that I remembered: voles winter over in the ivy. That heron had a feasible plan from the outset, and there would be at least one less rodent in my garden next spring.

With the advent of autumn, the red-tailed, red-shouldered, sharp-shinned, and marsh hawks return to our immediate area, and their appearance is heralded by the ubiquitous blue jays, who voice a cry imitating the "kee-you" of the red-shouldered hawk.

But why do they warn of the red-shouldered hawk, whose diet, like those of the marsh and red-tailed hawks, consists mainly of rodents, reptiles, and amphibians, rather than sound the call of that swift and deadly scourge of the songbirds at our feeder, the sharp-shin? It may be that "kee-you" is more frequently heard or easier to imitate, but in any event it is blue jayese for "hawk."

But even the sharp-eyed but gluttonous jays can be caught napping now and then, and often, as I sit at the kitchen picture window warming my palms with a cup of hot coffee, dozens of birds at the feeder will suddenly disappear as though expunged by a huge eraser. Then I have only to stoop and squint under the awning overhang to see a sharp-shin or two in a nearby tree, looking for stragglers and biding their time. On other occasions this small accipiter will thread its way swiftly through the orchard-size trees to slash like a scimitar through the feeding area and even press, full tilt with talons at the ready, into the bare, pliable branches of a bush where a straggler has taken refuge.

One winter afternoon we were alerted by a jarring thud from

the kitchen and rushed to the picture window to find a sharp-shin lying stunned in the grass beneath it. It might have been suckered into an awkward maneuver by a smaller, more agile bird and wound up crashing into a sheet of glass which reflected the open field to its rear. As our forms impinged on its addled wits, it pulled itself together and took off, leaving behind on the glass the dusty, cruciform image of its head, neck, breast and wings as evidence of its incautious foray.

A sharpie's swiftness is exceeded only by its tenacity. We have seen one come to rest on an abelia hedge, peer down intently through the twigs for suspected prey and, still unconvinced, descend to the ground to scrutinize the lower branches more carefully. As a matter of fact, its ability to hunt on foot seems, at this writing, to have gone largely unnoticed, and yet it appears to be one of the bird's most successful ploys. To my surprise, the hawk landed a short distance away and began slowly quartering the area on foot. When its prey broke cover, the sharp-shin took off and, with a furious burst of speed, made the kill after traversing only thirty feet. Obviously, persistence and speed make a lethal combination.

A less fortunate predator, a gray fox, first came to my attention when I sighted it one night in silhouette against the night light as it trotted down the causeway and melted as silently as its own shadow into the adjacent ravine. I spotted it again a few mornings later as it came pelting down a ditch, pursuer or pursued, to vanish in a thicket. When it appeared again, it was a headless, drawn, flayed carcass draped over a roadside fence post. The head, fur, and tail had undoubtedly gone to a taxidermist or furrier, and the display was intended as a warning to other foxes to mend their thievish ways; but I suspect, since a chicken or a suckling pig still disappears now and then, that it deterred the foxes no more effectively than a human head on a pike inhibited the pirates and brigands in humanity's recent past.

And so the endless round of birth, predation, and death continues, and in response to the age-old question, "Is Nature cruel?" one need only glance at the morning paper and ask, "Compared with what?"

*L*AWRENCE S. EARLEY (1944–) is the associate editor of *Wildlife in North Carolina* magazine, editor of the book, *North Carolina Wild Places: A Closer Look*, and co-editor of the book, *Wildlife in North Carolina*. The following selection, "Two Days in John Green's Swamp," is an article Earley wrote about the Green Swamp in Brunswick County, North Carolina, that appeared in *Wildlife in North Carolina*.

The North Carolina Nature Conservancy and several corporations have taken the lead in preserving some of the most important habitats in the Green Swamp. Lawrence Earley supplies an editor's note at the end of this article that recounts this success story: "In 1974, the Department of the Interior designated a 24,800-acre portion of the Green Swamp as a National Natural Landmark. Three years later, Federal Paper Board Company, Inc., which had acquired much of the swamp from Riegel Paper Corporation, donated 13,850 acres of the Landmark property to the North Carolina Nature Conservancy 'to be held in perpetuity for the people of North Carolina.' In December 1986, Federal Paper Board donated an additional 1,872 acres to the Conservancy. The highlight of the donation was 92 acres of longleaf pine-wire grass savannah called Big Island Savannah."

For another description of a magnificent savannah, although it is one that is now gone, see Edwin Way Teale's piece, "Prehistoric Trapline" (Document Seventeen).

"Two Days in John Green's Swamp"

from

Wildlife in North Carolina

by Lawrence S. Earley

Up Driving Creek

We had been pushing hard up Driving Creek, deep in Brunswick County's Green Swamp, when the canoe ran headup against a half-submerged log. It was a nice juniper log with the smooth cut of the saw visible at one end. It must have been snorkeling in the creek for the last fifty years or so, ever since the last of the big stands of juniper were logged out of this area.

It stopped us now on this warm March afternoon. There were three of us in the canoe—Manley Fuller, Sharon Grubbs, and my-self. Our plan had been to push up Driving Creek to the source, a place known as "the soups." There were alligators there, we had

Reprinted from *Wildlife in North Carolina*, by Lawrence S. Early. Chapel Hill: The University of North Carolina Press, 1987. Used by permission of the author.

heard. I wasn't as keen as Manley about this venture. Manley is used to alligators, having done his master's research on the alligator population at Lake Ellis, and having "wet his feet," as he put it, on Costa Rican crocodiles last summer. Alligators make me nervous. So do water moccasins. The last thing any human beings had said to us that afternoon was, "Now, watch out for moccasins. In this warm weather you're sure to run into them." That we had made it this far without one falling into the boat was an oversight I felt sure would soon be corrected.

"Guess we'll have to turn back," I said hopefully. Manley was delicately toeing the obstacle. It was not budging and I was glad.

We were approximately 135 miles southeast of Raleigh, 25 miles southwest of Wilmington, and 5 miles north of Supply. By our Green Swamp compass we were, as the crow flies, 7 miles southeast of Big Curve, 5 miles southwest of Big Bay Ridge, and 3 miles south of Honey Island. We were also about 2 feet from a thorny tangle of bay forest, titi (pronounced "tie tie"), and catbrier that had scratched our arms, snatched our hats, and punctured our good humors for the better part of an hour and a half. Above us a wrathful sky was boiling.

The swamp could use the rain, I thought. Two years before, on a broiling June day, I had seen the Green Swamp for the first time and frankly I was disappointed. I had expected something primeval and haunting, like the Okefenokee Swamp with its acres of standing water and cypress trees. What I saw was parched scrub land and pine plantations, more like desert than swamp. Nevertheless, the Green Swamp is considered one of the most valuable natural areas in North Carolina, with the best remaining examples in the Carolinas of pine savannahs, bay forests, and pocosin. Longtime residents will tell you that it's one of the most game-rich areas in the state, with good populations of bear, bobcat, deer, and raccoon. It's got every one of the fourteen carnivorous plants found in the state, and it's also got some stands of the rare Atlantic white cedar, or juniper as it's commonly called. A lot of people treasure the Green Swamp, including the folks at the North Carolina Nature Conservancy who have acquired 13,850 acres for a nature preserve.

Manley Fuller was stomping the juniper log with abandon even as thunder sounded. Suddenly the log broke from its underwater snag and bobbed gently in the black water.

"All right!" cried Manley.

"What's our plan if it starts to lightning?" I piped.

"We'll make out. It's so thick in here the rain'll never get to us."

"But we're in an aluminum canoe!"

"Then we'll just get out of the canoe." And he shot me a glance that said as clearly as words, "You've got a very unhealthy imagination."

He grabbed a handful of sweet bay and yanked the canoe over the log. As we pushed forward, deeper into the Green Swamp, I listened to the thunder and then, on my right, through the tangled pocosin . . . did I conjure it up? . . . I seemed to see a writhing row of water moccasins, their cottony mouths gaping open like faces in a boy's choir.

An unhealthy imagination? Me?

JOHN GREEN'S FIELD

As a man of science, Ebenezer Emmon's imagination was nothing if not healthy and progressive. And yet in the 1850s, as the nineteenth-century geologist studied the Green Swamp and other eastern North Carolina wetlands, it's likely that his idea of "swamp" was similar to the idea of "wilderness" that had been current ever since the first European settlements in America. Quaking at the edge of the great North American forest, seventeenth-century Massachusetts' Puritans described the dark miles of woods as a "howling wilderness," a "hideous wilderness." In much the same way, people recoiled from swamps. "Dismal" swamps, they were called, and not only the one that retains that name today. Unproductive and useless, swamps were wastelands, the source of a deadly vapor which was thought to cause fever and death. It would be several decades and a continent away before the mosquito was correctly identified as the cause of malaria.

Thus when Ebenezer Emmons saw the 140 square miles of Green Swamp, he coolly took note of its vast forests of cypress and gum, the Atlantic white cedar, the longleaf pines, and the beech, maple, ash, and poplars. Without benefit of an aerial view, he correctly surmised the swamp's round shape. Although he didn't comment on it, he probably understood that part of the swamp was drained by the Waccamaw River, while the southern half sloped gently toward the Cape Fear River.

And having considered the forests and other vegetation, he imaginatively swept them off the map. The soil, he wrote in his report, was superb! "The soil was found to be much richer than I anticipated. . . . The earthy matter is as fine as that of Onslow or Hyde county lands. . . . Hence the cost of drainage should be incurred, and these valuable lands reclaimed."

In place of the cypress-gum forests, he saw crops of corn. Cash-paying cotton or wheat grew where the longleaf pines waved in the summer breezes. The squatters who had made baskets on the sandy islands in the interior of the swamp became industrious farmers, and floating over the scene was a pale blue haze of progressive nineteenth-century chimney smoke.

Such was Emmons's vision, and such was the vision of men several generations before him. For the forests that the geologist saw in the 1850s had remained essentially unchanged since 1795, when three tracts of land totaling over 170,000 acres of the 200,000-acre Green Swamp were deeded to the three men for the scant price of $7,100. What Benjamin Rowell, William Collins, and

Stephen Williams had in mind with so much land is not known, but agriculture was then on the march up the Cape Fear River and no doubt this figured in the plans of these men.

Though practically impenetrable much of the year, the Green Swamp was well known to many travelers. It had been called "John Green's Field" at first, after an early settler, then "John Green's Swamp," "Green's Swamp," and finally "Green Swamp." Lake Waccamaw, on the northern border of the swamp, was an especial favorite of travelers. In 1734 the botanist John Bartram visited the lake, "as I had heard so much about it." Pushing inland from a Cape Fear River plantation, he swatted "large musquetoes" as he crossed pine barrens and swamp to get to the lake, which he found "the pleasantest place that ever I saw in my life." When his son, William, visited in 1773, he, too, was impressed, finding "the situation delightful."

It was a point of view that the Indian inhabitants would have shared, for archaeological evidence shows that the land was continually inhabited for several thousand years. And why not? It was thick with bear and deer and wild turkey. John Bartram remarked on the tameness of the deer, which looked on him as if they had never seen another human being.

And it had good soil, according to Ebenezer Emmons. Drain it, he said, and we'd put this unproductive swamp to work.

Easier said than done. What kind of machinery then invented could tackle 200,000 acres of swampland, much of it underwater? What kind of men would take on such a job with such evident dangers? In spite of little nips at its flanks, by the end of the nineteenth century the Green Swamp was just as massive and unsavory an obstacle to settlement and communication as it was at the century's beginning. The swampland forests that John Bartram had seen in 1734 and that Ebenezer Emmons had noted in 1860 were still pretty much intact.

Then in 1907 the Waccamaw Lumber Company lay siege to the Green Swamp. It railed in great steam skidders and it built a giant sawmill in Bolton. It laid 18 miles of rail between Bolton and Makatoka, and shorter spurs into the swamp off the main line. They might have called it the "Floating Railroad." Workers cut 8- or 10-inch wide gum logs for crossties, and lay them close together over the wet ground. Waist-high in water and moccasins, gangs of loggers used two-man saws and axes to fell the giant cypress and gum. They skidded out the longleaf pines. They took the maples, the beech, the ash, and the poplar. Flatcars hauled the wood to Bolton, and at night hauled the men to Makatoka where the logging camps were. For thirty-four years they cut virgin timber. When the Waccamaw Lumber Company sold 138,000 acres of the Green Swamp to Riegel Paper Corporation in the 1930s, the forest that Ebenezer Emmons had seen was gone.

By 1914 drainage operations had begun on the cutover land. In one district of 28,000 acres between Lake Waccamaw and Livingston Creek, 44 miles of canals were carved into the quaking soil. Dredgers, 30 feet long and 12 feet wide, driven by coal-fire steam boilers, dug deep into the swamplands. By the late 1930s much of the northern reaches of the swamp had been drained and were being farmed.

It had taken nearly eighty years, but Ebenezer Emmons's vision had almost been realized. The Green Swamp was nearly gone.

POCOSIN AND SAVANNAH

Manley Fuller has been trying to get me wet for the better part of two days. Yesterday we had grappled with shrub-choked Driving Creek, pulling ourselves along with fistfuls of vegetation until the creek had finally surrendered to the bay shrubs. Earlier today we had waded through muck in order to get into Layman's Pond, a sinkhole in the southern portion of the Green Swamp. I had returned to the car for my hip boots, obeying my undying conviction that there's no need to get your feet wet unless you can't help it. Of course by the time I returned and waded out to the pretty little cypress pond there were Manley and Sharon in the crook of a cypress tree, wet to their waists and smiling a little too smugly for my taste.

And now, midafternoon, with the storm clouds banished by a hot sun, we are about to push off into the pine savannahs—the most fascinating part of the Green Swamp tract that the Nature Conservancy owns. Separating Big Island Savannah, Shoestring Island Savannah and Bean Patch Island Savannah are long fingers of low-lying pocosin, and the rain has made them knee-deep in spots. My hip boots are back in the car again. And Manley is standing by the trail, with that familiar smile on his face. "Well," he is saying in his North Carolina drawl, "we're going to get wet."

I give him a wink. "You're a hard man," I say, and Manley turns and leads the way.

On aerial maps, the 13,850-acre tract acquired by the Nature Conservancy shows up as a broad swath of vegetation. Strikingly absent from this part are the parallel sliver scratches that strike east and west on the swamplands to the north—drainage canals. The Nature Conservancy's land, which we are entering here, is practically unaltered, although canals to the north, fire lanes, and Route 211 have changed some of the original drainage patterns. This intact micro-version of the original Green Swamp features three kinds of plant communities—bay forest, pocosin, and savannah. We ran into the bay forest yesterday as we tested Driving Creek. The pocosin that we're slogging through now consists of thickly growing evergreen shrubs overlying peaty soil. But the savannahs are the most interesting of the plant communities in the Green Swamp, and they are rapidly disappearing from the southeastern landscape. They crop up in the swamp as islands, sandy ridges that drain slowly.

As we break out of the pocosin, my boots streaming and my toes squirting water inside, I take a good look at Big Island Savannah. It's a broad, open area with irregularly spaced longleaf pines thrusting into the sky. A recent fire has swept the understory clear of everything but innumerable clumps of spring-green wiregrass a few inches above the blackened soil. There are scorched pine stumps about six feet high across the broad savannah. Longleaf pine seedlings have bronzed needles. In another two months the floor will be covered with flowers. But now, in early March, the savannahs are merely bright and airy and open, and I can understand why they were once used as pastures.

Although the savannahs have been studied carefully, there is a lot still to be learned about how they work and why certain kinds of things grow there. Elevation and hydroperiod, or the amount of time the vegetation spends in water, have something to do with it. We take a dogleg to the left and angle south where the savannah is being swallowed up by thick pocosin underbrush. Our feet swish through thick golden whorls of unburnt wire grass.

It's hard to tell, but the burned savannah we have been walking on is a ridge. From just about any angle, the savannah looks uniformly flat all around, but there is a slight elevation toward the middle—about one foot's worth—and that seems to make all the difference. At that "lofty" height longleaf pine grows. It will grow there because the savannah is wet in winter and dry in summer, and the longleaf can withstand both extremes. But now as we move toward the edge of the savannah, the vegetation changes. We pass through toothache grass, broomsedge with its wedge-shaped seed tufts. "Look what's happening," observes Manley ahead of me in the afternoon's orange light. "The ground is getting wetter. The longleaf is giving way to pond pines. There's titi, and fetterbush, too—typical pocosin vegetation." Not twenty-five paces from the higher and drier savannah we're in a wetland.

We begin to find relatively strange adaptations to the wet conditions. "Look—pitcher plants," says Manley. "*Sarracenia flava*." We have to bend down to see the dried stalks of last summer's pitchers, their tubular leaves still standing straight. These carnivorous plants are thought to have adapted to the nutrient-poor soil by taking nutrients from the bodies of insects that are lured inside their pitchers. There are all kinds of carnivorous plants along the wetter portions of savannahs. All four species of pitcher plant are found in these locations, and some hybrids. So are abundant numbers of Venus's flytraps, two kinds of sundews, two butterworts, and five species of bladderwort—all fourteen carnivorous plant species found in southeastern North Carolina.

The peculiar combination of soil and hydroperiod also produces an extraordinary diversity of other flowering plants. In summer the savannahs bloom with grass pinks, rose pogonias, rosebud orchid, and white-fringed and yellow-fringed orchids. There are milkworts, meadow-beauties, sabatias, snakeroots, trilesas, and goldenrods. Botanists have found over fifty plants in one square meter of savannah, an astonishing figure!

We're now mucking through the lowest point of the pocosin barrier between the savannahs. "You can see why they call these savannahs islands," Manley says as we break out of the pocosin and into the open pastureland once more. "This is Shoestring Island. Across from us there's another pocosin, then it opens up once more to another savannah, Bean Patch Island. Savannah, pocosin, savannah, pocosin—all because of elevation and soil."

And fire. The key to the savannahs is fire. Regular fires keep the understory low and maintain the open, airy effect. Without fires the woody shrubs like dangleberry, wax myrtle, and bitter gallberry would muscle in and take over. The orchids and wildflowers would lose light and disappear. The savannah would turn into a forest dominated by longleaf pines and evergreen shrubs. A woody shrub has no defense against fire, but wildflowers keep their stems underground and thus they can survive a fire. The pond pine releases its seed only after a fire scorches it, apparently nature's way of ensuring that the seed is dropped into fertile ash bed with little competition rather than into water where it might not germinate. The seedling of a longleaf pine keeps its bud armored within a thick coat of needles. Fires are essential to the botanical diversity of the savannahs.

We pass several pines that were once used for turpentining. One hundred years ago we might have seen large barrels sitting amidst the wire grass. From May through September, men would gouge V-shaped streaks into the wood. The raw sap would flow down these streaks and into a "box," or a small hollow cut into the wood below. Several times a season the sap would be dipped into the barrels and carted off. We stop by one of the old trees and notice that the deep scar is nearly closed. "Here's a turpentine tree that's about ready to close up," Manley says. "It's good to know they can heal themselves." We see several mounds in the savannah, evidence of the tar kilns that once were constructed here.

The trail to Bean Patch Island slithers through 100 yards of knee-deep muck. I know Manley is enjoying himself. He's far ahead of us. I try to keep pace with Sharon, although I'm extra cautious with cameras strung around my neck.

When we finally emerge Manley is holding out a tiny snake for our inspection. "I found it under the bark of that dead pine," he says, nodding to a fallen log not far away. A baby ring neck snake. "Bark is a real good place to find snakes. Look at the nice yellow belly on this snake!" We push our way through high wire grass.

Manley finds a Carolina anole in a tree and spies a gaunt cypress on the far side of the savannah. "Look at that big sucker over there!"

The Green Swamp is rich in wildlife. The longleaf pines in the savannahs provide good nesting sites for the endangered red cockaded woodpeckers. While you're looking for its nest holes you might hear the rattle of a canebreak rattlesnake; the wire grass is good habitat for this reptile. Some of the last of North Carolina's truly native white-tailed deer are found in the Green Swamp. Most were killed out of the state near the turn of the century and northern deer were brought in to boost the dwindling native populations, and have since spread and interbred to dominate the statewide herds. You might still find a native whitetail with a southern drawl here, however. Perhaps that's what we saw earlier today, dead in a ditch by the side of Route 211. Nearly fifty black vultures were sitting in a pine tree nearby, and they flew heavily into the air when we approached. Cautious field workers have avoided making claims that the American alligator is found in the Green Swamp, although they are fairly sure it is. Manley, Sharon, and I know at least two alligators who live in the swamp because we saw them in a drainage ditch north of Driving Creek.

"Here's the trail," Manley is saying.

"Bear? Where is it?" asks Sharon, lagging behind a little and not hearing. She is disappointed when Manley repeats his original statement. "I was hoping we'd see a bear," she says.

The mention of bear reminds me of my conversation with Joe Hufham of Delco not long before. Hufham is a longtime resident of the Green Swamp area and an energetic chronicler of its folk history. In articles for the Whiteville *News-Reporter* and in several books, he's shared stories from a lifetime of logging, trapping, and hunting in the swamp. He told me a story about the time he met a 350-pound bear in the Green Swamp.

"This happened when I was teaching school. I was walking the railroad track out there near Big Ridge, and it was raining. I had on my suitclothes, thick underwear, and a big overcoat, and everything was soaking wet. I was tired. And all of a sudden I heard something whistle. I sort of turned my head back. Not a thing coming.

"It was raining hard. The drops looked like sheets of sleet dropping. I turned my head back and exactly the length of one rail ahead of me stood a three-hundred-and-fifty-pound bear. I knew I couldn't outrun him because a bear can outrun a dog, for a short distance anyway. And something came to me: just stand still. So I stood there. And the bear challenged me. He had his hind feet and his front feet on the rail and he was shaking his head. My heart was beating so hard I could hear it. He finally got tired of looking at me—he must have looked straight at me for three minutes—and he went on across.

"As tired as I was I didn't want that bear to catch me unarmed again. So I picked up a log that was as big as a crosstie. I picked it up and put it over my shoulder. And I carried that thing to Big Ridge, about three hundred yards, I reckon, before I threw it down. My idea of that was to look bigger, but if he actually come up to me, to throw it on him."

Hufham has had other close calls in the swamp, one time with a cougar. Of course there's no proof that the native species of cougar still exists in the swamp, but like other places in North Carolina cougar sightings are still reported in the Green Swamp. "I heard it said that prior to the coming of the skidders and the locomotives there was many panthers in there killing up many deer in Columbus and Brunswick counties. The logging companies paid such a big bounty they killed them all out. Panthers and wolves."

Wolves? "Now I did know a very old woman—and she's been dead years and years—and she said that they used to hear wolves howling at night. . . ."

The Green Swamp is rich in stories like that. Stories of smart bears and alligators that hunt raccoons from the bottom of pits, like sanddoodles.

But on this unseasonably warm March afternoon, with the warm light of sunset staining the pocosin toward the west, we do not see any bears. . . . The snakes are still lethargic and the tough men who worked up to their waists in Green Swamp muck are gone. We are three visitors from Raleigh making our acquaintance with a distinguished bit of North Carolina landscape. Manley is ecstatic as we head back the way we came. "Tell you what," he says, "whenever I feel bad I just oughta come down to the Green Swamp. I just can't get enough of this place!"

JAN DEBLIEU (1955–) grew up in Wilmington, Delaware. She began her career working as a newspaper reporter and magazine journalist with an interest in science and medicine. Since 1984, the focus of her labors has been writing about ecology, oceanography, and wildlife biology. At the time she wrote the following essay on Bald Head Island sea turtles, she and her husband were living on Roanoke Island. This essay is titled "Loggerhead Rites," from DeBlieu's book, *Hatteras Journal.*

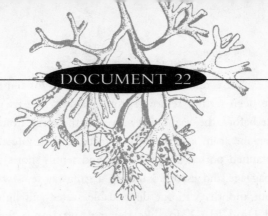

"LOGGERHEAD RITES"

from

HATTERAS JOURNAL

by Jan DeBlieu

O ne July evening just before dark I stood on a narrow, gently sloping beach two hundred miles south of Cape Hatteras with the hope of catching a glimpse of prehistoric times. A southeasterly wind tousled the sea oats, and a calm surf with thin coils of foam rolled across a mosaic of footprints in the sand. Next to me Cindy Meekins yawned, touched her toes, and did a spurt of jumping jacks in an effort to wake up. Behind us were two pale blue, woodframe houses with porches rimmed by short white railings, the kind of fusty, weatherbeaten retreats that tourist guides describe as charming.

The exclusive resort where I had settled in for the night could not have been farther removed from Hatteras and its gritty souls. An hour before, the yacht that serves as the ferry from Southport had taken me from a private parking lot to a private dock, where two suntanned porters in docksiders and tennis shorts relieved me of my baggage and escorted me up a gangway to a waiting tram. After four months without dependable water and lights, arriving on Bald Head Island was like being thrust into a foreign world where niceties can be taken for granted. But by the time I stood on the beach in the thickening darkness, I had forgotten the island's opulence and turned my thoughts to the activities of the night. At 9:30 I was to mount a three-wheeled, all terrain cycle and embark on a search for loggerhead turtles, a species of giant sea turtle that once nested abundantly in the middle Atlantic and is now threatened throughout its range. . . .

I had driven to Bald Head, the island that forms the tip of Cape Fear, in hopes of watching a loggerhead female dig a nest in the sand and lay a clutch of eggs. During the previous month I had helped the Pea Island National Wildlife Refuge run a daily patrol to check for loggerhead tracks on a thirteen-mile stretch of beach where only about a dozen sea turtles nest each summer. On several mornings I had found the tractorlike marks where a turtle had dragged herself across the sand. But I had yet to locate a nest. I knew I stood little chance of seeing a turtle on Pea Island, so I had decided to travel south to the most frequently used nesting ground in the state. Each year more than a hundred loggerheads lay their eggs on the beach at Bald Head between late May and late August. In mid-July it is not uncommon for ten or more two-to-three-hundred-pound reptiles to lumber ashore in a single night. I had timed my trip to Bald Head for what Meekins predicted to be the busiest week of the season, and now a storm threatened to steal the show. . . .

From the ferry an electric tram had taken me down a winding, washboard road past two pillar-trunked cabbage palmettoes and through a tunnel of live oak, laurel oak, and grape. The dwarfed, knotted trees pressed tightly against each other, clamping a hedge over the road. The forests of Bald Head are about six hundred years old—very old in terms of Atlantic maritime forests—and riding through them gave me the sensation of being deep within a maze. My brief passage into the culture of the wealthy began to fade; I imagined the tram winding me back to a not-so-distant past when Bald Head was unclaimed and undeveloped and giant sea turtles were more common on the beach than human beings.

Fossil records show that as early as 175 million years ago, the middle of the age of reptiles, a few species of giant tortoise developed ability to survive in the seas. Some paleontologists believe marine turtle fossils from 90 million years ago, the time of the largest dinosaurs, may have been early species of *Caretta*, the genus to which the loggerheads belongs. Other scientists argue that the fossils do not show enough anatomical detail to be certain. But it is clear that sea turtles evolved long before mammals, and perhaps as long as 160 million years before man.

The loggerhead and five other species of turtle—the hawksbill, leatherback, Kemp's ridley, olive ridley, and green turtle—bred prolifically in the Atlantic before humans began harvesting their eggs and relishing their meat. Loggerheads, the most abundant North American species, once nested on sandy beaches from Virginia to the Caribbean. They were especially prolific along the Florida Atlantic coast, which still is believed to be the largest rookery in the world.

The nesting ritual of the loggerhead is utterly common but difficult to observe. Sea turtles normally come ashore well after dark and re-enter the water before dawn. When a female turtle emerges from the surf, she crawls to the dunes, inspects the sand, and—if satisfied with the location—thrusts her front into a dune and uses her rear flippers to dig a round nest about two feet deep. A person who happens on her before she begins to deposit her eggs will almost certainly spook her back into the surf. Once she begins to lay, however, she goes into a trance; virtually nothing will disturb her until she has produced about 130 small, round eggs. She corks the nest with a lid of sand, rests for a few minutes, and returns to the surf.

Between sixty and seventy-five days later, the eggs begin to hatch. Bit by bit each turtle scratches out of its shell with a small spine on the tip of its nose. Not until all the eggs have hatched will the turtles begin to dig out of the nest, and then they will come in a burst. In the cool of the night the sand erupts with life, and a company of reddish-brown hatchlings two to three inches long scampers across the beach. A substantial percentage are snatched up and devoured by ghost crabs and raccoons. Those that survive crawl to the water and duck under the breakers, where they can still be eaten by fish.

What happens next is a matter of some debate. Most biologists believe loggerhead hatchlings swim frantically for the Sargasso Sea, the warm, salty gyre that lies just east of the Gulf Stream and reaches more than halfway across the Atlantic. The gyre's northern edge is roughly on the same latitude as the mouth of the Chesapeake Bay, and it is bounded on the south by equatorial currents. To reach it the turtles must swim at least fifty miles and cross the Gulf Stream. It is widely thought they achieve this without food or rest, although some biologists argue that the energy provided by the yolk of their eggs cannot sustain the hatchlings for the entire trip. . . .

Neither is it known for certain when loggerheads reach sexual maturity, although it is believed they mate for the first time between the ages of ten and thirty years. Thereafter, females become fertile every two or three years. In a fertile season a loggerhead female will lay four or five nests, and each time she must drag herself onto the beach. Scientists estimate that only one in every hundred hatchlings will live long enough to reproduce.

The reproduction rates were probably much higher before the widespread development of the southeast coast of the United States. Marine turtle meat was considered a delicacy by early American settlers, and turtle eggs, which have whites that do not harden when cooked, were used to make unusually moist pound cakes and breads. Hides were tanned for shoes and handbags, and the beautiful plates on the shell of the hawksbill were fashioned into tortoise-shell jewelry. However, it was not until the Florida coast was thickly settled in the 1940s and 1950s that the population of sea turtles began a precipitous decline. Turtle steaks and soups, always a specialty of the region, became increasingly popular in the 1950s, and bakeries began to market specialty products made with loggerhead eggs. At the same time, a wave of oceanside development severely decreased the areas where loggerheads could safely nest.

Despite an aversion to bright lights and developed beaches, turtles occasionally nest in the most populous areas, usually with disastrous results. When a loggerhead nest hatches, the young turtles instinctively make for the brightest horizon, which on dark, empty beaches is the starlight and moonlight reflecting off the surf. Before the establishment of turtle hatchery programs, beaches and streets in resort cities sometimes began to swarm with loggerhead hatchlings on still September nights. The hatchlings clambered toward the lights of restaurants and motels with resolute determination—even when turned around and placed in the surf. If they survived an onslaught by ghost crabs, the next day they were eaten by fish crows or they dehydrated and died.

Each year the number of nesting loggerheads on the Atlantic coast steadily decreased. Although no one is sure how many loggerheads live in the Atlantic, nesting surveys indicate that the number of turtles coming ashore to nest fell by as much as 75 percent in the thirty years after World War II. By the late 1960s southeastern states began to ban the killing of loggerheads and the harvesting of their eggs. Marine scientists began recommending that fishing trawlers, which accidentally catch and kill thousands of loggerheads each year, use nets with special doors that enable sea turtles to escape. And in 1978 the loggerhead was listed by the federal government as a threatened species.

Since the early 1970s wildlife biologists have started programs to monitor loggerhead nesting on federal and state preserves in North Carolina, South Carolina, Georgia, and Florida. Most of the projects are operated on slim budgets and staffed by students or volunteers who search for loggerhead nests and, when necessary, excavate the eggs and rebury them in areas safe from predators, encroaching roots, and high tides. Frequently the programs move the nests to fenced hatcheries.

The protection programs were heralded as a major step toward correcting the pressures of overfishing. Yet the earliest efforts unwittingly may have caused more harm than good. For several years some programs dug up nests and stored the eggs in styrofoam boxes that protected them from fungi and kept their temperatures from fluctuating. Wildlife experts believed keeping the eggs at a constant temperature of about 82 degrees Fahrenheit would increase the proportion that hatched. However, in the early 1970s a French biologist discovered that the sex of a marine turtle is determined not by the embryo's chromosomes but by the temperature at which the egg incubates. Biologists in the United States began checking the sexes of loggerheads hatched from eggs stored in styrofoam and found a disproportionate number to be male. They increased the incubation temperature of another group to about 90 degrees. All the hatchlings that emerged were female. The eggs kept above ground had been exposed to consistently lower temperatures than they would have been in sand—and the hatchery programs had produced nest after nest of males. If the practice of incubating eggs in styrofoam had continued, the species' reproduction rate might have dipped to an all-time low.

Ever since, the techniques for managing loggerhead stocks have been the subject of vigorous debate. Among North Carolina wildlife experts, Cindy Meekins is known for her adamant opinions on how loggerhead protection projects should be run. As I neared the headquarters of the Bald Head Conservancy program, I had the feeling I was in for a remarkable evening, turtles or no. . . .

I was to ride that evening with Jennifer Bender, a twenty-two-year-old intern from Norlina, North Carolina, who had graduated from Wake Forest in June with a bachelor's degree in biology. Bender was large-boned and strong, with a manner of speaking that was light and full of humor. She had also worked with the program the previous summer. At 9:25 we donned raincoats and long pants, then sprayed our wrists and necks with insect repellent. Two other interns, Kim Vanness and George Kosko, were to take a second three-wheeler.

We pulled out onto a narrow paved road, my back against the wooden box that contained stakes, wire, and a wooden rod used to probe the sand for air pockets surrounding the eggs. The Honda's red headlight barely illuminated the road. Loggerhead eyes do not detect red lights, so the interns had covered the lamp with a filter. From my position in back of Bender it seemed that the darkness had softened and shrunk in dimension. The butterflies in my stomach were inexplicable.

In front of us the scarlet beam from the other cycle bounced off the dunes. We passed the boxlike enclosure of wood and wire mesh that formed the hatchery and rode onto the beach.

"You're bound to see something tonight, even if it's only a false crawl," Bender said over her shoulder as she turned the cycle south toward the tip of Cape Fear. "I'll be surprised, though, if those two turtles that came in last night don't come up and nest immediately. You know they're out there, just waiting for the conditions to be right." I glanced toward the surf, which was calm and lit with pale blue-green phosphorescence. Without warning, Bender released the throttle and let the cycle glide to a stop. Before us was a set of deep slashes in the sand that led straight toward the dunes but doubled back in a meandering path. "I'd have stopped earlier if I'd only seen one set of tracks," Bender said, "but there she goes." A dark, oblong lump moved across the sand near the tide. We got off the cycle and silently approached from behind. The cumbersome animal paused, aware of our presence but presumably too tired to lunge into the waves. In the red flashlight beam her shell appeared black and lusterless. I stood close behind her, afraid to move lest I should scare her more.

"Go ahead and touch her," Bender said. I leaned over and placed my hand gingerly on her smooth, cool shell. She slid forward a few feet, then stopped. Bender followed her and wiped her hand across the crest of the shell, creating a swath of phosphorescent sparks. "These aren't particularly bright," she said. "Sometimes you can write your name in them." The turtle shoved herself forward with her flippers and disappeared into the surf.

"Off to a good start, even though it was just a false crawl," Bender said, remounting the bike. "Some people ride almost all night and don't see that much." I realized I had been holding my breath. Having convinced myself I would not see a turtle, the encounter had rendered me speechless. Bender turned the bike up the beach toward the dunes and traced the tracks. "That's so we know we've already checked it out. It gets confusing if we don't run over the tracks as soon as we find them."

"Was that one of the turtles that came in last night?"

"There's no way to know, but probably. She's got to be ready to nest."

We rounded the island's southeast point and drove west toward the Bald Head Inn and the Cape Fear River. The beach rose and dipped in red ridges before us. Peering into the soft night, I barely had time to brace myself for jars and bumps. Lightning continued to flicker on the south horizon, and the air grew moist. We had ridden for more than an hour when we came upon the other cycle parked next to a single set of tracks. Vanness and Kosko stood near a thicket of brush beside a large loggerhead that had thrust itself into the brambles. "Hey, Jen, look at this big mamma," Kosko called.

We scrambled off the bike and up the beach. "Good Lord, that's the biggest I've seen in a while," Bender said. And indeed the turtle looked much larger than I expected. Vanness had measured her shell length at forty-five inches. Patches of a thick, mosslike algae coated portions of her back, and flesh protruded in great pink folds from the bottom of her shell. Her flippers and neck were scaly, rough, and darkly blotched. A liquid the consistency of honey dripped from her eyes. "Those are the tears they use to keep sand out of their eyes and to excrete salt," Kosko said. "She's really crying." The turtle emitted a low groan. "Did she nest?" I asked.

"Yep. She's all through. See the depression?" I turned to see a shallow hollow about five feet by five feet. "The eggs are in there somewhere. Luckily we saw her just as she was finishing up, so we have a pretty good idea of where they are." The turtle groaned again and began moving toward the surf. At the back of her shell I could see a wide, fleshy stump of a tail. She moved her flippers alternately but quickly so that it looked like she was wiggling—if an animal with a carapace can wiggle.

Vanness and Kosko had already begun scooping out a hole in the shallow depression. Gnats swarmed in my eyes and nose, and I pulled up the hood of my jacket. Within minutes Kosko had located the eggs. He pulled two of them out and plopped them into my hand. Round and white, they were no greater than three inches in diameter, the size of Ping-Pong balls. One dented under the pressure from my thumb. "Don't worry," Bender said, seeing my sheepish look. "A lot of them give like that. It doesn't hurt the embryo's development."

It was time to continue our patrol. I positioned myself on the cycle and steadied myself for a long ride. I had begun to fear that my chances of seeing a turtle at her nest were growing slimmer with each passing hour. I began scanning the waves. The phosphorescence in the foam had intensified. With the blue of lightning to the west, the glowing waves to the east, and the wide beam of our diffused red light, the night was cast in two muted, jarring hues. We crested a ridge and Bender stopped.

"Aha," she said. "I see tracks going up, but there's none coming back."

Halfway up the dune I could see a dark shape. I got off the bike with the intention of walking toward it, but Bender cautioned me back. "Right now's a real critical time, because if you approach her before she starts laying she's likely to go back into the surf."

We leaned against the cycle, and I slapped a mosquito that had landed on my cheek. "Buggy tonight," Bender said. Overhead the lightning grew brighter, but no thunder sounded. I eyed the lump in the sand. It appeared to be moving to the north, parallel with the dune. Finally it stopped and I stood up, restless.

"Let's do it," Bender said.

She grabbed her flashlight and walked slowly toward the dark shape, but veered south well before she reached it. "Look at this," she groaned over her shoulder, "look at this. We've been watching a bush." To her left a turtle was positioned over the hole that formed her nest. To her right and farther up the dune was the shape we had been watching—a clump of myrtle.

"But it moved," I said.

"We just thought it moved. This red light can do funny things to your eyes."

We crouched in back of the turtle. Pure white barnacles that glistened with phosphorescence were strung down her shell like uneven strands of pearls. Through a gap between the animal's belly and the opening to the nest, we could look inside at the wet, round eggs. The turtle sighed a hard, raspy breath, curled up her back flippers, heaved her shell, and produced three eggs. She flattened her flippers, curled them again, and pushed out two more. The gap was about five inches wide, plenty wide enough for a person to reach inside. I remembered reading that raccoons had been known to steal turtle eggs as they were being laid. I watched closely as more eggs squeezed out. This was a sight from the archives of evolution, a sight too precious to be lightly forgotten. The sides of the nest were round and damp, and I could see scrapings where the turtle had pushed away the sand. Eggs fell from her in pairs and landed with a plop, forming a neat stack in the cavity's middle.

I put my hand on the turtle's shell. Unlike the larger animal we had seen earlier, her shell was clean of algae and sand. "She's an old girl," Bender said softly. "See how her shell is more dome-shaped than the others? That's usually a sign of age."

I walked around to the turtle's side and trained the red light on her eye, which stared straight ahead, unblinking and dull. She had thrust herself half into a dune, which had crumbled around her. Her front flippers and large, flat head rested on a shelf of sand. Her mouth was a jagged, tightly closed line. Loggerheads feed on crabs, jellyfish, and seaweeds, and their powerful jaws can crack a horse-shoe-crab shell in a single bite. To me, the mouth looked no more oversized than the rest of the beast. She let out a hard, grating breath. Her eye moved; her left back flipper scooped a lump of sand into the hole. "She's done," Bender said.

I walked back for a last look at the heap of eggs. Bender moved into the dunes to search for a spot to relocate the nest. Carefully, laboriously, the loggerhead shoved sand into the cavity with her back flippers, shifting her body from side to side with each swipe. She dug her front flippers deeper into the sand, presumably to keep from sliding down the dune. The motions were tediously slow; for me, knowing we would dig up her work within minutes of her return to the surf, the process was painful to watch. I flipped off my flashlight and sat down. The turtle heaved with another deep sigh and began breathing loudly, but with a more regular rhythm. The sound was harsh and resonant, like the sound of breath through a snorkel tube. Pulses of lightning outlined her shell. The irregular flashes tinted the seeds of the grasses, the ridges in the sand, the ghostly foam of the surf. We were miles from civilization, miles from anything resembling modern time. Without warning, she moved her front flippers, smearing sand over the area to camou-flage the location of her eggs. Finished, she rested and sighed.

I followed three yards behind when she finally turned and be-gan crawling back toward the water. Bender, strolling by with the tools she would use to move the nest, pulled a tape measure from her pocket and strung it across the turtle's carapace from front to back, then from side to side. "Thirty-seven by thirty-two," she said. "What you have here is Joe-typical turtle." The turtle resumed her laborious crawl, stopping every ten feet. The resonant breathing continued. She moved faster as she neared the water, pausing a final time as the first wave hit her, raising her head and remaining mo-

tionless for thirty seconds, maybe longer. I could still see her when the second wave broke over her shell, but by the third wave she was gone.

Bender had begun to dig with her hands when I climbed back up the beach to the nest. "This sand is full of oyster shells, which really makes it hard to feel for the eggs," she said. "Geez, if we hadn't seen this turtle laying, we might have been here looking for the eggs all night." She dug with her hands for several more minutes, until she uncovered the small, moist balls. Before extracting them she lined the bottom of a plastic ice cooler with sand from the nest. "Whenever we relocate eggs we always include a little sand from the original nest," she explained. "I don't think anyone knows for sure if it makes a difference, but it's something we like to do."

The eggs were closely packed, and Bender could bring out three and four at a time. I put my hand into the nest cavity and cautiously pulled out two eggs. They were covered with sand and a transparent liquid. "You need to handle them carefully," Bender said, "but remember that she dropped them down two feet into the nest. They're not as brittle as chicken eggs." Together we extracted seventy-eight eggs, an unusually small number. After Bender measured the nest's dimensions, I felt the rounded walls of the cavity with my hands and was surprised to find the air inside moist and warm, as if it had been heated by someone's breath.

We carried the cooler up a small dune to a flat area that seemed well out of reach of the tide. "This is the part that makes me nervous," Bender said, "because I feel a tremendous responsibility to make sure the eggs are in a safe spot." She began scooping out the sand to form a pear-shaped cavity twenty-three and a half inches deep and twelve inches in diameter—the exact size of the original nest. She arranged the eggs inside, packed sand over the top, and covered the sand with a wire netting with openings large enough to allow hatchlings to crawl through but small enough to keep out foxes and raccoons. I marked a stake with the numerals 167, the number of the crawl, and inserted it into a dune.

The lightning had intensified by the time we had loaded the gear back on the cycle and resumed our patrol. "Time for a midnight break," Bender said, flagging down Vanness and Kosko. We drove to the beach in front of the blue houses and went inside for snacks. . . .

I could not help thinking of the fury of that night two months later as I boarded the ferry for a second trip to Bald Head. The thinly overcast dome seemed a pallid version of the lightning-filled sky that had driven us from the beach. The air was damp and limp.

The hatching season was at its peak, but the interns had gone back to school. Instead of riding the beach all night to watch for loggerheads erupting from the sand, I would join Meekins on her nightly check of the hatchery at 9:30. If none of the nests in the enclosure happened to be ready to hatch I was out of luck. And even if some of the clutches had broken out of their eggs, the turtles would not catapult through the sand covering the nest. As we waited for dusk, Meekins explained that for some reason most of the nests in the hatchery had developed pockets of air at the top of the cavities. When the hatchlings were ready to dig out, they could not reach the sand overhead. To compensate for the problem, she had started opening nests by hand after the eggs had incubated for seventy days.

"Usually if I just stick my hand down four or five inches—not enough to disturb the eggs, if they haven't hatched—I can see a head or two," Meekins said. "Then they all come pouring out. It looks like we may have built the hatchery on an overwash fan. The sand is very coarse, and that may have affected the way the nests held their shape. The nests in the state park are hatching out with no problem."

I had half-hoped to be able to see the hatchlings from the eggs laid by 167, the number assigned to the turtle that had nested as I watched. But barely sixty days had passed since that visit, and a nest laid by turtle 127 had hatched only the night before. "We're almost halfway through," Meekins said. "Every time a turtle makes a crawl, we give her a number. We had more than two hundred crawls and a hundred and thirty-three nests, a few more than last year. We thought we had a hundred and thirty-one, but the interns missed two nests that were laid near the inn."

Since Meekins and the interns hadn't known about the nests, they were surprised when someone called to tell them baby loggerheads were crawling in the roads, the yards, and the marshes near the inn. "They were everywhere, even back in some of the freshwater ponds. People helped us collect them as fast as they could. I have no idea how many there were. That's what it would be like all the time if we didn't run this program. Absolute chaos."

It was time to go. A quarter-mile off the beach a trawler rocked with its outrigger extended in a wide V. "There's the enemy," Meekins said. She was not joking. Most of the fisherman I knew scoffed at the notion that the species needs federal protection, because loggerheads are still common sights in southeastern waters; the turtles chew up crab pots and rip holes in fishing nets, and many fishermen would welcome a decrease in their numbers. As I mounted the Honda behind Meekins, I was surprised to see the headlight shining white against the trees. "I just ripped the red cover off one day," she said. "We don't need it anymore. We even use a white flashlight to lure the turtles down to the water."

There were no sightseers at the hatchery to witness the night's release of baby turtles. As Meekins opened the pen door, she shined her flashlight around the edges in a search for hatchlings and tracks. The short wooden stakes that marked the nests gave the pen the look of a cemetery. A hundred yards to the east I could see that the phosphorescent waves were even brighter than on my previous trip. "Any activity in here?" Meekins asked, stepping into the pen. "Aha. I see some tracks. There he is. . . ." A dull brown turtle three inches in length crawled toward the beam of her light. She scooped up the animal and handed it to me. Cool and smooth, it wiggled in my hand. Its flippers moved alternately as it tried to skitter across my palm, but when I held it aloft by the shell its movement changed to the rhythmic butterfly stroke it would use in the surf. At Meekin's direction I placed it inside a wooden frame that surrounded nest 149.

"None of these are sinking in, so I guess we'll have to check the ones that are farthest along by hand." She bent over and began gently scooping out sand. About eight inches down she uncovered a turtle head. "Okay, these are ready to go." She pulled out the lead turtle and two others, then shined her light into the small cavity for me to inspect.

The sand below was writhing with life. Tiny flippers appeared from all directions and sank beneath tumbling grains of sand, rising and squirming in a wild attempt to break through to the top. Heads gaped and stretched toward me as rivulets of sand poured down. I reached in and brought out four of the animals. Four or five more immediately filled in the gaps. "They've been patient for so long," Meekins said. "Now every ounce of energy is geared toward getting out." Hurrying to free the leaders so those at the bottom would not be injured, I pulled dozens of turtles to the surface. Sand clung to their moist limbs and shells. Until hatching they had maintained a fetal position, and their shells, although stiff, were slightly curled. Each had a small yellowish nodule on its belly, the last of the yolk. I lowered my cupped palm into the warm sand and let it fill with turtles. Gently I pulled the hatchlings out and again curled my hand into the nest. I could feel turtles squeezing in between my fingers, like water seeping through cracks. Scraping at the edges of the hollow, I uncovered six hatchlings that seemed to be having difficulty digging out of packed sand.

At length they stopped breaking the surface, and I could feel no more wriggling limbs. In less than five minutes I had extracted seventy-five turtles. They bumped against each other in the frame, following the flashlight beam like a school minnows rising to the surface for food. A few that had turned over on their backs pressed their tiny rear flippers together in a gesture of self-defense. They looked like miniature versions of Winnie the Pooh's friend Piglet. I had difficulty imagining them as three-hundred-pound adults.

We put the hatchlings in four buckets and started toward the beach. It is Meekin's custom to release hatchlings at a different point every night in hopes of reducing predation by fish, and we walked north to a wide stretch of beach. "Someone asked me the other night if I didn't feel horrible releasing these poor baby turtles into the surf to fend for themselves," Meekins said. "I said, 'listen, if I can get them this far I feel like I've done them a big service'."

The sand near the water lit with sparks beneath our steps. Fifty yards north of the hatchery Meekins stopped and set down the buckets. "I'll get in the water with the light to make sure the turtles head in the right direction. Try and release as many of them at once as you can." She kicked off her shoes and strode ankle deep into the surf, leaving me to dump four buckets of turtles simultaneously.

I gathered the buckets around me and watched her dark silhouette. The flashlight beam turned toward me. "Ready?" she called.

I lifted two buckets and tipped out their contents gingerly, spreading turtles across the sand. The ones that landed upright fanned out immediately, and not all toward the surf. I emptied the last two buckets and began righting turtles that lay on their backs and turning others toward the surf. Their frenzied movements never stopped, even when I picked them up, as if the purpose of their lives was to get somewhere, anywhere. I reached for a turtle to my right, lost my balance, and stuck out my foot to save myself a fall. "Watch where you step," Meekins called sharply. I couldn't blame her; I could have easily killed six or seven hatchlings, maybe more.

The majority of the turtles were toddling toward the surf. Dark shapes dotted the sand as Meekins played the beam of light across the beach in a search for stragglers. I moved carefully up and down a five-yard area, collecting wayward hatchlings as quickly as possible. Within minutes the final turtles had scampered to the water's edge. The surf was rising and strong, and the spent waves swept sharply to the south, carrying the turtles in a wide arc. I took off my shoes and waded out beside Meekins; pricks of light dotted the foam that surrounded my feet. Despite the coolness of the night, the ocean was as warm as it had been in midsummer. A small hatchling ventured down toward the water, only to be caught by a wave and deposited neatly back on the beach. Again it crawled down, and again it was knocked back. Meekins and I chuckled. The turtle's struggle had all the comic appearances of a small child trying to tackle a giant. "If they can get out a little ways and then stay low, the waves will break right over them," Meekins said. The straggler caught a wave on the ebb and rode past us stroking furiously, a baby on a water slide. Another wave broke over it, but it did not reappear.

I watched the phosphorescent breakers silently for several minutes.

A T HER HOME on the Outer Banks, Jan DeBlieu is a keen and sensitive observer of nature. In this essay, she considers the pervasive influence of the wind. Like the stunted, warped trees, humans in the area must adapt to the relentless force. The essay is titled, "Into the Dragon's Mouth."

"INTO THE DRAGON'S MOUTH"

by Jan DeBlieu

*I*t begins with a subtle stirring, and the falling of sunlight on the vapors that swaddle the earth. It is fueled by extremes—the stifling warmth of the tropics, the bitter chill of the poles. Temperature changes set the system in motion: Hot air drifts upward and, cooling, slowly descends. Knots of pressure gather strength or diminish, forming invisible peaks and valleys in the gaseous soup.

Gradually the vapors begin to swirl as if trapped in a simmering cauldron. Air particles are caught by suction and sent flying. They creep across mountainous ridges and begin the steep, downward

Reprinted from "Into the Dragon's Mouth," by Jan DeBlieu. *Orion* Magazine (Fall 1993). Used by permission of the author.

descent toward the barometric lows. As the world spins it brushes them to one side but does not slow them.

Tumbling together the particles of air become a huge, unstoppable current. Finally some of them rake against the earth, tousling grasses and trees, slamming mountains, pounding anything that stands in their way. By now they are a force unto themselves, one that shapes the terrestrial and aquatic world. They bring us breath and hardship. They have become the wind.

I stand on a beach near sunset, squinting into the dragon's mouth of a gale. The wind pushes tears from the corners of my eyes and across my temples. Ocean waves crest and break quickly as I have ever seen them, rolling onto the beach like tanks, churned to an ugly, frothy blue-brown. The storm is a typical March northeaster, most common in spring but just as apt to occur in January or June.

Where I live, on the North Carolina Outer Banks, the days cannot be defined without wind. The roar of the surf would fall silent as the ocean grew as languid as a lake. Trees would sprout wherever their seed happened to fall, cresting the frontal dune, pushing a hundred feet up with spreading crowns. We would go about our lives in a vacuum, as content somewhere else as here. That is how it feels in the few moments when the wind dies: ominous, apocalyptic. As if the world has stopped turning.

I lounge on the beach with friends, enjoying a mild afternoon. A light west breeze lulls and then freshens from the east. Its salty tongue is cooling and delightful at first, but as the gusts build to fifteen miles an hour we begin to think of seeking cover. We linger awhile—how long can we hold out, really?—until grains of sand sting our cheeks and catapult into our mouths. As we climb the dune that separates us from the parking lot I am struck anew by the squatness of the landscape. Nothing within a half mile of the ocean grows much higher than the dune line. Nothing can stand the constant burning inflicted by salty wind.

On a thread of soil twenty miles from the mainland, every tree and shrub must be designed to tolerate wind that is both laden with salt and ferociously strong. Gusts of sixty miles an hour or more will shatter limbs that are any less pliant than rubber. Weather is not normal here; we are too far out to sea. There is nothing between the coast and the Appalachian Mountains, 250 miles inland, to brake the speed of building westerly breezes. There is nothing between the Outer Banks and Africa to deaden the blow of easterly gales.

Any weather book will tell you that winds are caused by the uneven heating of the earth. Pockets of warm and cold air circle each other, create an air flow, and *voila!*, the wind begins to blow. Air moves from high pressure to low pressure, deflected a little by the Coriolis effect. It is a simple matter of physics. I try to keep that in mind as I stand on the beach bent beneath the sheer force of the air being thrown at me, my hair beating against my eyes. Somehow, out in the element, conventional wisdom falls a bit short. It is easier to believe that wind comes from the roaring breath of a serpent who lives just over the horizon.

The wind, the wind. It has nearly as many names as moods. There are siroccos, Santa Anas, foehns, brickfelders, boras, willywaws, hurricanes, northeasters, chinooks, monsoons. There are bands of wind and calm that girdle the earth. At between thirty-five and thirty-six degrees parallel, the Outer Banks lie just north of the Horse Latitudes, in which, legend holds, light winds slowed the sailing ships of European explorers and hot weather killed many of their horses. But in winter the weather of this coast is shaped by the prevailing westerlies that scream across the continent, pushing calmer, milder air far south.

Offshore, the wide, warm Gulf Stream ropes its way north past Cape Hatteras and turns back out to sea after a close swipe at land. It mingles briefly with the cold tongues of the Virginia Coastal Drift, a spin-off of the southbound Labrador Current. In terms of weather, the junction of these two flows is enough to stop the show. In winter when a dome of high pressure from the arctic drifts southeast, it may come to the edge of the Gulf Stream and stall.

Will it linger or be pushed over the Gulf Stream and out to sea? Suppose there is a core of warm air off the coast, just to the east of the stream. At the same time, suppose the jet stream has grown unusually strong and is flowing to the northeast. The two air masses bump against each other like huge bubbles, the cold air fighting to move east, the warm air prodded north by the jet stream. A pocket of turbulence develops in the crook between them. Wind flows east, then is bent quickly to the north. Unable to resist the centrifugal force, it begins to move full circle, creating a system of low pressure that deepens violently.

The barometer plummets; rain descends in torrents. Up north snow falls thick and fast. The edge of the Gulf Stream is where great winter storms are made. They drift north, bequeathing to the Outer Banks rain, usually, but sometimes snow. And wind.

In the spring of 1962 an explosive low pressure system developed unexpectedly over the Outer Banks. In the wake of fierce northeast winds the ocean pounded the shore for three days, spilling over the dunes and through the little towns tucked behind them. During that particular meteorological episode, known as Ash Wednesday storm, people woke to find the ocean sloshing into their beds. This cycle of weather has been repeated many times since, though never with equal force.

Such sudden, lashing northeasters have always intrigued the forecasters at the Cape Hatteras Weather Station, who as recently as a decade ago were at a loss to explain them. Now, with the help of sophisticated probes and satellite photos, meteorologists can often tell when a winter low pressure system threatens to form over the coast. They can warn island residents, with some confidence, to buckle down for a squall.

More typically the wind blows fickle, and its swings of mood are devilishly tricky to foretell. At the center of a pressure system wind speed slows, but at the edges it quickens. A strong core of high pressure, sliding over the coast, may bring light wind that lasts for days. The system may stall long enough to dissolve, or it may venture out to sea, stirring up gales as it passes.

How much wind tomorrow? The technicians at the weather station make their educated guesses, knowing all along that the wind may fool them. Knowing that, whatever else it does, the wind will call the day's tune.

Before the advent of sophisticated forecasting equipment, islanders watched for subtle changes to predict the behavior of weather and wind. They studied the sky and the animals the way a mother might look for the tell-tale signs that her young child is growing tired and cross. If, in a light, variable wind the gulls stand facing north, watch for steady north wind by nightfall. If clouds form a halo around the moon, count the stars within the halo. If there are three, expect bad weather for the next three days.

A mackerel sky—one with thick clouds that look like fish scales—means rain is on the way. A sun dog at sunset foretells a bad storm. A mild spell in December or January is a "weather breeder;" it brings penetrating cold before winter's end. "A warm Christmas," an elderly island man once told me, "makes a fat cemetery."

Only fools lived on the ocean, back before hurricanes could be spotted on radar. The houses of Outer Banks natives nestled together in wooded sections just off the Albemarle and Pamlico sounds. The sound side was considered the front of the islands, and the ocean beach, where the fury of storms hit hardest, was thought of as the back. It was the jumping-off point, the place where swimmers could venture from the encircling arms of a continent into an ocean of uncertainty and terror. Islanders spoke of their homeland as if they were intent on keeping their backs, figuratively speaking, to the wind.

The cattle that ranged freely across the Outer Banks in the late nineteenth and early twentieth centuries seemed to know when a weather shift was imminent, and they anticipated changes in the wind to escape biting flies. If they moved to the "back of the beach," east wind was on the way. If they migrated to the marshes, the easterly breeze would swing west. Most of the time the range stock stayed in open grasslands and dunes. When they wandered into the villages, residents began boarding windows for a hurricane.

The intensity of the weather always depends on the wind, and Outer Banks saws impart more homespun knowledge about gales and breezes than any other facet of life. A heavy dew in the morning means heavy wind by afternoon. If a swarm of biting flies shows up on a fishing boat far offshore, a land breeze is bound to shift to an ocean breeze. When the wind swings hard to the northeast, it will most likely blow itself out in a day:

A Saturday shift, come late or soon,
It seldom stands till Sunday noon.

Once or twice a winter, however, a northeaster lasts for most of a week. No matter how it begins or ends, local wisdom holds that the blow will always diminish on the third, or fifth, or seventh day, never on an even-numbered day. Normally the wind migrates slowly from northeast to east to southeast to southwest, moving clockwise in the anticyclonic pattern typical of high pressure systems.

There are exceptions, of course, when the wind moves backward or counter-clockwise. For generations native islanders have known such shifts to be harbingers of the most violent storms. The weather change might come as a localized thunderstorm or a devastating hurricane, but a backing wind is always to be feared. As an old saying suggests, "I'd rather look at Grandma's drawers than see a backing wind."

Wind is culture and heritage on the Outer Banks; wind shapes earth, plant, animal, human. It toughens us. It moves mountains of sand as we watch. It makes it difficult to sleepwalk through life.

The spring I moved to the islands I lived in a house beset by wind. Air seeped easily through the decayed siding and whistled through the roof. The constant clatter made me lonely and chafed my nerves, but I gladly sought the shelter of those rooms rather than stand exposed to the chilling breeze. I developed a ritual for going out: Before opening the door I pulled on my coat and gloves, yanked down my hat, and braced myself for an onslaught.

I conditioned myself slowly, taking walks in steady wind for twenty minutes at first, with the hope of working up to forty-five. An appreciation for wind was not in my nature; I had to learn to like the feel of air pummeling my chest and roaring across my skin. "Light" wind, I learned, blew less than fifteen miles an hour. Anything less than ten miles an hour was not worth mention.

Walking with my hood pulled hard against my scalp, I began to notice how animals coped with wind. Terns, the kamikazes of the bird world, seemed oblivious even to hard gales. I remember watching them one spring afternoon at Oregon Inlet as air howled down on us from the north and waves sloshed against each other. Together wind and tide made a mess of the landscape; with the frothing water and the whipping branches of oceanside shrubs, it seemed like the world was being shaken at its foundations. Yet the terns hung steady in mid-air, flapping their wings quickly and chittering to each other, their beaks pointed downward as they scanned the ocean for fish.

Not many animals come out in such a wind. Those that do may find the normal parameters of earth redrawn. In a sustained east wind the water in the sounds is pushed toward the mainland, so that vast stretches of bottom are exposed. Islanders refer to this as the tide running out, and indeed it is the only kind of falling tide to be seen on the banks' western shore. The water level in the estuaries here does not respond to the pull of the moon. All sound tides are erratic and strictly driven by wind; they ebb in northeasters and flow during westerly blows.

Soon after I moved here I learned that water swept east by wind for twenty miles has a way of suddenly spilling over its normal banks, like a bowl tipped sloppily to one side. One morning after several days of hard west wind I parked in a lot near a fish house on Pamlico Sound. An islander casually warned me, "You might ought to move your car, 'case we get some tide." Translated this meant, "Move it or lose it." I parked on higher ground. Within an hour three feet of briny water filled the fish house lot.

Water ripples like a washboard in heavy wind. Its malleable surface shows approaching gusts long before they can be felt. Riding in a sailboat, trying to safely harness the Outer Banks breeze, you can watch the front edge of a gust push across the water as it sweeps toward you, takes hold of your sail, and keels your boat hard to the side.

Even the more docile winds affect the shape of the water and the distribution of creatures within it. East winds send the surf pounding against the beach; west winds slow the shoreward roll of breakers and make them stand erect. The best surfing waves are sculpted by a northeast blow that shifts cleanly to the west. But if the west wind blows too long, the breakers are knocked flat. Surfers disappear, replaced by commercial beach fishermen who row dories just offshore to set their nets for bluefish.

We all have our favorite winds. Outer Banks surf casters like a land breeze because, as they say,

> *Wind from the east, fish bite the least*
> *Wind from the west, fish bite the best*

A westerly breeze draws bluefish, trout, mullet, and other species to the calm waters in the lee of shore. During duck hunting season it also pushes waterfowl from the middle of Pamlico Sound toward the islands, putting them in easy range of hunting blinds. A friend of mine, an avid hunter and fisherman who lives on Hatteras Island, grew so enamored of the soundside breeze that he threatened to name his firstborn son West Wind. His wife's wisdom prevailed; they named the child Teal.

Good fishing or poor, the light summer easterlies are dearest to my heart. West winds muddy the ocean waters, but east winds clear them. West winds bring biting flies to the beach, but east winds banish them to the marsh. The most pleasant summer days are those with an ocean breeze strong enough to set up a little surf but not too strong to make swimming dangerous. Waves roll lazily ashore as wind gently fills my lungs, caresses my skin, and sweeps cobwebs from my brain. I lie in the sun, hot but cool enough for reading. I slip noiselessly into the clear green surf and float on top, watching as sparkling grains of sand tumble out to sea between waves.

I live in an island forest now, where tree trunks slash the winter wind before it can hit the house full force. At night I listen to the loblolly pines pitching back and forth, high overhead, and wonder how many more years the cottages on the ocean will be able to stand against the forces that batter them. I do not bundle up as carefully when I go out; to tell the truth, I have come to look forward to the cleansing power of heavy blows. But unlike the old-timers I will never think of the ocean as the back side of the islands. It is the front line of battle, the front line against the wind.

In eight years I have been in more gales than I can count. A few have stayed in my thoughts. One of my clearest memories is of an August day when I stood on the back porch of my little wind-haunted house and waited for a hurricane to blow through.

It was 1986, the year of Hurricane Charley—a runt, as hurricanes go, but with gusts to eighty-five. A friend had come over to visit my husband and me with his dog, a Chesapeake Bay retriever. The storm, passing offshore, was throwing off east wind and was not expected to do much damage. Even so, no one wanted to be out in it. It was enough to stand on the leeward side of the house and watch the myrtle bushes being shaken like rag mops.

That summer a pair of Carolina wrens had built a nest in the pump house and raised several broods. There were still chicks in the nest when the storm hit. In the excitement I had forgotten about the wrens when I saw a quick movement under the dilapidated table we used to clean fish.

An old beach chair was folded and stashed beneath the table. Leaning over, I could see an adult wren clinging to the chair. He was soaked from rain and, judging from his hunched posture, too exhausted to move even as far as the pump house. We had caught him off his home base and he knew it but did not seem to care.

The others noticed the wren the same second I did. Nobody moved, not even the retriever, although he eyed the wren with a lazy spark of interest. Nobody did anything except look out at the wind and rain. We stood on the back porch, an unlikely alliance— two men, a woman, a dog, a bird—each of us snagged, momentarily, from the flow of our normal lives, refugees from the wind.

H ARRY MIDDLETON (1949–1993) was a gifted writer, particularly on the subject of trout fishing. Middleton lived in Birmingham, Alabama, and wrote the "Outdoors South" page for *Southern Living*. He was also the author of several award-winning books and numerous articles in national magazines.

The following selection is from Middleton's book *On the Spine of Time: An Angler's Love of the Smokies*. It's apparent from this piece that, as he surveyed the impact of industrialization and consumerism, Middleton viewed the future of wilderness in the United States with great pessimism. Perhaps, because he believed wilderness was endangered, if not doomed, he viewed his moments in the wild as precious and poignant.

Selection from
ON THE SPINE OF TIME

by Harry Middleton

S een at a distance, as a range of peaks and ridgelines and shadow-filled valleys, the Smokies look as though they have been violently compressed, an accordion of worn-crested peaks and thin, gnarled valleys. Many of the knuckled ridges covered with great slicks of mountain laurels give way suddenly, precipitously, to nearly vertical slopes that tumble at air-gasping angles into valleys and gorges so narrow that even shadows find scant comfort there. A missed step along these slicks and it's a one-way adventure down the mountainside, beat-up and bruised, down among stones and weak light where only the toughest roots sink in and hang on.

Along the entire ridgeline of the Smokies large, garish outcrops of stone are rare. These are thick-coated mountains, heavy-browed with forests and undergrowth, tulip trees and white oaks, lush cucumber magnolias, hemlock in the damp shadows and glorious sugar maples, knots of goatsbeard, dog hobble, wood sorrel, and mountain laurel, galax looking like polished greenstone, irrepressible thickets of Catawba rhododendron, while higher-up sunlight goes gold among stands of yellow birch. The liquid sound of calling black-throated blue warblers gets lost in the rush of mountain streams, and the wind high up among the trees smells of spruce and hemlock and wild onion, sharp and fresh. Higher still, up along the ridgeline, the sky shimmers, a thick liquid of blues as the light comes off bent Fraser firs, their needles flat and blunt and unforgiving, like the worn summits they occupy.

The highest peak in the eastern United States, the apex of the ragged Appalachians, is Mount Mitchell. Its summit has the look of a heavy fist, jutting through smoky-blue clouds and perpetually chilly mists. Mitchell, like all great mountains, is a place of wrenching extremes. Its summit makes up the firm belly of the high Appalachians' intriguing, haunting Canadian Zone, a land that is closer in character to parts of China than to North Carolina. Life in this high country, in this land above the clouds, is perpetually pressed by hard times, hard, unforgiving weather. Another mountain paradox: a place that is at once exceptionally fragile and yet doggedly enduring. Like trout in wild mountain streams, what survives above 5,000 feet does so on its own terms, without compromise. The press of civilization, of man's coughing, wheezing, pneumatic world, brings death more than adaptation.

A raw cold wind blows hard atop Mount Mitchell. A constant wind, merciless. Trees are gnarled, twisted, stunted, bent in grotesque attitudes like galleries of violent sculpture. The summit is a place of harshness, an environment where death is a common resident. For as long as I have been coming to these mountains, the crown of Mount Mitchell has always been marked by dead trees, great stands of them, hard, honest evidence of the vagaries of life above 5,000 feet. They were part of the fabric of the mountains and I paid little attention to them until the winter of 1984 when it struck me that their numbers were growing, that the small stands of dead and dying trees had become a bulging, swelling host. I studied the summit of Mount Mitchell through powerful binoculars and the dead and dying trees piled up before my eyes like massive gray shoals of dust-colored bones. A sweep of the binoculars showed that almost the entire crest of the mountain seemed to have taken on the aspect of long, rippled, grimy scar pinched against the sky.

And the trees, the great stands of spruce and fir on Mount Mitchell, go on dying. The mountain today looks like death's gray land, wearing the despair of a plague's vile kiss. The once thick forest that crowded the ridgelines lies fallen and falling, as though laid down by some sudden killing wind. No matter the month, no matter the press of weather, Mount Mitchell knows only death's touch and its dull gray color.

The death atop Mount Mitchell has fueled argument among scientists and environmentalists for years. The common explanation for the great number of dead trees along the summit was the mountain's severe climate and the sudden appearance in the 1950s of a number of insects, especially the wooly balsam aphid, that feed on the spruce and fir trees. The wooly balsam aphid, it turned out, is a recent immigrant, just another insect that had been accidentally imported into the country. After its arrival, it eventually made its way to the Appalachian Mountains and found there its favorite meal, Fraser firs. Nothing has as yet stopped the aphid. It, too, knows no compromise. It seems as irrepressible as the chestnut blight. But Dr. Robert I. Bruck, a plant pathologist at North Carolina State

University in Raleigh, refused to lay all of Mount Mitchell's troubles on a single aphid. There was just too much destruction. He sensed that the mountain's deepening ruin went further than the appetite of the woolly balsam aphid. After all, the aphid ate mostly fir trees, yet the destruction on the mountain swept through all the trees above 5,000 feet. Indeed, in many places the red spruce were dying out even faster than the firs. Bruck believed that something else was killing the trees, or at least contributing to their deaths, and he believed that that something else was airborne pollution and acid rain. He studied the mountain's air, soil, and its water, and his findings portray an atmosphere atop Mount Mitchell that is more toxic than the worst smog-bound summer days over downtown Knoxville, Nashville, Charlotte, Birmingham, and Atlanta combined. Yet another irony: the lure of fresh, invigorating mountain air, the clean winds blowing over the rim of the highest point of stone in eastern North America, when in fact the air swirling about the summit of

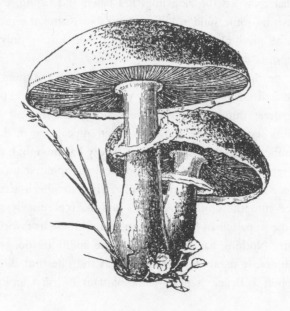

Mount Mitchell is only slightly less foul than the brown, congestive, ruinous automotive emissions floating stiffly above Los Angeles. . . .

I still go to Mount Mitchell, though it is not easy. I hesitate, grapple for excuses to stay away the way I might hesitate about visiting a dying friend because I know that going will seal the truth of things, make me hold death's hand yet again. So I go to the mountain and stare at the dying trees that now cover nearly its entire summit and below, and I understand that even setting aside a wild land, a mountain or a river, any piece of remnant wildness does not guarantee its survival. Against winds heavy with ozone and toxic metals and acid rains, laws that call for protection cannot begin to ensure preservation and survival.

Sometimes as I walk along the bony ridge of Mount Le Conte, I am reminded of Mount Mitchell the way I first saw it more than a decade ago—crowded stands of fir and spruce dripping with tattered wisps of cold mountain clouds, tendrils of fog, sudden icy mists. Often I will taste this cold rain, let it sit for a time on my tongue, waiting for that first bitter metallic taste of acidic rain, while the rain runs off my face and hands and down among the layers of spongy moss that spread among the rocks and fallen trees looking like lush green islands in a vast and bleak gray sea. Still the view of the Smokies from the summit of Mount Le Conte, especially looking north from Cliff Top and east from Myrtle Point, when the daylight is nearly spent and is the old red color of faded roses, is like looking into great sheets of red rain pouring out of the sky and slanting off Clingman's Dome and Thunderhead and the worn hobble-headed crown of Siler's Bald where the headwaters of Hazel Creek gather. The knotted dome of Mount Guyot is clearly visible, too, and beyond the vaporous shapes of the Plott Balsams and Great Balsams, even the rocky thumb of Water Rock Knob.

Enjoying this country's remnant wild places is a touchy issue.

The Great Smoky Mountains National Park covers more than 500,000 acres. In the half century since the park's creation, conservationists, state governments, the federal government, lumbermen, and developers have argued about the proper use of the park. In 1988, in a unanimous vote, the House passed a bill that would have permanently set aside 419,000 acres of the Smokies as primitive wilderness area. So far only Senator Jesse Helms of North Carolina has stood in the way of the bill making its way through the Senate.

If the bill does pass it will only more or less validate what has been happening to the park for a long time. There is not enough money or manpower to keep the entire park tidy and groomed, ready to embrace the public at all times. Making most of it wilderness would mean the Park Service could stop spending its time maintaining trails and other facilities that so few people use. Most of the park, and especially the great wild North Carolina sections of the park, is already wild and has been for years.

Let the trails go to hell. Don't improve the roads. Make anyone wanting to expose themselves to the hard beauty of these mountains get a permit. Keep all cars at a distance. Pass laws that will stop anything like a Gatlinburg or Pigeon Ford from happening on the North Carolina side of the mountains. Do all of these things. I am for all of it, and more, selfishly so. These are the kind of things that will keep the streams open and wild and the trout alive and uncompromising and me trying with fits and starts to hook into them both, hoping they will pull me into the soft, warm cathedral light that comes off mountain streams just at dusk.

I walked the trail down Slickrock Creek in a hard rain that tasted cold and clean, innocent, free of toxic metals and the sharp taste of acid. Knowing that the creek made a wide bend ahead and that there was a nice pool above a gallery of stones, I stood in a thick grove of sheltering trees, rigged up the Winston rod, and noticed a tiny pool of rainwater gathering in a green fold of my jacket, the drops of rain as firm and regular as cells. On the creek, the light eddied and spilled and rushed with the water and the water took on the moody character of light until they mingled so completely that I could no longer separate water from light and light from water. Everything drifted in a warm, rainy harmony of motion. I worked the green 4-weight line out through the guides of the willowy rod and tied on a fetching nymph. I cast and watched the small nymph go down in the fast, cold water.

On the sixth cast a small brown took the nymph and ran. I could feel its weight and its anger and its determination as it bent around stones and submerged roots and limbs trying to free itself, to escape line and hook. It spent its energy in a great rush and I pulled it close, bringing the line in with my hands, not even using the reel, and as it rose just out in front of my rod tip I could see its head and eyes—eyes raven black, a blackness as wide as a clear night sky and drenched in wildness, a wildness of trout and creek and rain; everything seemed liquid, a welcome stream that reached for me like a spring tide, flooded around my calves and thighs, pulled at the muscles of my legs and stomach. I felt the full weight of the fish in my hands and arms and I gave it line, not wanting it to die as it fought. Near the surface I saw it still tossing its head violently, folding and unfolding its deep brown body like a coach whip. Its muscled back was mottled with dark blotches of deep red, the red of dried blood, dark and melancholy. Call it Slickrock Red because there is no other name for it, because I have seen it mark no other trout save the big browns of Slickrock Creek. I lifted the fish slightly, just so its back would break the water, and the rain on its back flashed red, ran down its flanks like tiny streams of claret. I held the trout for an instant, then freed the hook from its lip, let it go, slowly, gently, carefully. For an instant there, knee-deep in the creek with the rain falling and that brown trout's seared-red back disappearing in the deep water, I was absolutely certain of the interconnectedness of all things, the cold touch of time against my chilled skin.

The rain came down harder in great pounding sheets, grinding torrents that churned up the creek bottom, made it look like some storm-tossed sea, hell's own boiling ocean, and still the red-backed brown trout took the little nymphs and wet flies and fought fiercely, more aware, it seemed, of their lineage than their size. Trout. *Salmo.* No compromise. None at all.

I took two more while it rained, neither any bigger than the first, their dark backs laced with jagged pools of bitter red. As I let them go, I could feel the heavy rise and fall of their flanks and bellies, the deep pull of their near total exhaustion. They had held back nothing. Nothing. Part of the great allure and fascination and temptation of mountain streams is that everything about them seems so fully alive, so completely caught up in the rush and motion of life. Motion twitches against every flash of light, no matter how dim, just like the speck of light widening in a rising trout's endlessly black eyes.

The last brown slipped out of the landing net I had eased under it to hold it steady in the water while it regained its strength. It moved off slowly, deliberately, and sank like a wet leaf into deeper, darker water. Mountain storms have a tendency to reach biblical proportions, pounding and ripping at the sky and earth, vibrating the very atmosphere, but by midmorning the apocalyptic-looking storm clouds had broken up, moved on, pressed by a fresh wind out of the southwest. Sunlight came up off the creek like a sudden mist, and the creek seemed a whirlpool of process and form, time and energy, a whirlpool that feeds the imagination and gets it good and drunk. Moments like this are wild and rare and are, like just the thought of trout, what lasts, endures, lines the membrane of memory rather than the fleeting excitement of rod and reel, the near-perfect cast, the set hook. The best experiences are those that are earned, even if, like me, you happen to be an angler of modest skills.

A mist fringed in tendrils of green light drifted just above the trees, and the wind smelled of birch and hemlock. Large drops of rainwater hung languidly from leaves of wild hydrangea, falling, finally, and exploding against the backs of dark stones. I packed up the rod and reel and sat in the middle of the trail and made lunch—a can of Spam, crackers, and cool root beer, all bought that morning up at the Crossroads of Time grocery, gas station, and motel up on U.S. 129 at Deals Gap near Peppertree Fontana Resort.

Slickrock Creek is part of the Slickrock Wilderness Area tucked back in the hard and devastatingly beautiful reaches of the Joyce Kilmer Memorial Forest, a stretch of woods that covers 11,000 rugged acres of the Little Santeetlah Creek and Slickrock Creek watersheds defined by the high ridgeline running between Stratton Bald and Haoe Lookout. From Stratton Bald, the crenelated backs of the Smokies are to the north just across the Little Tennessee River. To the west is the great expanse of the Cherokee National Forest.

Established by law in 1935, the Joyce Kilmer Memorial Forest is dedicated to the memory of the young soldier and poet Joyce Kilmer who was killed in World War I. I cannot say I care much for Kilmer's poems, but his forest is beautiful indeed, wild and unsettling and heartbreaking as any enduring rhyme. Although lumber companies logged vast tracks of these woods before 1900, there are islands of virgin timber still here, groves of giant trees that give the woods a dark and alluring character. Like fragile strands of spiderwebbing, more than twenty-six miles of them, move through this magnificent forest. Many of the trails are rocky, unkempt, difficult, poorly marked. Slickrock is not a place that is easily stumbled on; rather it is discovered, slowly, gradually, like a distant star carefully brought into focus through the powerful lens of a telescope.

Here I walk slowly, deliberately, taking it one step, one trout, one sunset at a time. Shadows drift about the woods like a dark fog and there is mystery under every stone.

There is a strange comfort in a forest, along a trout stream, where mystery hangs on, where not everything sits out in the bright sunlight completely revealed. In these woods I fight the urge to define and order what is about me, what is in and out of the light. And I attempt only to raise a trout or two, and accept what each moment brings, even what pants and growls in the dark shadows at dusk, what moves beneath the water, what thrives beyond man's rules and categories, his expedient designs and explanations. Too often we explain the world to suit us, to ease our own uncertainties, even though, in truth, it often suits us not at all. Watching the creek run hard with the afternoon's rain, feeling the olive-colored mist on my face and arms, listening to the trill of warblers far back in the thick trees, looking hard at the creek's surface for any sign of fish, it seems to me that I am fated always to see the world as it rushes by and that I can never outrace the moving universe, feel it moving toward me rather than forever sweeping over me, by me, through me, leaving me behind, seeing not where it's going but where it's been.

My view, it seems, is that of every modern man—the sight of the so-called natural world, the natural earth, in full retreat, like watching the faint glimmer of an exhausted comet's tail. Time, like certain ranges of light, is not fully appreciated until it's spent, a mend of memory instead of reality's immediate ache. Which is another reason for my journeys here: to be closer still to the ghosts I willingly carry about of the old men I spent some of my boyhood with in the Ozark Mountains. The present is the past impacted, swelling moment by moment. Here my moments, all of them, are clear and fresh, energy, light, and wind, and every trout a reminder that I am, for better or for worse, only what I choose to remember, what I choose to haul about.

There are several ways to walk into Joyce Kilmer Forest and the Slickrock Wilderness. I like going, when the weather holds, by way of Big Flat Gap and the old Cheoah Lake Dam bridge. The Slickrock Wilderness offers anything but a genteel and accommodating character, which is one of the reasons why the place is so completely admirable. Well into these woods and a man is pretty much on his own.

BLAND SIMPSON (1948–) grew up thirty miles from the Great Dismal Swamp. He now teaches writing at the University of North Carolina at Chapel Hill.

The following selection is "Songbird Swamp," from Simpson's book, *The Great Dismal*. The essay describes Simpson's trip into the Great Dismal with ornithologist Brooke Meanley and his wife. No one knows more about bird and plant life than Meanley. His references to famous early birdmen like the Bartrams, Thomas Nuttall, Alexander Wilson, and John J. Audubon, indicate his awareness of, and participation in, a great tradition.

"Songbird Swamp"

from

The Great Dismal: A Carolinian's Swamp Memoir

by Bland Simpson

*A*t the heavy, iron-pipe National Wildlife Refuge gate, I met an old-time birdman, ornithologist Brooke Meanley, who has studied wildlife and Southern swamps all his life and who with his wife Anna comes down from the Shenandoah Valley several times a year and wanders his favorite of them all, the Great Dismal. I parked my station wagon and went into the wilderness with the Meanleys. . . .

The day was crisp, not yet fifty degrees, and patches of the snow that had fallen across Virginia earlier in the week lay along the road beside Jericho Ditch. As we walked north up Jericho towards the Williamson Ditch, our footfalls noisy on the wet sand road, Brooke spoke easily and steadily about the Swamp world we were moving through.

"There's a pileated woodpecker," he said, when we heard the big bird's cuk-cuk cry. I thought of all the hopeful people who have mistaken pileateds for ivory-bills, and of Audubon's T. Gilbert Pearson, who unsuccessfully sought the ivory-billed woodpecker here in the Dismal nearly a century ago.

"Mistletoe," Brooke pointed up, "a lot of the birds eat that—bluebirds, mockingbirds, cedar waxwings. Red bay, swamp magnolia in here too. This little green vine, that's one of the smilaxes, greenbriar. We've got a lot of the prothonotary warblers, they like the ditches—the number one breeding bird, or nesting bird, in the Swamp. Lot of the birds feed on poison ivy berries. Almost any bird in here that feeds on smilax likes poison ivy berries much better. And the holly berries are a great food, robins love those. That's a red-bellied woodpecker, very common, hear that?

"I think that's a horse-sugar, or sweet pea—good deer foraging plant. Now we're getting into a mesic forest, sort of between swamp and upland forest, lot of white oak in here, and beech. This is a red oak. Swamp chestnut oak, water oak, sweet gum. This north end of the Swamp is drier than the rest of it, an exceptionally dry area compared to the rest of the Swamp. And you get a change. See those pines? These hardwoods, and the loblolly, that means you've got a drier area. Not too dry, cause there's quite a bit of beech right in here, and beech grows where there's a little moisture.

"The pine warblers hang around here. The yellow-throated warbler, which is the earliest warbler to come in from the tropics, comes in here in the middle of March. You usually find them singing in the loblolly pines."

We stopped beneath a tall tulip poplar with a great elbow in one of its upper branches, and Brooke laughed and recalled the classic encounter he had had here. "End of that limb out there is where there used to be a beehive. I was walking down here and I didn't see the bees, I didn't even notice the cavity there. But these bushes were just dripping with honey, and I couldn't figure it out for a while. Then I looked over at the scratch marks, claw marks where a bear had gone up and just pulled out the honey and the comb and everything else—this place was just dripping with it! Little later on I saw the bear a number of times. It was a yearling bear, that sort of had a loafing place in that tree. Big hole, can't see it now, but at that time it was a big opening where he went in. I saw him about half a dozen times—course he'd get out of the way when I'd see him. It's exciting, exciting to see them."

I remembered the story of a surveyor out in the Dismal in the early 1930s, who got some odd and unanticipated excitement from another honey-tree. Maywood Rabey came upon a great cypress, twelve feet in diameter, with a recently defunct bear impaled on a cypress knee, and then he discovered nearby the jungle-twined remains of half a dozen more, all their skeletons with bones broken. There were bees swarming around a hole in a hollow limb high above, and the surveyor realized that these dead bears had slipped, fallen, and died in their quest for honey.

Wandering the Swamp a generation or so ago was a solitary pursuit, said Brooke Meanley, who first came into this wilderness in 1957. "In those days you'd never see anybody in here, except the caretaker, Mister Lynn, would come down occasionally in a jeep, check the water structure, open a gate. Never see a soul. And I'd be in here all day long."

When we started back down Jericho towards Five Points again, I asked him about some borings we had seen in the peat just over a footbridge across the ditch, something about carbon dating.

"Well," he said, "I can't tell you much about that, but it's pretty accurate. I haven't kept up with a lot of peripheral stuff that I should have, but I've read about it. I'm an old-time naturalist."

It was after noon now, and the day had warmed enough for us to unzip our coats. There was a frequent thrumming of small aircraft, our steady footfalls in the wet sand, and tiny ice raining down out of the trees and sounding briskly upon the bushes and vines below like shot.

"The Great Songbird Swamp, I call it," Brooke said. "There're about eighty-five species of breeding birds in here, and it's more of a songbird refuge than anything else. Most of your refuges, or certainly a lot of them, were originally set up as waterfowl sanctuaries. Oh, you get some large waders, like herons, egrets, occasionally along a ditch, a few down at the Lake. Course you get some waterbirds on the Lake, ducks, loons, gulls, not too many. You know, the Lake's pretty sterile. Doesn't have any submerged aquatic vegetation, which is duck food. No emergent vegetation. Just water surrounded by forest, so it's more of a resting place for waterbirds."

"What about raptors?" I said.

"Well, you have two basic raptors: the barred owl and the red-shouldered hawk, they're Swamp birds. You get others coming through in migration, few others nest in here sometimes. I've seen a great horned owl in here during nesting season. You get a good migration of hawks across this Lake later on in October: sharp-shinned hawk, Cooper's hawk, broad-winged hawk, and some others. But this is mainly a songbird swamp."

"Why," I finally asked, "is the Dismal your favorite of all the swamps and bottomlands?"

"I don't know. It's an emotional thing, I guess, partly. The fact that it's the northernmost of the great Southern swamps, and all this Southern stuff kind of comes all the way up, is dumped in here. See, these plants are up in here because of the moderating influence of the Gulf Stream offshore. Comes up almost to the Carolina-Virginia line, then it swings over out in the ocean towards England. But I think it's the history of it, the mystery of it, fact that it's the northern limit of so many Southern plants and animals. And it's right next to this huge metropolitan area, a million, maybe several million people. Sort of a special thing, don't you think? To have this area so close to civilization, this great wilderness.

"Plus the fact that one of my favorite birds, the Swainson's warbler, that I've spent more time studying than any other bird, lives in here. In good numbers. . . ."

As we first entered the Swamp that February day, Brooke pointed at the small, twiggy cane along Jericho Ditch Lane and said, "Well, we call this 'switch cane.' It's more in the peat soils, whereas the giant cane—the fishingpole cane—it's in the floodplain marsh, whole different soil type. But the switch cane is important here as cover, and the bird specialty of the Swamp, the Swainson's warbler, usually nests about four feet above the ground in the cane, but off a little bit from you, not right along the edge, but back in a hundred, couple hundred feet where there's a lot of cane."

And near the bear honey-tree up north Jericho Ditch he said, "That's pretty good Swainson's warbler territory. Dense, not too dense, but fairly dense, lot of cane. And then there's a lot of sweet pepperbush goes back in there. The cane, the sweet pepperbush, and the greenbriar form most of the understory through an area like this, which is prime Swainson's warbler habitat."

Seventeen species of warblers fly back from the tropics in the spring and nest in the Great Dismal, and another dozen or more migrate through the Swamp going farther north. Swainson's warbler is the last of the resident warblers to return, arriving here after the middle of April until the first part of May. Their nesting season lasts till late June or early July, and it is during this stretch that the old-time birdman has staked them out, netted and banded them, defined their territories—their individual home grounds.

"Whenever it sings, you go to a spot . . . you just pace all through there, pace maybe to that big tree where you heard it singing. You pace all around them, you plot these points on a map, and after a while you get so many points—you've done it maybe a hundred times—and you get a pretty good idea of the area that it's using, its territorial home range.

"You may be working with a bird for a month, couple months off and on. Come down here, spend three days, come back two, three weeks later, spend three or four more days—all during their nesting period. You usually find the nest, too, at the same time. And you find a nest, you can pretty well nail down the territory. Wherever you hear them singing, then they're on an established territory, and they're defending. . . ."

Though birdlife was his first love, his interests were catholic, and nothing was too small or slight to escape his careful eye. It was here twenty ears ago that he discovered the dwarf trillium, growing scarcely above the leaf litter in the woods of north Jericho Ditch, abloom in late March. Nearby he found another rarity, the wild camellia that blossoms the last week of May.

"Wild camellia is a very small tree, ten or fifteen feet, something like that. And that's in the same family as the extinct *Franklinia*. The third species in that family is a plant that doesn't come quite this far north, called *Gordonia*—loblolly bay is a common name for that. But it is very common in the pocosins of eastern North Carolina. *Stewartia* is the generic name of this tree here.

"Bartram discovered the *Franklinia* down in Georgia along the Altamaha River during the Revolutionary War period—it's never been seen since. Except, he took some slips back to the botanical garden, Philadelphia, so there's some growing in cultivation."

A little later, when he was talking about the nesting habits of the golden mouse, how it will put a roof over an old Swainson's warbler nest and there make its home, he mentioned its Latin name:

Peromyscus nuttali. "You've heard of Nuttall, Thomas Nuttall, famous naturalist and botanist way back, Colonial times? All those fellows started around Philadelphia, the latter part of the 1700s, early 1800s, that was the center of early naturalists. Audubon was there. Alexander Wilson, famous ornithologist. Nuttall, the Bartrams, John and William, and a host of others. All lived in Philadelphia."

There was something affecting about the way Brooke Meanley mentioned these men's names, something that bespoke not only a respect for them, but also a strong tie to them, a keen sense of fellowship with them. He spoke fondly, too, of an old National Museum naturalist he had known when he worked at the Smithsonian, before he went with the Interior Department, a man named Paul Bartsch who had come into the swamp in June of 1897 and June of 1899, and spent a week each time in the white rough-board hotel at the mouth of Jericho Ditch into Drummond, touring the Lake taking specimens of birds and mammals with a .22 pistol.

"He found a lot of bats nesting in those big old cypress trees out in the Lake," Brooke said. "Something else I remember: we were out at Doctor Bartsch's place on Pohick Creek—that's a tributary of the Potomac, near Mount Vernon—a bunch of us one time, and we found a Bachman's warbler, rare bird, right near his house, but he was too old, too weak, to come out and see it. It was kind of sad."

A sad thought, indeed, and a very real concern for Brooke Meanley, who in 1986 was in an auto wreck and, in a separate incident in Beaufort, North Carolina, while staying in an inn and going out by day to study the Croatan woodlands, broke both his knees in a fall down a stairwell. The birdman knows well that he cannot forever go down into his beloved swamps and bogs and pocosins. What else has he seen, does he remember from all his days in the Great Dismal?

He recalls the dark-leaved cross vine creeping up the trunks of tall timber, likewise the climbing hydrangea, both vines at or near their northern limit. And he recalls the otters that go sleek and fleet in the ditches below, one otter in particular that he once watched working underwater, leaving a line of bubbles for him to trail it by, and bringing crayfish back to its two near-grown pups, waiting with their heads just out of their den on North Jericho Ditch. And he recalls the snakes of the Swamp.

"Well, you don't see many snakes. There're a lot of snakes here, but you don't see them. I've been here for a week at a time without seeing a single snake. But you have the canebrake rattler, the copperhead, and the cottonmouth—the three poisonous snakes. The copperhead's the most abundant of the three, and the canebrake rattler and the moccasin are at their northern limit right in this general area."

I reminded him of the popular impression of the Swamp as a snake-infested morass, and the oft-repeated tales and warnings about snakes dropping like ambushers from trees and cane into boats passing beneath.

"Yeah," he laughed, "that's fable. The thing about the poisonous snakes, the one *good* thing about them, they're sluggish, much slower than the nonpoisonous snakes. The snake you see the most is the black snake, which is harmless. Man, they can take off! Very quick, very fast! But you don't see many snakes wandering around here all day long, middle of summer."

Once, walking, Brooke and Anna and I stopped and studied some tracks in the road along Jericho. "This looks like a bob-cat, very much like a bobcat, fairly fresh. You hardly ever see a bobcat, but you do see the bear." Then he stood still a moment, and wondered and worried over the fate of bear in the Great Dismal.

"You're not allowed to shoot bears in the Swamp, but they go around the edges, and a hunter will come on one sometimes and shoot him. I think the Virginia game man in charge of this section told me they killed nineteen around here this year. The farmers get a permit, bear goes out in his cornfield, they shoot him. Some are going to be killed by automobiles, not too many, a few.

"This friend of ours, the mammalogist Don Schwab, has a collection now of forty skulls of bears taken here or right around the Swamp, killed by automobiles, hunters, farmers, and this is just in the last three or four years he's collected these. Right north of here, up in Magnolia, a village up above the Swamp, someone had some beehives. A bear was getting into the beehives, and he got a permit and shot that one.

"So they keep picking away at them."

Just before sunup one frigid January morning years ago, along east Corapeake Ditch, Brooke Meanley watched line upon line of robins flying out of their roost in the evergreen shrub bog. The Swamp was covered with snow, a very light frosting, and during the day he saw thousands of the birds feeding on gallberries, or inkberries.

One million robins, he estimated, the most he has ever seen in the Great Dismal.

They are common here, if not in such magnificent numbers. At the Wildlife Refuge headquarters on Desert Road, former manager

Jim Oland has watched clouds of robins fly over for an hour at a time. And Brooke and Anna and I saw some in a wintertime band of birds working the woods of Washington Ditch.

"They're not a member of the regular band, usually," Brooke said. "But birds attract birds, that's what it's about, and the bands are a stable thing in the wintertime. It's real interesting in the fall, these bands begin forming. Then the warblers, fifteen or twenty species, and some of the other birds from the North start coming through—they'll join these bands too. And it's the Carolina chickadee and the tufted titmouse that are the key birds holding this band together, because of their constant calling. Robins are hanging by themselves most of the time, though."

Or almost by themselves. Robins often roost with blackbirds, the old-time birdman said, but not in the same section of the roost. If the robins go to roost first, blackbirds sometimes displace them—and it is the blackbird that was the subject of Brooke Meanley's most astounding avian activity in the Great Dismal.

Twenty-five years ago, farmers after pulling the vines from the ground were still putting their peanuts up in shocks to dry. These big brown mounds, ten or twelve feet high and nearly as broad and with a central stake round which they were wound protruding from the top, were everywhere in the Down East fields. And in the fall, great swarms of blackbirds—redwings, grackles, cowbirds, and starlings—were coming out of an enormous Swamp roost that straddled the Virginia and Carolina line at East Corapeake Ditch, and they were tearing up the peanut shocks there in the fields.

Several students from Virginia Polytechnic Institute, working with monies granted them by the Fish and Wildlife Service, set about solving the blackbird-peanut problem, and Brooke Meanley occasionally came down from Patuxent Wildlife Research Center to help them. How many birds were they up against? they needed to know. The blackbirds would return to roost nightly along the same flightlines, and Brooke and his fellows positioned themselves with large-negative aerial cameras and took big pictures from which they could count this fabulous flock:

Thirty million blackbirds.

Fish and Wildlife had had success trapping blackbirds in Arkansas with a light-trap, a huge tunnel of netting forty feet tall and a hundred wide at its mouth, funneling down to a small tent with several thousand-watt lights inside to attract the birds from the roost at night. One night's catch of starlings and blackbirds was 120,000, and Brooke Meanley's team decided to try the light-trap technique in the Great Dismal.

By day they worked cutting lanes in the dense shrub cover, hundred-yard trails that fanned out from the mouth of the net. A cousin of one of the workers paid the team a visit one day, crawled into a tent where the floodlights were stored to take a nap, and got a visitor of his own. When the lanecutters returned, they discovered beartracks all around the tent—the cousin had slept right through it.

Once the trails were cut and the netting strung, ten or twelve men would go out in the Dismal dark to the end of the lanes and attempt to herd the roosting birds into the trap once the floodlights were turned on. All those millions of birds were in that pocosin, but they were all spread out. The beaters coming down the lanes awakened and impelled very few to their doom, and the low density of the great roost was defeating the operation.

"That's when we went after the helicopter," Brooke told me.

"See, all the fellows had given up and gone home except two of us, a V.P.I. boy and myself. My partner, Joe Hardy, went to the Elizabeth City Coast Guard Station and talked them into having a helicopter pilot take Joe over to the roost to try to herd the birds. They flew up above Highway 17, then cut into the Swamp when they saw the light beam I pointed up towards the sky, then flew around above the roost for about an hour—and *still* no birds to speak of came into the trap."

"Was the propwash supposed to blow them into the trap?" I asked.

"No, we thought the headlights would push them in there, and the noise. But there was a light on the underside of the helicopter that was directed towards the ground. The blackbirds were attracted to that light and were flying up and hitting the belly of the copter. The pilot was afraid his communications might be knocked out, so he got *another* helicopter to come up from Elizabeth City. Now two helicopters—one behind the other—tried for another hour or so.

"Still didn't catch any birds."

In August we went back into the Swamp together, and Brooke said the water was about as low as he had ever seen it. Just below Five Points there was a big outbreak of sweet pepperbush, abloom with little white flowers and growing into the ditch, and partridge pea and the red-stemmed Hercules'-club (bear food, Brooke said of it) were along the road there too.

We spooked a green heron, and watched it moving about in the Swamp, its yellow legs standing out against the green jungle. We heard a white-eyed vireo, and a cuckoo—the rain crow. Down Jericho Ditch the road doglegs across the ditch, and there near the brick-rubble in the woods we saw an Arcadian flycatcher.

"It often nests over the road," Brooke said. "They like an opening, they fly out and catch stuff. It's easier out over the road than it is in the Swamp."

I had my old friends Jake Mills and Tommy Thompson along on this outing, and Tommy focused on the birds while Jake remarked upon the Swamp's "odor of eternal rot." It had rained a good deal in the past twenty-four hours, and butterflies and dragonflies crowed the mudpuddles in the road. By midday the Swamp was steamy and fetid again.

We followed the Meanleys back out of the Swamp and on south to Washington Ditch and into the Lake. Morning glories, pink and purple, wound around corn in the fields, and down Washington Ditch there was much pokeweed and orange and yellow jewelweed along the ditchbank. The ditch was extremely muddy, and there was trumpet vine hanging beyond the waters, locusts grinding out across the way.

Lake Drummond was so low there was a sandy beach on the north side, and Tommy and I walked around looking at bolts, nails, pieces of plates, and linoleum, all of which were scattered about the Lake-bottom shallows where a hunt cabin or two had been. "I woke up on the edge of Lake Drummond in the middle of the Dismal Swamp," Tommy had written in his 1984 play, *The Last Song of John Proffit*, adding, "I can't tell you how I got there, but it's a hell of a place to wake up." Now at high noon he was seeing the real thing for the first time.

One of the Refuge rangers told us the Swamp was so dry that not only was a lightning-set fire burning over on the west side of the Lake, but also that a small aircraft had come down into Drummond and landed on that northern beach.

"Who was fool enough to pull that?" I asked.

"We never knew. Never saw the plane," he said. "Just saw the tiretracks in the sand."

Cycles of the ocean's elevation and subsidence created the collection of ancient seabeaches underlying the Lake, the peat, all of this Swamp, that has its own, far shorter, cycles of wet and dry. Not too many years ago, firefighters extinguished a lightning blaze burning only two hundred yards from the Lake's edge with water that had to be brought in from outside the Swamp, so dry was Drummond.

One winter's day, when Brooke and I talked about the question of the Swamp's drying out, he said that he just could not tell, by his eye, whether it was or not.

"Come down here in the spring sometime, maybe March, and it'll be dry. Come down next March, and it's full of water, so you can't tell that way. Only the hydrologists can answer that question." Not much later that same day we stopped at a turn in the road, near the head of Washington Ditch, where Brooke thought he saw a little activity. He quickly spotted a myrtle warbler—"A hearty warbler that winters here"—and a hermit thrush. And then he turned back to our earlier talk, saying, "You know, a lot of folks, when I show them a bird list of the Swamp, are very surprised to see the ovenbird so high on the list. Because it's a bird that likes upland woods, a lot of leaf mantle, and a dry ground cover.

"So maybe the ovenbird being so common, that's enough to tell you that the Swamp really *is* drying out."

Late in a February day we rambled down into North Carolina to see the largest cypress Brooke had ever encountered in the Great Dismal. The tree grew about a hundred yards into the Swamp, just south of U.S. 158 at the boundary between Pasquotank and Gates Counties. It was about six feet in diameter, with huge two- and three-foot bulbous knees all around it, extending to as far as forty feet from the tree itself.

We flushed the same woodcock twice as we stomped through the switch cane going in, and a third time after I tripped and fell over a half-submerged barbed-wire fence. Then we went nearly a mile west, back into Gates County, to look for catbirds in a long jasmine and greenbriar hedge on Weyerhauser Ditch.

Before we had gotten very far, two hunters in a pickup truck drove in past us, parked, and let their rabbit dogs out. Seven beagles started yelping and working a viny thicket where two roads came together at an angle, and the hunters thrashed about noisily at the edge of the thicket. The Meanleys and I moved steadily south down Weyerhauser Ditch, a good half mile below the hunt.

The last fall's hurricane had left a good many windfalls all over the Swamp, and I highstepped through a bramble to a broken juniper, wresting a piece loose from the trunk's sharp stalactite splinters—it smelled cedar clean, like all the very old beach cottages I remembered from my young days down at Nags Head and Kitty Hawk.

We turned two corners and headed back for our cars. No birds were moving, and the Meanleys thought we had seen about all we were going to see.

"Ah, yeayeayeayea yea yea yea!" one of the rabbit hunters cried, exhorting his dogs, his calls carrying up the road to us on the wind that had risen. "Whee! Whis, whis, whis!"

When we were about forty yards from the hunter, and walking towards him, the rabbit finally flushed—midway between us and the man with the shotgun—and ran our way. The hunter raised his twelve-gauge about halfway before he saw us, and his disappointment was evident in his dropped shoulders. He lowered the shotgun and called gamely our way:

"Don't worry, I wadn't gon shoot you."

It was our long day's end in the Great Songbird Swamp, and if the hunters ever got another chance at their prey, we were never to know. Back out at the highway, the Meanleys and I wished each other well and parted company and drove our separate ways west. It does me good whenever I think of them, at one with each other and with the great wilderness, their hearts filled with the melodies of these big boggy woods.

MARY A. NARBY (1943–) is a writer in Charlotte, North Carolina. An avid horseback rider, Narby's rides along the corridors of power lines has revealed a remarkably rich natural world. Even around Charlotte, the most developed area of the state, a discerning seeker has found a rich plant life. This piece is titled "Power Trips: A Highly-charged Ride Into Charlotte's Longest Nature Preserve."

"POWER TRIPS: A HIGHLY CHARGED RIDE INTO CHARLOTTE'S LONGEST NATURE PRESERVE"

by Mary A. Narby

*W*hen I first got my palomino horse, Nugget, I got cowboy-hooked to the saddle. I hadn't ridden in eight years. The idea of dismounting—"what, me walk? I have a fine hoss, here"—was downright repugnant, if not flat embarrassing. Fortunately, I got over this phase of my juvenile celluloid indulgence, mostly due to my curiosity about the butterfly pea.

Although I still ride Nugget on the broad median of the four-lane highway, the scenery there is mostly mowed greenery, and with the horse moving forward, two tracks of cars passing front-right-fast and the opposite way back-left-fast, my vertigo glands were going a little dizzy. Besides, on the side-roads, the narrow space on the berm sometimes gave us a gut-sucking sensation as hard-metal cars swooped past inches from my rather soft left knee.

I trusted Nugget, because the horse had apparently been born on an equipment dealer's lot, so ho-hum was he about screaming machinery. But I certainly didn't trust the drivers, who sometimes nearly ran into us just staring at the odd phenomenon of a horse and rider walking about.

Naturally, dirt roads were a lot less traveled, and it was at the end of one of these and through the woods a bit that I discovered the ethereal "Aisle of Grass" that was a new sewer line, heavily sewn with fescue, a chin-high swath of feathery green that led us down a private corridor of beauty indescribable.

To add to this delight, we broke out onto the Duke Power Company right-of-way one sunny day, and a whole new world of exploration was opened to us. Multiple lines converged toward a major electricity-producing plant located a half-dozen miles from Nugget's barn at the edge of North Charlotte. As we paced happily along this wide cut, with draped tower cables strung above us like guide wires, I noticed that there were huge towers, medium-sized towers and then just single poles, on the side lines. Later I learned the difference between "transmission" lines (the biggies—525 kilovolts) and "distribution" lines, which carry lower volumes of electricity to the transformers near your home. Plus, "switching stations," those metal boxes and tangles of wires and insulators with signs warning "DANGER—stay away," and other ominous stuff.

Actually, at the time, I wasn't much interested in all this Thomas Edison laboratory detail, and certainly Nugget was not, with his heavy-equipment background. Both of us were more interested in what was passing beneath us—myself because it was so varied and new and Nugget because a lot of it was horse-edible.

Thirteen thousand miles of these swaths of greenery crisscross

Duke Power's service area, creating ribbons of a nature preserve throughout our community. Some of these are as narrow as an office building corridor, others as wide as the Catawba River. Some are mowed and trimmed, but many of them are left to grow wild.

These are the ones that produce a profusion of pretty flowers and vines I wanted to call by name. My describing finds to most of my friends and co-workers did little good—either my descriptions were inadequate, or else they had been in such slight contact with Mother Earth, they just did not know. Grabbing books off the library shelves, I soon discovered that common names for the same plant in even the same area can number in the dozen, and I have heard daffodils called "buttercups" by some individuals. The wild azalea, for instance, had always been referred to by my mom as "honeysuckle," a term she'd been taught as a child, and it is still co-listed as "pink honeysuckle" in reference books.

Establishing order was a challenge that greater minds than mine had tackled. "It looks like a part of a giant sweet pea," I'd go on, "pale lavender, about eighteen inches tall." This turned out to be the butterfly pea.

"It's an iris. It's a maypop." They were trying . . .

I later found that the "maypop" is the fruit of the passionflower, that there is a small and delightful dwarf iris in North Carolina, and everyone, in their own learning and own way, was sorta right . . .

Rather than give up, I got more books, began learning the names, and educated myself to classify by family of plants, to sharpen my eyes. This actually worked, because families of plants, like people, do resemble their aunts and cousins and brothers—just sometimes, you have to wait until it blooms to see if it inherited "Uncle Morty's nose."

So I learned that, seeing the blooms of butterfly weed resembling the flower of milkweed, I was in the family. Joe-pye weed belongs there, too. Butterflies love the whole family. I was off and running on a galloping tour of who-looks-like-who.

My slight observations that the blooms of the redbud tree looked like sweet pea and the butterfly pea all came together in the family, even though the redbud tree is an exception to the rule that this family are legumes, with nitrogen-fixing nodules on the roots. Great fun.

No wonder wild sweet-potato vines (also called man-of-the-earth) bloom like white morning glories—they are Ipomoea, they are family.

Discoveries . . . the resemblance of the little ground-creeping sensitive brier flowers and the sweetly scented bush or tree, mimosa, brought into my realm a whole new family group. To say nothing of the striking contrast of the magnolias.

Ah, the magnolia. . . .

To a northerner with romantic ideas, the words jasmine, bougainvillea, honeysuckle, and magnolia are teasing tortures, that, with endless descriptions—"floating fragrances of magnolia and wisping mimosa, gently floating through the southern night"—are designed to drive snow-ridden, cooped-up Yankees stark-raving mad. And should be put on a list of controlled literary substances.

Magnolias, so out of my reach and imagination before, were now everywhere. Big, tall magnolia. Magnolia that hid saucer-sized, waxy blooms above even bigger green-sheeny leaves. The magnolia of hundreds of years of southern-fried, hot-and-steamy literature.

As I rode Nugget smoothly beneath the real magnolia trees, that which he had taken for granted, southern-born, I drooled for . . . magnolia. Now, my magnolia.

It had distressed me when, in Tennessee, I had chosen to cut down two small trash trees on the lot in Holston Hills. They were only three or four inches through, but as they swayed and fell from their thirty-foot, spindly height, crashed to the ground, I saw the huge blooms of the magnolia, which had been hidden from sight below by the leaves. I was inconsolable, for days. I had killed, out of ignorance. Surely my soul would rot in some small and slimy magnolia hell. I determined never again to be so stupid.

Yet, in North Carolina, trying to clean out the hedgerow to keep it from choking itself, I very nearly cut down two thin but respectable paw-paw trees. My paw-paws seem to be really persimmons, and these most wonderful, fruit-bearing thinnies have so much to offer, it's amazing.

I cooked the fruit into a custard pie, with hickory nuts gathered from the streets of metropolitan Charlotte, from a recipe given in Sue Hubbell's book, *On This Hilltop*, and regardless of the name, the pie is out of this world.

As I identified the lovely, gentle butterfly pea, I began to realize I was seeing species and individual small stands of plants that once were common, becoming more and more crowded out by the advancement of civilization. Once, I read, my peas were all over the place. So was ironweed, joe-pye weed, and marshmallow. Marshmallow . . . the foam candy of our grandparents. We eat a semblance of it now, but we don't even know why we call it that. In fact, what we eat now at Easter is a gelatin-sugar-foam-whip, but it's still called marshmallow.

The real marshmallow still grows in Charlotte, and I intend to gather some of the root, pound it up in water, mix it with sugar and boil it down. Then I'll whip it, and if past experience serves me, it will be the taste treat of a lifetime, just as the persimmon pie was.

As my butterfly pea (which still to me looks like an orchid) turned out to be the once-commonest of plants, I also saw those that had always been somewhat rare and were now even more endangered. Having noted a small place where the dwarf iris grew, I always walked the horses carefully around it when riding the back lot. Yet within one season, and without any notice, plows came in and wiped a wide swath, squashing not only the delicate native iris (which I could have tried to transplant, had I known) but everything else in its path—dogwood, redbud, silly little delicate salamanders—blam, crush. Not a damn second thought. I'd have spent tons of hours moving that stuff, if they'd spoken a word.

As I walked the early spring path of the sewer line that had changed so much, so fast, I came out on the power line. Here, much stayed the same or got better. The sewer line has to have a water level. It is molded in a completely different way—the land must conform to the fact that water seeks its own level.

The power line, because it is suspended in the air, can walk over the landscape and not be so disruptive. This point may seem minor, but in the end, it gains something. In the way that it marches through the countryside, the power line seems to be greater than the sum of its parts—because of its elevated permanence, and slight land maintenance requirements, it may actually contribute to the continued wildness of the landscape. This observation caused my heart to leap, and I longed somehow to aid it in the fact. As I watched the plantscape evolve beneath the massive towers, I felt greatly encouraged.

People abandon that from which they cannot profit—gardening efforts, horse-pasturing efforts. The right-of-way that at first seemed so attractive eventually came under the realm of "there's a little more there than I can handle." Thus, as the power line crews came in and slightly maintained and mowed, they spread Mother Nature's efforts around, and within a few years, the whole thing began to bloom, as it was meant to.

Because they did not move the little streams but just lightly rode over them, the ironweed spread and flourished, the cattails grew better, the queen of the meadow got reseeded.

Jewelweed, which I use for a quick-and-certain cure for poison ivy, was spread even better by the light fall mowing, which is done every third or fourth year. Frogs had time to lay eggs and make new freshly wrapped frogs. Box turtles had a couple of years to lay eggs and produce mini-carton turtles.

Fairly delicate fungus sprang up all over, because the power line workers didn't mash everything into the ground. Beneath the spreading steel armor-arms of the giant towers a lot was safe, I saw. A lot was growing, and growing better.

Gleams in my eyes. The ironweed where, six years ago I saw three plants, were now twenty-three. I collected the seeds, wanting to see if there were soggy, sunny places I could also introduce and nurture them. A wet place here, a watering-trough advantage there, yes . . .

My French "bronzie sunflowers," surely they would do well on the power line and feed the finches. I began to wonder if my "fairy-wing" poppies from England could be naturalized here. It began to occur to me that, in the permanence of the giant towers of the power line with its minimal maintenance, ten or twenty years from now these plants might grow and present a new wonder to this overly-pressured, crowded-out, I-don't-need-you-anymore landscape.

Joe-pye weed nourished and healed our ancestors, dandelion fed our grandma, sassafras "tonicked" my father, and now they are being pushed aside like red-headed stepchildren.

This spring, I will go up there and collect the seeds of the jewelweed, mayapple, passionflower. And put them back down for the day that will come when I need them to heal myself from the noxious insults of my modern society.

INDEX